The African Called Carr

The AFRICAN CALLED CARR

THE ANCESTRAL JOURNEY FROM THE SLAVE SHIP *Wanderer* TO FREEDOM

Velma Maia Thomas

NewSouth Books
an imprint of
The University of Georgia Press

NSB

Published by NewSouth Books,
an imprint of the University of Georgia Press
Athens, Georgia 30602
https://ugapress.org/imprint/newsouth-books/

Designed by Melissa Buchanan
Set in Adobe Caslon Pro

Printed digitally

EU Authorized Representative
Easy Access System Europe—Mustamäe tee 50, 10621
Tallinn, Estonia, gpsr.requests@easproject.com

Library of Congress Control Number: 2026023915
ISBN: 9781588385833 (paperback)
ISBN: 9781588385840 (epub)
ISBN: 9781588385857 (PDF)

Until the lion has a storyteller,
the hunter will always be the hero.

—AFRICAN PROVERB

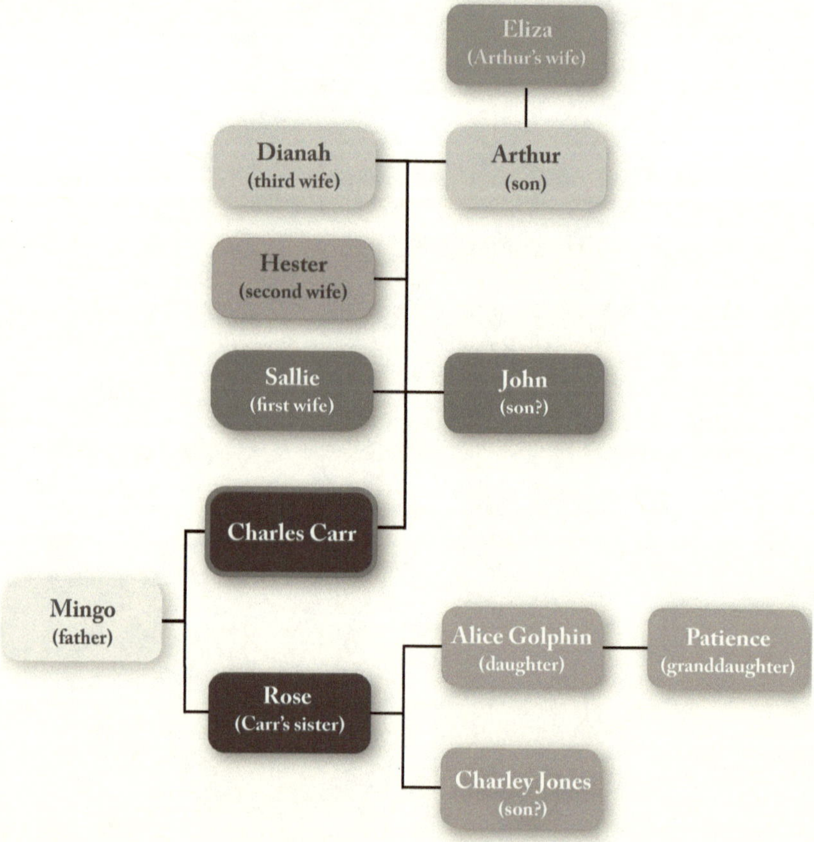

CARR'S FAMILY TREE

CONTENTS

ILLUSTRATIONS

A WORD ABOUT THE LANGUAGE OF SLAVERY

Recently, historians have begun to rethink and ultimately reject the word "slave" when referring to Black people held in bondage during our nation's history. Referring to people as slaves reduces their entire humanity to their social and economic position, as chattel. Historians are choosing instead the word "enslaved." They were people held in bondage.

And yet, throughout this work, I, an African American, use both terms.

I use the word "slave" because it is an ugly word. For many of us, the word brings up a pressed-down rage. "Slave" makes us angry, makes us look around and demand, "Who said that?!" We need to keep that edge. "Slave" means we were someone's property to be bought, sold, used, and disposed of. Some words need to cut to the core, lest we become complacent. When we forget, we are headed for trouble.

At times, I use "enslaved." I do this because just as it seemed life could not change, our ancestors realized that they could throw off the yoke of oppression—if not in their lifetime, then soon and very soon. "Enslaved" says, "This dehumanizing condition in life is temporary. It is not who I am." Had my ancestors accepted they were slaves (which by law, they were) instead of believing they were *enslaved*, they would not have fought for and believed in their freedom.

Both Black and white America have tussled with what to call us since we were forcibly brought to these shores. We were slaves, niggers, colored, negro, Negro (with a capital "N"), black, Black (recently capitalized), Afro-American, African American, and people of color. That is what happens when people are stripped of their heritage and brutally punished for being who they are. We grapple to define ourselves, to choose words that strengthen and soothe us. Certainly, we were human beings who were enslaved. But make no mistake about it: We were treated like slaves.

I use both "slave" and "enslaved" when writing about our history because each word tells a truth. "Enslaved" attests to who we say we were. "Slave" describes who they said we were. I invite you to choose the word that allows you to remember how far we have come and reminds you that the struggle is not over. Let the words swirl in your subconscious and your soul. When you hear them spoken, they will make you feel a "certain way," and you will know from deep within how to respond.

AUTHOR'S NOTE

When I began my research on the life of an African illegally brought to the United States in 1858 aboard the slave ship *Wanderer*, I shared my findings with Glenn Eskew, PhD, professor of Southern history at Georgia State University, whom I admire and respect. He read my synopsis and gave me this sage advice: "Don't write about the slave ship *Wanderer*, write about the African." His counsel confirmed my desire to write into history people whose names we may never know, but whose strength and faith paved the way for future generations.

This work reconstructs what I uncovered about the African called Carr. I knew when I took on this search that I might find just bits and pieces of Carr's life. I checked estate papers of his former enslavers. I ordered a copy of his military record and his pension application. I checked the records of the Bureau of Refugees, Freedmen and Abandoned Lands for labor contracts with former plantation owners. My quest took me to Savannah, Georgia, and Hardeeville, South Carolina, and surrounding communities, to churches white and Black, to archives, online databases, and the records of Tennessee and Florida. Although the written documents I uncovered captured only a few sentences spoken by Carr, he, his family, and community gave testimony and eyewitness accounts to history that I was able to reconstruct.

The case of the *Wanderer* and the trial of the masterminds behind this clandestine voyage are chronicled in two works: *The Slave Ship Wanderer* by Tom Henderson Wells (University of Georgia Press, 1967) and *The Wanderer: The Last American Slave Ship and the Conspiracy that Set Its Sail* by Erik Calonius (St. Martin's Press, 2006). Both masterfully recount the voyage, capture, and landing of the Africans and the federal trial to convict the coconspirators who carried out the illegal operation. My work not only speaks of the *Wanderer* and the trial, it also gives a rare account of the life of one enslaved man on the ship. The tale of the *Wanderer* is not just about a vessel but about a life uniquely different yet eerily representative of the millions of Black lives seeking justice in America.

In these pages I will lead you as Carr led me—to places near and far, through joy and disappointment, through Black life in America, from slave ship to freedom to a Black community that equipped freedmen and women to survive and even thrive. When I would hit a dead end in my research, Carr would ease open a new door. When I thought I would never find answers, I knew Carr was with me as I stumbled upon information in unexpected places to better understand him and the everyday life of enslaved people. I seek to honor and tell their untold stories, to have their accounts guide us. We will see how that Black history is everywhere, woven into the fabric of American and global history to remind the world that the often forgotten, nameless Africans in America, too, have something to say. With some digging, our stories emerge and give us an understanding of critical issues today. That is the beauty of our legacy.

This is a dual journey, mine and his. I intertwine my perspective with his. As you come to know more about Carr, you will also learn about me. The nineteenth and twenty-first centuries aren't so far apart. African Americans have gained much, but much still resides beyond our reach. You may find yourself nodding your head, noting that the struggle for Black equality in America continues. And yet today as in yesteryear African Americans press forward, ensuring tomorrow is better if not for us, then for the generations to come.

ACKNOWLEDGEMENTS

A heartfelt thank you to my agent Adrienne Ingrum, who walked with me, guiding me and assuring me through this process. To Uwimana Olabisi—your humor, boldness, and your "you can do this" to your "you better do this!" directives kept me on track.

To my ancestral guides, Ewa Ife Omo Oba and Milton Ahdwele Dakarai Fann, thank you. I felt you and I heard you. To my family, and especially Eleanor Davis and Deborah Thomas, you have always believed in and supported me, your little sister. I look up to both of you and love you both, dearly. To my son, Olu Fann, "Johnny Venus," you have made me and your dad so proud! To Dennis Williams Sr., you bring joy, so much laughter, and wisdom. Thank you, for being in my life.

Thank you to my big family, the Pan African Orthodox Christian Church. I see clearly now because of your teachings. Thank you to New South Associates, Inc. You supported my extracurricular activities, giving me room to be me and to write about, speak about, and represent my community.

Finally, to Carr—correction: to the African *called* Carr. I bet you thought the world had forgotten you! Your insistence paid off! You remembered the dark days aboard the slave ship *Wanderer* and told of them. You fought for your freedom, loved, and lost. Yet enough people left enough clues enabling me to find you and to get to know you, your family, and your community.

My sincere appreciation to employees at the National Archives and the South Carolina Department of Archives and History! Thank you for your diligence in retrieving documents. Yes, you were only doing your job, but whenever I inquired, you made me feel as though it was your pleasure to help. A big hug to lieutenant colonel Emma Hamilton, genealogist extraordinaire! Thank you for your assistance and cheering me on with "write the story, sister, write!"

To the University of Georgia Press, thank you for saying yes!

TIMELINE

1565	In August, enslaved Africans form part of Spanish expedition to establish a first outpost in present-day South Carolina. In September, enslaved Africans brought to Spanish Florida.
1619	Captured Africans brought to Point Comfort in Hampton, Virginia, and traded for food.
1787	United States Constitution signed, extending importation of "such Persons" (wording used for Africans slated for enslavement) for twenty years
1808	Date importation of Africans to enslave was to end
1858	Arrival of the *Wanderer* and the young African later named Charles Carr
1861	Civil War begins
1863	Emancipation Proclamation
1865	Carr escapes and enlists in the United States Colored Troops
1865	Civil War ends with Lee's surrender
1865	Freedmen's Bureau founded
1866	Carr opens account at Freedman's Bank, providing first documentation of his life
1870	First census that records all Black people by name, not as property of white enslavers
1883	Dianah and Charles married
1886	Arthur Carr, son, born
1890	Carr applies for disabled pension

1894 Carr describes horror of Middle Passage

1895 Carr dies

1896 Dianah applies for widow's pension

1901 Community of freedmen and women provides details of Carr's and Dianah's lives

1911 Dianah dies

1915 Arthur petitions to reopen widow's pension application on behalf of his deceased mother

1920 Arthur's widow, Eliza, pursues application on behalf of Arthur

1936 Charley Jones, Carr's uncle, petitions for Carr's pension; Pensions Bureau denies claim, closes case

2008 Jekyll Island Authority unveils *Wanderer* Memorial

2018 Jekyll Island Authority opens *Wanderer* Memory Trail

The African Called Carr

CHAPTER 1

The Journey Begins

Anyone who has ever taken on the exhilarating challenge of solving a mystery knows that often the mystery chooses you. The greatest mysteries for many African Americans have involved digging up our history, much of which has been overlooked by our education system. Unraveling our stories is one of my biggest passions as a historian. When I work in a library or archive, a compelling person, place, or event often catches my eye. I am pulled in by the facts and narrative to delve deeper. *The African Called Carr: The Ancestral Journey from the Slave Ship "Wanderer" to Freedom* is a book about one of my most memorable discoveries. While preparing to teach a summer course at the historic Penn Center on St. Helena Island, South Carolina, I stumbled upon a record of a man who had been part of enslaved and freedmen communities in South Carolina and Georgia, an African called Carr. He is perhaps the only survivor of the slave ship *Wanderer* whose life from slave ship to Civil War soldier to freedom and citizen can be told now, more than 150 years later. Carr's story exemplifies a triumphant legacy of Black people in the United States who continue to push for human and civil rights, despite tremendous odds.

This one man's life story offers a view of American history as told through the African American experience. Carr's life offers a glimpse of the trauma experienced by Africans caught by slave traders. His story confirms the well-known horrors of the Middle Passage and slavery, from auction blocks to rice and cotton fields. It also documents the lesser-known agency of Black men taking their freedom as soldiers on Civil War battlefields and reveals the dream-crushing freedom at the war's end. While these aspects of Carr's story are plenty to make it special, it captivated me for yet another reason: It provides firsthand accounts of the Black community that bridges post–Civil War America, Reconstruction, all the way to Franklin Roosevelt's presidency. From Carr's history—and that of his wife Dianah and son Arthur—I've discovered many lessons that matter today, and I've discovered what ordinary Black people had to say about themselves in their own words, as distinct from what has been written *about* us.

It was 2007 when I started on this journey of looking at Carr's life. Penn Center is among the most significant African American historical and cultural institutions. It is in the heart of the once-remote Sea Islands off the coasts of South Carolina and Georgia, a portion of the Gullah Geechee Cultural Heritage Corridor, designated in 2006. It is here where African culture was most preserved by descendants of West Africans in America. Portions of the classic film *Daughters of the Dust* were filmed here. It is also the site of one of the first schools in the South for formerly enslaved men, women, and children. The focus of my course was how to use primary sources—such as letters, diaries, legal documents written at the time of an historical event—to illuminate African American history. I used one of my previous books, *Lest We Forget: The Passage from Africa to Slavery and Emancipation*, as a textbook. My students were white high-school teachers, mostly from the Northeast. They came to Penn Center to learn more about teaching Black history and about the unique Gullah culture.

While spending time in libraries and archives preparing for the course, I scanned microfilm, reading through enslavers' wills, letters, and estate papers. This research method preceded the availability of many online databases and usually involved a great amount of work for researchers and history lovers like me. I knew enslavers' records could be found on microfilm, but I became obsessed with finding something beyond the words and accounts of those who held power over the enslaved. I needed the testimony of those whose experiences under slavery are less often heard: the enslaved themselves. I wanted documents that let the enslaved speak for themselves. Based on my thirty-year research on African American history, I found that these are rarely available. Most of what we know about slavery is written by the enslavers or gleaned from public documents focused on Black people as property.

To solve this problem, I turned to the records of the Freedman's Savings and Trust Company, commonly known as the Freedman's Bank. It was chartered by Congress in May 1865, one month after the Confederate surrender at Appomattox, which effectively ended the Civil War.

The Freedman's Bank provided a safe place for Black men and women to deposit wages and save a portion of their earnings. When the newly freed Black people deposited funds into the bank, they completed and signed or affixed their mark on signature cards kept in the branch register. Should they lose their bank books, the signature cards served as a form of identification. Signature cards recorded personal information: age, place of birth, occupation, military service, spouse, children, physical marks, and in some cases the name of their former enslavers. These cards contained firsthand accounts of slavery as told by those formerly held in bondage.

I focused on the Savannah branch of the Freedman's Bank, as I wanted to catch a glimpse of the lives of freedmen and women along the coastal area near St. Helena Island. Their responses on the cards intrigued me. They revealed what the recently emancipated had endured and also served as evidence of their experiences. Their answers to the questions were direct, and many of them were heartbreaking: "brothers and sisters sold away," "all dead," "father unknown."

And then I came across the signature card of Charles Carr. Dated April 21, 1866, it read:

> Name of Master, Capt Aiken
>
> Name of Mistress,
>
> Plantation, Savannah
>
> Height and complexion: 5ft 5¼ Black
>
> Father or mother? Married? Sallie in Savannah
>
> Name of children, John 6 yrs
>
> Regiment and Company, K. 34 U.S.C.T.

I had to catch my breath after reading the next lines.

> Place of birth, Congo, Africa
>
> Residence,
>
> Occupation,
>
> REMARKS:
>
> Father Mingo (Dead), Sister Rose, Mother My Dear
>
> Brought over in Slave Ship *Wanderer*

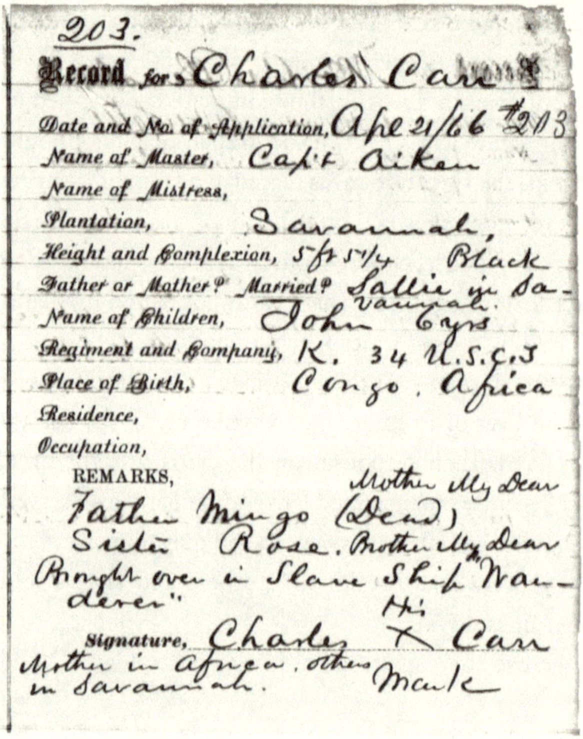
203.
Record for Charles Carr
Date and No. of Application, Apr 21/66 #203
Name of Master, Capt Aiken
Name of Mistress,
Plantation, Savannah,
Height and Complexion, 5 ft 5 1/4 Black
Father or Mother? Married? Sallie in Savannah.
Name of Children, John 6 yrs
Regiment and Company, K. 34 U.S.C.T
Place of Birth, Congo. Africa
Residence,
Occupation,
REMARKS, Mother My Dear
Father Mingo (Dead)
Sister Rose. Brother My Dear
Brought over in Slave Ship Wanderer"
Signature, Charles His X Mark Carr
Mother in Africa. others in Savannah.

Carr's Freedman's Bank signature card

SOURCE: *Registers of Signatures of Depositors in Branches of the Freedman's Savings and Trust Company, 1865–1874*. Microfilm Series: M816, National Archives in Washington, D.C., Charles Carr, Savannah, Ga., Record 203, April 21, 1866.

Words written beneath his mark gave clarity about his mother:

> Mother in Africa, others in Savannah

In answering the questions, Carr did more than complete his application. He told the story of the Middle Passage, slavery, struggle, and freedom experienced by him and other Africans captured and brought to these shores. Through Carr, millions of enslaved Black men, women, and children speak.

I knew I had found something and someone special. In November 1858—less than a handful of years before the outbreak of the Civil War and fifty years *after* Congress had closed the door on the transatlantic slave trade—the *Wanderer* secretly offloaded more than four hundred Africans on the coast of Jekyll Island, Georgia. The illegal voyage captured the attention of the nation, stoking fires leading to the Civil War.

The *Wanderer* was a swift, sleek, racing yacht, operated by men of status and means. They were enslavers, dealers in the enslaved, cunning ship captains, men consumed with reopening the transatlantic slave trade despite a constitutional ban on importing Africans for labor. They were men who believed they were above the law. History remembers the slave ship *Wanderer* and its coconspirators. It has recorded their crimes of enslaving Africans and importing them into the United States on the eve of the Civil War in flagrant violation of the United States Constitution and federal laws, in a case tried in federal court. Minutes of the court case against them can be found in the National Archives.[1] Until the recently discovered *Clotilda*, the *Wanderer* was believed to be the last slave ship to smuggle Africans to America. While much is known of the case of the *Wanderer*, less is known of the victims who were its human cargo. Carr's story was a hidden gem, tucked away in Civil War pension applications filed more than one hundred years ago.

As I researched the *Wanderer* and Carr, I found the name of the slave ship in historical newspapers and journals. Newspapers occasionally carried stories on the death of an aged *Wanderer* survivor, describing him or her as a slave and servant faithful to their enslavers. In 1908 *American Anthropologist* published an interview with seven survivors of the slave ship, who shared words and memories of their native country. In a ceremony on Jekyll Island in 2008, descendants of Africans brought over on the *Wanderer* spoke their names and honored the sacrifices of their ancestors. But Carr had no one to celebrate him. No one has chronicled his story; in 2008, there were no known descendants to call his name.

With the Freedman's Bank signature card as my guiding document, I began discovering and uncovering Carr's life—his haunting memory of the Middle Passage, his service as a Union soldier, his appeal for a Civil War veteran's pension, and the community that supported him in difficult times during freedom. Carr's story adds to the rare, firsthand accounts of the enslaved. His story also bears witness to the strength of the African American community that allows us to rise up, rather than crumble, as we push for freedom in America.

CHAPTER 2

The Slave Ship *Wanderer*

Creating the Black Holocaust Exhibit at the Shrines of the Black Madonna Cultural Center in Atlanta started me on my journey of discovering and writing about untold Black history. I first heard of the *Wanderer* long before I learned about Carr. Because the exhibit, a collection of documents and images on slavery and resistance, garnered local and national media attention, I received a call in the early 1990s from a man who asked, "Do you know about the *Wanderer*?" He then shared bits of information about the slave ship's illegal voyage in 1858 and how it tested relationships already strained between North and South on the issue of slavery. I admitted that I had not heard of the *Wanderer*, but now the slave ship caught my attention. As time passed and my interest in telling the story of our enslavement and resistance grew, I learned more about the *Wanderer*. Never did I expect to connect so closely to it, more accurately to an African called Carr whom the ship held bound as it slipped onto the Georgia coast.

In researching ships, the logs kept by ship captains are valuable primary documents. They contain captain's notes of navigation, wind direction, hull speed, latitude, and longitude. They also may contain records of daily activity aboard a ship, including deaths of crew and acts of resistance by the enslaved. Much of what we know about enslaved Africans aboard slave ships was chronicled in personal journals by ship captains, physicians, and crew. However, unless we have firsthand documentation by Africans, the stories of those who were crammed in the horrid holds of slave ships can never be told from their perspective. As a descendant of enslaved Africans, I became fascinated by this survivor of the Middle Passage when I came upon the long-overlooked primary document among the Freedman's Bank records directly connecting Carr to Africa. I could begin to tell the story of the *Wanderer*, with Carr at the center.

The *Wanderer* coconspirators were men of wealth, influence, and prominence who knew no bounds. Among them, Charles Augustus Lamar of Savannah should be signaled out as the mastermind behind the clandestine enslaving affair. Lamar invested in slavery and recoiled at the thought of Northerners determined to bring the institution to an end, even as this future drew ever closer: The United States Constitution stipulated that the transatlantic slave trade would end in 1808. The Slave Trade Act of 1818 prohibited the introduction of slaves into any port or place within the jurisdiction of the United States. In 1820 transatlantic slave trafficking was deemed as piracy—a crime punishable by death. Nonetheless, the illegal trade continued.

Charles Lamar was a "fire-eater"—a proslavery extremist who advocated secession from the Union over freeing one's human property. A son of Gazaway Bugg Lamar, one of the wealthiest men of the South, Charles revered success. He handled his father's enterprises—his plantation, commission house, cotton press ships, insurance company, and shares in several banks and railroads. Lamar reasoned that since the enslaved traded domestically had originally come from Africa before the constitutional ban, then buyers should be able to go directly to Africa for more. He bolstered his argument with the religious tenet that slavery was ordained by God. He posited that if slavery was good for the master and the slave, as ministers taught, then one was obligated to bring more Africans to America.

In early 1858 Lamar eyed the *Wanderer*, a swift yacht owned by Colonel John Johnson, a Louisiana native and member of the prestigious New York Yacht Club, as it sailed from Southern ports to Long Island. Perhaps this is when Lamar devised his plan to spirit Africans to Georgia. He figured no one would guess the *Wanderer*, one of the finest vessels of the New York Yacht Club, was a slaver, and if she were discovered, no one would catch her before she offloaded her human cargo. If he could bring Africans to Georgia and sell them for a profit, breaking federal law would be worth the risk.

Lamar found men of like mind who dared to capture and transport Africans into the United States in defiance of federal laws, initially partnering with Henry DuBignon and his brother John DuBignon, a

Slave ship *Wanderer*

SOURCE: *The Yacht "Wanderer"* (ca. 185–), photograph, Library of Congress, https://www.loc.gov/item/2023640761/.

wealthy enslaver who along with his two siblings owned the fifty-seven-hundred-acre Jekyll Island off the coast of Georgia. Jekyll was a private island, where John ruled, warning trespassers to keep out. Soon, Lamar brought others into the fold: John S. Montmollin, a slave trader who advertised from August through September 1858 in the *Savannah Daily Morning News* that he would pay the highest cash prices for Negroes—either singularly, in families, or gangs; Richard F. Aiken, a member of the Savannah Jockey Club; and John Tucker, an enslaver and Lamar's confidante. He also persuaded William Corrie, a Charleston planter and D.C. lobbyist who boasted he "knew the exact sum for which each member of Congress could be purchased," to join him in his nefarious plan.[1] All would dip their hands in the trade for flesh.

By late 1858 Lamar found himself in financial trouble. Having failed in several of his own ventures, he convinced Corrie to travel to New York and purchase the *Wanderer*. While in New York, Corrie and others retrofitted the yacht for the slave trade, adding storage and a tank that would hold fifteen thousand gallons of water. It was difficult to maintain secrecy: Rumors circulated that the luxury yacht was being converted into a slaver. The surveyor S. S. Norton grew suspicious when seeing the *Wanderer* undergoing repairs, the number of water tanks going on board, and the unusually large load of provisions for a small crew that included foreigners of rough appearance. Corrie welcomed inspectors aboard for a luncheon, where they were taken in by the *Wanderer*'s beauty. The décor included mirrors and satinwood furniture, lace curtains, a library of choice books, carpeting, and expensive nautical instruments.[2] New York officials may have had suspicions, but finding no conclusive evidence—no handcuffs, chains, large cooking pots, huge supply of rice or beans commonly fed to African captives—they allowed Corrie to depart.[3]

Corrie took on the role of the *Wanderer*'s "captain." Joining him in a supporting capacity were J. Edgar Farnum and Nicholas Brown. Under the pennant of the prestigious New York Yacht Club, Corrie and crew left New York on June 18, 1858. They arrived days later in Charleston, where Corrie continued preparing for the clandestine journey to Africa. Amid the dinner and high society welcoming Corrie home, he had arranged to load the *Wanderer* with supplies for the slave trade, including pans, tins, food, and Georgia pine to construct a second deck to hold the captives. Corrie secured papers for Trinidad, leaving port on July 3. In Trinidad he visited his family and the governor. To cover up the fact that he was headed toward Angola and the Congo River, Corrie announced he was traveling to St. Helena, a remote island near South Africa, to visit Napoleon Bonaparte's tomb. On July Fourth, as the nation celebrated its freedom, Captain Corrie prepared to deny Africans theirs.

CHAPTER 3

Clandestine Voyage to Congo

Captain Corrie never intended to go to St. Helena to visit the tomb of Napoleon Bonaparte; instead, he veered toward Africa's Cape Padron on the south bank of the Congo River, bordering the countries of Congo and Angola, the center of the region's slave trade. Carr, whose African name is unknown, was about eleven or twelve years of age when the *Wanderer* arrived at the Congo River. Men, pale as though covered with ash, emerged on the shore speaking a foreign language, understood only by those who would serve as translators.

The transatlantic trade consisted of middlemen—Africans who ventured into the villages, snatched children, bound warriors, and left behind mostly women and the weak. It relied on chiefs willing to sell their enemies. It was contrived by whites ready to inflame dissention, deplete villages, and disrupt cultures to secure Black laborers for the West Indies, Europe, and the Americas. The captives were likely held in barracoons—thatched huts where they were kept alive and sorted for the trade.

When speaking about the slave trade to African Americans, I often sense uneasiness in the room. They often ask, "Didn't we sell each other?" It is a question that confirms how this society thinks we should feel about our history: guilty—as though Africans were the ones who initiated and benefited from the "trade."

I remind audiences that slavery is as ancient as civilization. Many civilizations enslaved captives of war, criminals, or the poor needing to cancel their debts. Yet, crucially, the transatlantic slave trade was different from any form of slavery the world has known. Families were ripped apart, people were born and died in bondage. On America's shores, Africans were deemed inferior because of the color of their skin. Black became evil, less than, feared, and despised. The enslaved were dehumanized, brutally treated, worked to death, sold, bartered, and sexually violated. This set slavery in America apart from slavery in Africa and other parts of the world. Its brutality and lingering effects from generation to generation are unmatched.

Some Africans did join Europeans in the nefarious slave trade, and the African continent suffered. The pain of separation and lives snatched was felt by those captured by enslavers and those left to mourn. Europe and America built their economies on the knowledge and backs of Africans. Africa lost its strong, skilled laborers to the trade, even as Africans likely had no perception of slavery in the "New World." Africa's participation in no way exonerates Europeans from their exploitation and greed. Cannons mounted on top of the walls of slave fortresses controlled by Europeans pointed toward the Atlantic Ocean, not inward at villages. The great weaponry was aimed outward to keep competing European slave trading nations from entering. The "trade" was about economics, and if Europeans had to swindle, conquer and divide, kidnap, pour liquor, or push guns to get Black bodies they needed for free labor, so be it. This does not excuse African involvement, but it sheds light on it. As the African Ottobah Cugoano, kidnapped and sold in 1770, crucially pointed out in his autobiography, *Narrative of the Enslavement of Ottobah Cugoano, a Native of Africa; Published by Himself, in the Year 1787*, "if there were no buyers, there would be no sellers."[1]

On September 16, 1858, the *Wanderer* reached the mouth of the Congo River. The crew's greatest challenge rested in outwitting British and American squadrons patrolling the coast of Africa to catch illegal slaving ventures. The *Wanderer* faced this test soon after arriving at the mouth of the Congo, in an encounter with the captain of the *Medusa*, one of the fastest vessels of the British squadron keeping watch on the Congo River. It would take sophisticated sportsmanship to win over the British officers. Corrie invited them on board. For reasons that remain unknown, the British officials did not seize the ship, despite accounts that they heard hammering as the Americans worked to construct a second deck for holding captured Africans. With British suspicions assuaged, Captain Corrie continued his journey toward a coastal town in Angola. On October 4, 1858, he entered into his log, "Arrived at Benguela."

For nearly two weeks, Captain Corrie remained in the Congo. He

Entrance at Benguela to Angola and Congo, West Africa

SOURCE: J. C. M. Reinecke, *Charte von Africa: Nach den neuesten astronomischen Beobachtungen und Reisen berichtiget und gezeichnet* (Weimar: Geograph. Instituts, 1804), map, Library of Congress, https://www.loc.gov/item/2010587000/.

demanded mostly male captives—those strong and youthful enough to make fine slaves. The trade, then nearly three hundred years old, was well established. Portugal was the first European country to capture Africans, taking them from west central Africa and shipping them to Europe and Brazil in the fifteenth century. Between the mid-1500s and the 1860s, more than 10.5 million Africans (some researchers report 12 million) were chained and loaded on slave ships crossing the Atlantic. Nearly half came from two regions, the west coast and west-central Africa, which includes the Congo, the place Carr knew as home.[2] While Britain and the United States outlawed the transatlantic slave trade in the early nineteenth century, Portugal continued the trade with Brazil until 1842, the last country in the Western Hemisphere to abolish slavery. The *Wanderer*'s leaders took advantage of Portugal's centuries-old business of shackling and selling humans: Captain Corrie and crew called on African rulers at their compounds and entertained Portuguese traders at their outposts, to trade the enemies of the local rulers for cloth, firearms, and rum.

Determined to get the most for their effort, Corrie and crew crammed perhaps five hundred Africans into the *Wanderer*'s tiny hold before their venture was cut short. On October 12 the crew spotted the American vessel *Vincennes* patrolling the area, seeking to catch ships engaged in the trade in human cargo. In haste, the *Wanderer*'s crew cut loose the last canoe of captives and set sail. Luck again was with them. The *Vincennes* gave chase, but the *Wanderer* outmaneuvered her, carrying nearly five hundred shackled Africans with her.[3]

Filled to the brim with illegally captured Africans shelved on the floor and the added deck, the *Wanderer* sailed toward Georgia. An African called Carr, along with his father, his sister, and other countrymen, suffered the dreaded Middle Passage voyage across the Atlantic.

CHAPTER 4

The Hellish Middle Passage

I can only image the heart-wrenching Middle Passage experienced by Carr and other Africans crammed in the *Wanderer*'s hold. Writing about it hurts me to my core. Call it racial memory, the feelings and experiences transmitted from generation to generation that influence memory and behavior. It may explain why when I'm digging into this research my heart beats faster and I take time out to remind myself, "breathe, Maia." I didn't experience the traumatizing effects of the Middle Passage, but my foreparents did. Among them were the parents of Winnie Minter, my grandmother's great grandmother on her father's side, and the first known member of my Minter family born in the United States.

I learned of the birthplace of Winnie's parents when I found her listed in the 1880 federal census for Dallas County, Alabama. She more than likely was enslaved on a plantation in or near Selma, Alabama, a place that my mother's people call home. Winnie's parents were born in Africa, just like Carr. The census taker listed Winnie's birth year as 1803 and her birthplace as Georgia. He then filled in the place of birth of her mother and father: reported as Africa. No family memories have survived about Winnie, and I probably will never know the names of her parents. Their life experiences, like those of most of the estimated ten to twelve million other captured Africans, have been lost over time. This is what makes Carr's story so important. It provides a rare account of life in slavery and freedom told by a survivor of the Middle Passage.

Africans from the interior were terrified upon seeing the ocean, the ships, and the white men who chained and beat them into submission. Slave ships like the *Wanderer* were floating death ships. Several eyewitness accounts written by ship captains and crew tell of the inhumanity of the Middle Passage, but only a relatively few accounts exist written by Africans enslaved on board. One captive, Olaudah Equiano, described the horror on a slave vessel in *The Interesting Narrative of the Life of Olaudah Equiano or Gustavus Vassa, the African*. His autobiography is one of only fifteen narratives written in the eighteenth century by victims of the slave trade. Aboard the slave ship he described strange men with "red faces, horrible looks, and loose hair," whose language was far different from his. Equiano wrote:

> The first object which saluted my eyes when I arrived on the coast was the sea, and a slave ship, which was then riding at anchor, and waiting for its cargo. These filled me with astonishment, which was soon converted into terror, when I was carried on board. I was immediately handled and tossed up to see if I were sound, by some of the crew; and I was now persuaded that I had gotten into a world of bad spirits, and that they were going to kill me. . . . When I looked round the ship too, and saw a large furnace of copper boiling, and a multitude of black people of every description chained together, every one of their countenances expressing dejection and sorrow, I no longer doubted of my fate; and, quite overpowered with horror and anguish, I fell motionless on the deck and fainted.[1]

British surgeon Alexander Falconbridge wrote in his journal, published as *An Account of the Slave Trade on the Coast of Africa*, about the torturous conditions aboard slave vessels. In rough weather, crew closed the portholes and covered the grates, cutting off the flow of fresh air into the hold where captives were chained. Africans wedged in tight spaces grew sick, falling ill to the flux and fevers. The floor of their filthy quarters was so covered with blood and mucus that it resembled a slaughterhouse. Some of those who had fainted were carried up to the deck, where several were revived. Others who were brought up found relief in death. There was not a sight, Falconbridge wrote, more dreadful or disgusting.

While some of the enslaved fell into melancholy, others fought for their freedom. The crew aboard the English slaver *Don Carlos* learned that lesson with their lives. On the afternoon of August 5, 1701, the Africans revolted, killing several crew members before the uprising was put down with firearms. The captives armed themselves with knives the crew had carelessly given to them days earlier, not thinking the seemingly passive Africans would use them as weapons. People who wield power fail to realize, then and now, that at some point Black people pushed to the limits—oppressed people the world over—will one day declare, "No more!" On the *Don Carlos*, the Africans wielded bits of iron they had torn off the cabin doors and shackles they had broken off their countrymen's feet. The captives stabbed one stout seaman fifteen or sixteen times and cut a petty officer's leg to the bone. They slit the cook's throat and wounded three other sailors. When the crew managed to fire their guns to subdue the uprising, some Africans fled below for safety while others jumped overboard, preferring death to enslavement. The next day, the ringleaders of the revolt were severely whipped in front of the other captives. For the remainder of the voyage, the crew searched every corner of the ship daily, looking for wood, nails, tools, or anything that the Africans could use as weapons.

When we are taught Black history, rarely are we told of the rebellions aboard slave ships. We know about Demark Vesey's rebellion in Charleston in 1822 and Nat Turner's rebellion in Virginia in 1831 and learn in grade school about the heroic escapes to freedom led by Harriet Tubman. But we need to know that as a people we fought our captivity and enslavement every step of the way. Just as on slave ships, there comes a point in the streets today, when oppressed people wrap themselves in defiance and risk all for freedom. That fighting spirit was finally acknowledged in some way by media during the summer of 2020, in the wake of the protests over the killings of Eric Garner, Breonna Taylor, Trayvon Martin, Ahmaud Arbery, Sandra Bland, and George Floyd, just to name a few. Our community, joined by others, let it be known that we would not sit idly and "endure." Our call "no justice, no peace" echoed the cries of those who rebelled on the slave ship, those who for generations have fought for their freedom. That spirit brought to my mind the words of poet Claude McKay, written in response to racist, brutal attacks on Black people during the "Red Summer" of 1919:

> If we must die, let it not be like hogs
> Hunted and penned in an inglorious spot,
> While round us bark the mad and hungry dogs,
> Making their mock at our accursèd lot.
> If we must die, O let us nobly die,
> . . .
> Pressed to the wall, dying, but fighting back!

Ours is a fighting spirit that cannot, will not, die.

To keep the Africans alive and to maximize profits in the slaving business by minimizing the number that perished, enslavers brought the captives up on deck once or twice a day to exercise their stiff limbs. They fed them horse beans when food from Africa ran out and gave them a daily pint of water. Often the Africans were forced to dance—to jump sometimes until their ankles bled from being cut by the leg irons. Men resisted, women gave birth on ships, and the melancholy stopped breathing, willing themselves to death. Dysentery, smallpox, and scurvy raged. Blood, vomit, and excrement covered where they were forced to lay.

As I researched the *Wanderer*, I came across an article in the *Atlanta Chronicle*, dated 1888, reprinted from the *Augusta News*, titled "One of the Last Cargo of Imported Slaves."[2] The journalist spoke to Lucius Williams, whose African name was Umwalla, a survivor of the *Wanderer*. According to Umwalla, at one point the *Wanderer* was caught in a storm, and for days, the Africans were shut up in the hold. The foul air and sickness overtook the living and several Africans died. The fearless were held in chains. For Carr, Umwalla, my ancestors, and others taken against their will from Africa, this is the trauma of the Middle Passage. Carr would remember the Middle Passage and later in life utter these words: "Sometimes fifteen were picked up dead in the morning and thrown overboard."[3]

For forty-five days, the *Wanderer* steered across the Atlantic. Amid the stench and sickness, death claimed scores of the captured, their bodies brought up from the hold and flung overboard. Of the nearly five hundred Africans on board, an estimated 407 survived, many whose names we will never know.

CHAPTER 5

Strange Land

On November 28, 1858, in the predawn hours, the Middle Passage ended for the tortured Africans when the *Wanderer* dropped anchor in St. Andrew Sound, south of Jekyll Island, Georgia, owned by the DuBignon family. Just as the British and American squadrons patrolled the coast of West Africa to enforce anti-slavery laws, the southern coast of the United States was monitored to prevent illegal activities. Corrie left the *Wanderer* the evening of November 28 in a rowboat, seeking to find a pilot who could guide the slave vessel ashore. It was imperative that he bring the Africans on land before the *Wanderer* was detected by the crews of other ships in the area or customs agents and patrols in charge of ports in nearby Brunswick.

Arriving on Jekyll, Corrie knocked on the door of John DuBignon, whom I earlier identified as a partner in the *Wanderer* conspiracy. An elderly enslaved African answered the door, and with DuBignon's approval, welcomed Corrie in from the evening chill. James Clubb, the lighthouse keeper on Jekyll Island, soon arrived. Corrie pleaded with Clubb to guide the *Wanderer* ashore, telling him the vessel was running low on food and water. Clubb balked at guiding a ship to shore in the dead of night. He agreed to guide the *Wanderer* ashore in the morning, but for a price—five hundred dollars, a fee fifteen to twenty times what he normally charged for his services. He may have known there were Africans aboard, as rumors swirled about the area. DuBignon, desperate and anxious to get his human cargo ashore, agreed to pay.

In the dark early hours of the next morning, Corrie and Clubb rowed out to the *Wanderer*. When dawn broke, Clubb saw the Africans on a deck below. He was in shock. He had never seen Africans like these, later describing them as "weird" looking, with strangely shaped heads, filed teeth, and tattoos on their foreheads and chests. They were filthy, half naked, and huddled together like pigs. Many of them were sick; one dead African was thrown overboard. Cockroaches swarmed the vessel. The stench of sickness, excrement, and death rose from the yacht. Upon touching land, another African dropped dead.[1] Corrie and his crew hastily filled small boats and transported the Africans to shore. For the first time in more than a month, Carr and the others touched ground. The land must have been as much of a relief as it was a shock for Carr and his people. This new place was neither the Congo nor Angola, nor any place they knew. Some Africans came ashore in quiet anticipation and warmed themselves by a fire. Some devoured raw corn found in the fields to soothe their hunger. The old African who had answered the knock the night before at the DuBignon plantation recalled that several Africans looked at their strange surroundings, let out a loud shriek, and ran back toward the sea. They returned to the water, their last act of self-pride: suicide. They drowned seeking home and freedom.

When the lot of Africans was on shore, DuBignon called on his brother-in-law, a physician, to examine Carr and his countrymen. He diagnosed them as dehydrated but nothing more. He would later boast that none of the captives died in his care. Having offloaded his human cargo on the island, DuBignon called two elderly enslaved Africans brought from the Congo area to Georgia years earlier to talk to Carr and the other arrivals. Following the prevailing method of acculturating the newly enslaved, the two would teach those who remained on the DuBignon plantation valuable lessons—how to speak enough English to be understood, how to adjust to a new culture, new food, and especially the new rules: Never run away, never disobey a white man, never stand as the white man's equal. Black men and women have passed down a similar message for generations: from slavery to Jim Crow to the Civil Rights era, even to our current day. It is the "talk" Black parents have with sons, and now—since Breonna Taylor, Sandra Bland, and others—their daughters, as they come of age.

Today, older Black people prepare younger ones to survive racist police or other authority figures, including self-appointed white vigilantes who believe they have the right to serve as judge and executioner. We tell Black youth, "Assume a submissive role. No sudden moves. Don't try to reason or defend your point of view. Answer 'Yes, sir' and 'No sir.' In the moment of confrontation, *they* are always right, even when they are wrong. Failure to comply could lead to your death." I imagine the young African, whom I would come to know as Carr, received a survival talk in this vein from an older enslaved person.

Informed that the *Wanderer* had anchored, Lamar and other coconspirators headed toward Jekyll Island to join with Corrie and DuBignon. Getting the Africans from the Congo to Georgia was one feat. Hiding them from authorities would be another.

DuBignon kept some of the human cargo on Jekyll Island, and over the next few days the Africans were disbursed, with Lamar rewarding his fellow conspirators with enslaved Africans as payment. Each African could be sold for five hundred dollars or more—easily equivalent to more than twenty thousand dollars in 2025. About half of the captives initially were taken to the plantation of John S. Montmollin, a few miles up the Savannah River on the South Carolina side. Later, they were divided between Montmollin and his neighbor and coconspirator John Tucker. One hundred or more were taken to the South Carolina towns of Hamburg and Edgefield. Some reportedly were carried overland south to southern Georgia, Florida, and westward to Louisiana, Alabama, and Tennessee. Other *Wanderer* captives were given to Richard Aiken or seen in possession of other enslavers in Savannah.

First torn from their families, villages, and life in their African homeland, now Carr and the Africans who together survived the forced Middle Passage were torn from each other. Black history is full of sorrowful goodbyes. Separated from the continent of our birth, we were separated again on the auction blocks and courthouse steps from which we were sold. As already mentioned, Carr had been captured with his father, Mingo, and his sister. Given the name Rose, she survived the Middle Passage; later, I would discover that Rose was sold and carried to another state and that Montmollin, Aiken, and Lamar would factor again in Carr's life.

By the time the *Wanderer* landed in 1858, the importation of Africans to enslave had been outlawed for more than fifty years. The arrival of "fresh" Africans fanned conversations in Savannah and its countryside. Curious onlookers gawked at the Africans, easily identified by their filed teeth and tattooed breasts. They roared with laughter as the *Wanderer* Africans struggled to understand the white man, mimicking his gestures and speech. White viewers never hesitated to humiliate the Africans for sport and amusement. A January 12, 1859, *New York Times* article reported that a group of enslaved Africans transported to Alabama by rail refused to board a steam ship to Montgomery. They were terrified of the water and the smoke emanating from the ship. No doubt, they still remembered the harrowing Middle Passage journey. To force them to board the steam ship, the slave driver snatched an enslaved Black man from the crowd and slapped him several times with a leather strap. He yelped, ran on board, and beckoned the other Africans to follow, which they did, to the entertainment of the onlookers.

Carr and the other Africans brought to the United States were forever changed. They became novelties in this foreign land—sights to be ridiculed, pitied, or looked upon with disdain. They, like their descendants, became the "other," viewed as less than human, always watched and held in suspicion, always burdened with proving their worth.

CHAPTER 6

Flying Africans et al.

Not every African settled into the new way of life. Not everyone had forgotten freedom. Some longed for their homes in Africa. I read about Mingo of Brunswick, an African brought over on the *Wanderer*. I was searching for accounts about the *Wanderer* in online newspaper databases when I came across an article titled "King Mingo. A Story of the Slave Ship *Wanderer*," by Montgomery Folsom in the *Atlanta Constitution*, dated February 23, 1896. The African was "christened" Mingo. Because Mingo was a common name among the enslaved, I don't know if this Mingo was Carr's father. Carr never revealed much about him.

Folsom wrote that Mingo was an old man who had been a warrior and chief in his African village. The enslaved who knew him called him "King Mingo." After some time, the once rebellious King Mingo adopted a conciliatory stance under restraints and became submissive. King Mingo was known to "chant some weird lay in an unknown tongue while the big bright tears started from his eyes when he thought himself unheard." No doubt, he was thinking of home. Enslavers along St. Simons Island heard of Africans who drowned themselves rather than live enslaved and gave strict orders not to allow Mingo near the seashore.

One day while the enslaver and his family were at church, King Mingo seized his opportunity. He stole softly away from his cabin and, coming across some enslaved children, beckoned them to him. He carried them in his arms to a high bluff over the river, stripped, and bid the children to do the same. Three fishermen watched in disbelief as Mingo grabbed the children, let out a triumphant yell, and jumped into the swirling waters. Twice their heads appeared at the surface of the water, the third time they were swept under by the current. For years to come, fishermen called the spot Murder's Leap and avoided it at nightfall. Whenever passersby heard a strange sound, they were told that it was Mingo calling the children home to Africa.[1] King Mingo knew there was a better life. He had lived it before the capture.

I culled clues as to the location of Murder's Leap. According to the newspaper article, the site is a bluff that hangs over Savannah's "Back River," near a plantation on St. Simons Island. When traveling inland from St. Simons one reaches Mackay River and Hutchinson Island. Savannah's "Back River" flows behind Hutchinson Island, joining Mackay River and the East River at the St. Simons Sound. A piece of land called Retreat Plantation rested on the southwest tip of St. Simons Island. Enslaved Africans are listed on the 1860 estate of Retreat Plantation owner Anna Matilda Page King. However, the name Mingo does not appear. If he did "belong" to Anna Page King, he may have chosen his freedom before the appraisal. Without more information, I could not, with a measure of certainty, pinpoint Murder's Leap. I would have loved to locate the place where Mingo could be found calling us back to our history, helping us to feel and understand the importance of our freedom, the magnificence of where we come from.

St. Simons Island, six miles southwest of Jekyll Island where the *Wanderer* landed, also has a history of Africans choosing death over enslavement. The island is home to Ebo (also spelled "Ibo" or "Igbo") Landing, named for the Igbo people in present-day Nigeria. People have told different versions of what took place on the landing of the island's Dunbar Creek, relying on legend, folklore, or spiritual beliefs. A white overseer recounted that in 1803, more than fifty years before the *Wanderer* dropped anchor, African captives rebelled while being brought to shore in a small boat. The white handlers were thrown (some accounts say they jumped) overboard, drowning in Dunbar Creek. As soon as the Africans reached shore, several took to the swamp. They waded into Dunbar Creek until the water consumed them, affirming in their native tongue, "Water spirit brought us. Water spirit will take us home."

In later years African Americans remembered the event differently. An elderly man interviewed by the Federal Writers Project during the Great Depression said about Ebo Landing that Africans, tired of being beaten, rose up in the sky, turned themselves into buzzards, and flew right back to Africa. The old-timer assured the writer of the truth of his story: "Ev'rybody know bout um."[2] Accounts vary whether the captured Igbo walked or flew back to Africa. What matters most is that they chose freedom over bondage, home over a strange land.

I wanted to pay my respects to the Africans who walked into the water. One day I stood on St. Simons Island, as close as I could to Dunbar Creek at Ebo Landing. The landing site is not easily accessible from the street, being located on private property adjacent to a Glynn County sewerage plant, a facility that filters human waste. As with much on St. Simons Island, the name Ebo Landing has become commercialized: It is also the name of a posh residential and vacation section on the island near Dunbar Creek and MacKay River, where homes are listed for half a million dollars or more. Today a historical marker on Stable Street near Market Street on the island honors the tale of the Africans who chose death over enslavement.

While scanning a newspaper database, I found an article in the *Weekly Sumter Republican*, dated June 27, 1884, about the death of two countrymen of a deceased enslaved man called Squash, who was held in high regard. The three had been kidnapped in their youth and forced aboard the *Wanderer*. The journalist wrote that "pining for the native jungles," the two "dressed themselves in their best attire and returned to Ebo Landing, and waded in . . . muttering as they went, 'We will get there Eli, and herd the cattle'."[3] The article's author added that he hoped the two would carry the news that many were sorry that Squash was dead. No doubt Squash's companions longed for their friend, their village, and the lives they had known before falling victim to the brutal slave trade.

Sure, tales of flying Africans are hard to believe. So are accounts of Africans who walked on the floor of the Atlantic Ocean back to Africa. But we as a people want to believe them. We want to believe that all things are possible—even freedom for the enslaved. Director Julie Dash honored the history of Ebo Landing in her film *Daughters of the Dust*. Toni Morrison illuminated the folklore of flying Africans in the powerful prose of *Song of Solomon*. Virginia Hamilton wrote and Leo and Diane Dillon beautifully illustrated the legend in *The People Could Fly*. These are myths that some people consider truth, until someone proves them wrong.

I understand why Mingo took his life, or more correctly took back his freedom. We who are shackled physically, socially, economically, or metaphorically often feel the need to lay down our burdens and run free. I know I do. I'll continue to look for Murder's Leap, and even if I never find it, I know King Mingo is there. His spirit presides over us, along with the spirits of all the others who returned to the waters to go home to Africa. Choosing the liberty of death, they watch over us, as do the descendants of those who stayed in the United States—like Carr—and made this foreign land their home.

CHAPTER 7

Caught, Tried, Acquitted

Once the Africans were off-loaded, Corrie had the *Wanderer* scrubbed and the slave deck removed. A local seaman was given one hundred dollars to sail the yacht to Brunswick, Georgia, about thirteen miles from Jekyll Island. But despite Lamar's success in dismantling the evidence on the *Wanderer* and disbursing the human cargo of Africans that had been smuggled ashore, time and the authorities would catch up to him.[1]

Soon after the ship was sent away, three members of the *Wanderer* crew were overheard talking in a Savannah hotel. The hotel clerk became suspicious because the crew—Nicholas Brown, a "swarthy Greek," Juan Rajesta, and Miguel Arguirir, both Spaniards—had returned to the hotel with suits from the finest shop in Savannah. Officials began to home in.

Authorities in Brunswick discovered the *Wanderer's* papers were flawed. A closer look revealed the stamp from Trinidad, where Corrie supposedly traveled upon leaving Charleston with the *Wanderer*, was a fake. There was no stamp from St. Helena off the coast of South Africa, where Corrie allegedly stopped to visit Napoleon Bonaparte's tomb.

Lamar's plan had been too ambitious to go unnoticed or unchallenged. Officials swung into action, seizing the *Wanderer* and indicting Lamar, Montmollin, Aiken, and others. Although they contrived the illegal transportation of the Africans, an offense that included the serious charge of piracy, the coconspirators Lamar, Montmollin, and Aiken were charged with the lesser crimes of violating the slave acts. Charges included holding African Negroes, importing Africans, and the rescue of a jailed inmate. Lesser charges, of course, meant the potential for less severe punishment, if found guilty. In contrast, Captain Corrie and three crew members—Brown, Rajesta, and Arguirir (who spoke little or no English)—were charged with the serious crime of piracy, punishable by death, and of importing Africans.

In the wake of growing suspicion, Corrie fled to safety in his hometown of Charleston, South Carolina. His connections with officials in high places (a benefit of privilege) paid off, as twice South Carolina officials refused to extradite him to Savannah. Through legal wrangling, the case against Corrie was eventually dropped.

When I read about the accused crew members, I questioned, "Was this racial or at least class profiling?" I doubt that if Lamar, Aiken, or Montmollin had worn pricy suits to the hotel in Savannah, they would have raised alarm. Just like slavery has existed since this country's founding, so has racial profiling. If you are Black or a person of color, then you know what it is like to be judged immediately because of your skin color, the way you wear your hair, even the sound of your name. If you are Black, you will find that you often get more attention from salesclerks who are watching you—just in case. Job seekers with "Black sounding" names are less often to get a call from recruiters, even if their qualifications match those of people with "traditional names." Black youth have been told to cut their locs in order to participate in extracurricular activities or even to walk in their own graduation. Black professionals driving luxury cars have been stopped in affluent "white neighborhoods"—the police just making sure they belong there.

This experience has hit home with me. On one unforgettable occasion, my second-oldest sister, Deborah, now a retired judge, and I were driving in broad daylight in Detroit where we grew up and where she still lives. We decided to take a ride through an exclusive suburb of the city. She noticed that we were being followed by the police. Then suddenly, the police officer stopped trailing us and drove off. "He ran my tag and found out I was a county judge," she said with a measure of disgust. "That's why he stopped following us." We were lucky. The story could have turned out worse.

The three men who were not the wealthy, well-connected masterminds of the *Wanderer* conspiracy were pinned with serious charges and considered suspicious because of their fine jackets, trousers, and shirts. Had they stayed in their frumpy, seafaring clothes, they might have gone unnoticed. The criminal (in)justice system favors the wealthy and the white. People of color are arrested at higher rates than whites, and if convicted, they are given harsher treatment than whites who commit the very same crimes.

The rich dodge taxes, the poor are penalized for failure to pay. The wealthy make mistakes, the poor go to jail. It seems that Justice, despite its blindfold, is not blind. Things are not so different now than they were in the nineteenth century.

The trial of those indicted for crimes involving the *Wanderer* became headline news. It was a watershed moment, pitting slaveholding states against free states. President James Buchanan, the last president before the Civil War, became involved: The *Wanderer* coconspirators violated federal laws and the United States Constitution, leading the U.S. Senate to pressure the president to take a strong stand against a bold South that disregarded the laws of the land.

The stakes were high. *Wanderer* coconspirators exemplified men who challenged the North for meddling in the South's business of slavery and resisting the latter's expansion westward into new territories. Southerners pointed to the hypocrisy of the North for condemning slavery when it, too, benefited from the institution. Textile mills in New England manufactured products from cotton grown in the slaveholding South. Clipper ships from New York carried cotton to textile mills in Great Britain. In 1860 cotton amounted to 60 percent of all exports from the United States.

I found this context important to understand. The purpose is not to exonerate the South (or the North) for holding my people enslaved or to excuse Lamar and the other culprits. It's to remind us that this country as a whole benefited from the forced labor of Carr, other *Wanderer* captives, and others among millions of Africans and their descendants for nearly 250 years.

The federal trial was held in the courtroom of the U.S. Custom House in Savannah. As no verbatim records of the trial were kept, historians have relied on newspaper accounts to piece together the court proceedings. Helpfully, newspapers in New York and across the country reported the trial of Lamar and other coconspirators. Lamar enjoyed the publicity from the North, believing that the more he was vilified in the Northern newspapers, the more sympathy he would draw from his Southern jury. He was correct: Juries returned verdicts of not guilty for all those associated with the *Wanderer* affair. As a slap on the wrist, Lamar was sentenced to thirty days of house arrest at his place of business—for assisting in freeing a coconspirator from jail. It was a victory for the South and the fire-eaters, further straining the relationship between the North and South, soon to be embroiled in the bloody Civil War.

The acquittal of the *Wanderer* coconspirators was not the first or the last such verdict in favor of those who have committed a hate crime against Black people. The nation's history is full of lynchings and other killings for which no one was arrested, much less charged or convicted. It took three trials and nearly thirty-one years to convict Byron De La Beckwith, who had bragged about killing civil rights activist Medgar Evers in his own driveway in Jackson, Mississippi. Recall the murder of fourteen-year-old Emmett Till of Chicago, accused of whistling at a white woman in a store in Money, Mississippi. It took the all-white jury only sixty minutes to return a verdict of "not guilty," despite clear evidence that the two accused white men brutally beat Till, tied a seventy-five-pound cotton gin fan around his neck, and dropped him into the Tallahatchie River.

Yes, justice prevails once in a while. In 2021 a jury returned the verdict of guilty in the trial of Derek Chauvin, the police officer accused of killing the unarmed George Floyd by pressing his knee on Floyd's neck, cutting off the flow of oxygen for more than nine minutes. That same year, a jury found three white men guilty of killing the unarmed Ahmaud Arbery as he jogged through a white neighborhood in Brunswick, Georgia. But for every "guilty" verdict there are scores of "not guilty" that leave us stunned and angry. As important as criminal justice work is, undoing four hundred years of injustice will take time and relentless demands. Until then we must remain vigilant in speaking for those who cannot speak for themselves. For me, at this time, it means telling the story of the African called Carr—a *Wanderer* survivor whose guilty captors walked free.

CHAPTER 8

Carr, Aiken, and the Weeping Time

Now that I understood the history of the slave ship *Wanderer*, the trial, and the acquittals, I was determined to learn more about Carr. Several questions swirled in my head. Who was the "Captain" Aiken who held Carr in bondage? Where was the plantation on which Carr was enslaved? Did Carr ever run or strike out on his own for freedom? Could I discover more about his family and comrades? As a free man, did he ever come face-to-face with his enslavers? Was freedom as sweet as it sounded?

I focused again on portions of the document that had introduced me to Carr: his signature card for the Freedman's Bank in Savannah.

Name of Master, Capt Aiken

Plantation, Savannah

Father or mother? Married? Sallie in Savannah

Name of children, John 6 yrs

Place of birth, Congo, Africa

REMARKS: Father Mingo (Dead) Sister Rose, Mother My Dear,

Brought over in Slave Ship *Wanderer*

Mother in Africa, others in Savannah

Carr's life and ties to the *Wanderer* became clearer when I realized that Captain Aiken was Richard F. Aiken, one of the *Wanderer* coconspirators with whom Lamar left a group of *Wanderer* captives. I later learned that Aiken served in Company F of the 2nd Cavalry Regiment, Georgia, during the Civil War, where he held the of rank of captain. I also learned that just months after the landing of the *Wanderer*, Aiken and Charles Lamar were again connected to the business of selling the enslaved—this time on the grounds of Savannah's Ten Broeck Race Course, where more than four hundred men, women, and children were sold in the largest sale of enslaved people in Georgia's recorded history. The auction became known as the "Weeping Time," as it rained during the two-day event. African American lore tells that the heavens cried during the sale, mixing with the tears of the enslaved torn away from family and community.

I knew that to find out more about Carr under slavery, I had to find out more about Richard Aiken, his enslaver. I searched online databases, including federal censuses, slave schedules, and tax records. In the 1850 census I found R. F. Aikin, age thirty-five, in Chatham County, Georgia, of which Savannah is the county seat. He resided in a hotel; his occupation was listed as "none." Aiken did not appear in the 1860 census. As Carr was brought over on the *Wanderer* in 1858, I searched for Richard Aiken in the 1860 slave schedule. I found him in the White Bluff community near Savannah, where he was listed as holding four enslaved persons. They were males, ages thirty-two, seventeen, sixteen, and thirty-eight.

Slave schedules grouped the enslaved by family unit, gender, and age. Because of this, I would not find Charles Carr or any enslaved African listed by name. I could only note that he may have been one of those enumerated as belonging to Aiken. This is one of the challenges and frustrations of conducting African American genealogy. During slavery, our enslaved ancestors' names appeared in deeds, wills, estate appraisals, or in runaway slave notices in newspapers. Even then, they were identified by first name only or by description such as "Katie, Sarah's child" or "Old Jim." This leaves most African Americans with little alternative than to make an informed guess or lean on family oral history to trace our ancestors and the places they were enslaved. As Aiken's enslaved were listed only by gender and age, I found it impossible to know for sure if Carr were among them, but it is likely that he was.

I next turned to the tax digests. In 1859 Aiken was listed in the Georgia property tax digest as owning 110 acres in White Bluff, Chatham County, valued at twenty-three hundred dollars. He held three slaves valued at nine hundred dollars.[1] Although Aiken enslaved people and owned more than one hundred acres, his property in White Bluff could not be defined as a plantation. Historians reserve the description "plantation owner" for persons owning at least five hundred acres and holding in bondage twenty or more enslaved people. The popular image of antebellum plantations is that of large plantations, like the fictional plantation Tara in *Gone with the Wind*. The historic reality for most enslaved persons was far different. Aiken was an enslaver who wasn't very rich the way plantation owners are usually portrayed. If Carr were among those whom Aiken held as his property, Carr lived as did the majority of slaves—on a small farm with ten or fewer persons in bondage.

With the information I found in census, slave schedule, and the tax digest, I decided to take a road trip to Savannah and the White Bluff community. My journey to uncover elements of Carr's life took me to small cities and towns between Savannah, Georgia, and Beaufort County, South Carolina, time and time again. My eldest sister, Eleanor, and I often traveled on these roads together. Eleanor (we call her Rosy, taken from her middle name, Rose) is the only family member adventurous and fearless enough to go with me through small Southern towns, courthouses, and cemeteries in search of little-known facts about Black folk. These were leisurely trips, often on two-lane roads that twisted and turned and were quiet enough to allow me to think and piece together information as my sister drove.

Rosy had been my guest at Penn Center on St. Helena Island, South Carolina, the summer I taught my second class on using primary documents to teach African American history. At the end of the course, we drove to Savannah, specifically to Coffee Bluff, a Savannah community four miles from White Bluff, where Aiken had most likely enslaved Carr. The trip was a one-hour drive from Penn Center. Our excursion served two purposes. Rosy would finally meet Arthur "Pete" Dilbert (now among the ancestors), the African American whose hand-carved walking sticks have been on display at the Telfair Museums in Savannah and the Smithsonian American Art Museum in Washington, D.C. I would look for clues to find the location of the property where Carr labored near Savannah.

My sister would have more luck. She met the artist she had long admired. I found nothing more in my search for where Carr had been enslaved. We chatted with Mr. Dilbert, as we would on several more weekend trips in the Savannah area. He was friendly, wise, and innocently flirtatious. I am glad that I had a chance to meet him. During our visits, my mind often drifted to Carr. He had been enslaved in White Bluff just a short distance from where Mr. Dilbert lived. The 1860 slave schedule listed 580 men, women, and children held in White Bluff. Other than this, I could find little information about the community. *A Historical Record of Savannah* published in 1869 related that White Bluff was a popular resort with summer residences, however, this account admitted there was little written history about the area.[2]

After visiting Mr. Dilbert, my sister and I stopped in Savannah at the site of the former Ten Broeck Race Course, the location of the Weeping Time auction. Ten Broeck was home at the time to the Savannah Jockey Club, which held the purse for those who gathered twice a month to race or bet on sleek, swift horses. In the 1850s Charles Lamar rallied to refurbish the race track and had served as president of the club.[3] In 1856 and 1857, Richard Aiken, whom Carr named as his "master" on the Freedman's Bank application, served as secretary of the Jockey Club. In 1859, the year of the slave auction at Ten Broeck, Lamar served again as president and also as secretary of the Savannah Jockey Club. The two men were as tied to Ten Broeck as they were to the *Wanderer* and the capture of Carr and his comrades. In March 1859, four months after the *Wanderer* off-loaded approximately four hundred Africans on Jekyll Island, Lamar and Aiken gave the nod to allow four hundred enslaved Africans and their descendants to be sold at Ten Broeck.

The enslaver and seller at Ten Broeck was Pierce Butler, a wealthy rice planter and grandson of one of the signers of the Declaration of Independence, Senator Pierce Mason Butler, an enslaver from South Carolina. A gambler, Butler found himself in tremendous debt. His financial advisors arranged a sale of some of his property, taking more than four hundred enslaved men, women, and children from Butler Island Plantation in McIntosh County, and Hampton Plantation in Glynn County, both in Georgia, to Ten Broeck Race Course to be auctioned.

I thought about families on auction blocks. During a sale, children were often sold with their mothers, although there are numerous accounts of enslavers wrenching a child from its mother's arms. Husbands and wives often did not fare as well and were separated. Enslavers did not consider marriage among the enslaved as binding or sacred unions. Our marriages in bondage were not legally recognized and therefore not legally protected.

The enslaver could decide whom we would marry, forcing an ideal "wench" of childbearing age to have sex with a strong Black "buck." If a couple who loved each other won enslavers' approval, they would be united in a simple ceremony, performed by the enslaver. And just as he could join couples, he could also separate them.

In 1866 Carr told the Freedman's Bank agent that he had a wife named Sallie and a six-year-old son named John. This would mean that John was born while Carr was enslaved, just two years after the landing of the *Wanderer*. According to the records I found, Captain Aiken never held a female slave. If Sallie was Carr's wife, she may have lived on a different property. To visit wives and family, enslaved Black men needed a written pass from the enslaver to travel, lest white patrollers grab and confine them or worse. If lucky, husbands were able to visit their beloved at mid-week and on Saturday. Some Black men preferred not to marry a woman on the same plantation, as they could not bear to see her abused. Moses Grandy, who escaped from slavery in 1833, wrote in his autobiography *Life of a Slave*, "No colored man wishes to live at the house where his wife lives, for he has to endure the continual misery of seeing her flogged and abused without daring to say a word in her defense."[4] If Sallie and Carr united in slavery, they may have renewed their bonds upon his return from the Civil War, or they may have met and married for the first time as a freedman and woman.

I turned my attention back to Ten Broeck. The sale was the largest in Georgia, but other sales were just as heartbreaking. I still stare in disbelief when I read of people selling other people. Scanning historic newspapers, I read announcement after announcement of auctions or estate sales that included men, women, and children as items to be purchased.

> From the *Savannah Daily Republican*, February 20, 1851: "Rice Negroes Private Sale Nine negroes for sale low. Warranted sound, healthy of good character. . . ."
>
> From the *Savannah Daily Republican*, April 14, 1856: "For Sale. Two Young Negro Men ages 20 and 21, tall and strong. Intelligent, first [c]lass field hands."
>
> From the *Albany Patriot* (Albany, Georgia), January 19, 1860: "Twenty or more Negroes for sale, under the special direction of the will of the late

Joseph Bond will be sold before the Court House door in Albany . . . well trained to the cultivation of Corn and Cotton."

From the *Southern Confederacy* (Atlanta, Georgia), April 25, 1863: "65 Likely Negroes for Sale . . . consisting of families, field hands, house servants, cooks, washers, ironers. . . ."

These are just a few of the thousands of advertisements in newspapers where our ancestors were appraised, marketed, and sold at public auction.

For several days the enslaved at Ten Broeck were corralled in stables, as slave traders rode into Savannah. In smoke-filled rooms, speculators pored over the catalog that listed the slaves by name and age and posted remarks. Negro brokers educated themselves as to who was a good purchase. They struck marks by the names of those they wished to physically examine and contemplated how much they would spend:

103—Wooster, 45; rice hand, and fair mason

104—Mary, 40; cotton hand

111—Anson, 49; rice—ruptured, one eye

112—Violet, 55; rice hand

356—Smith's Bill, aged; sore leg

357—Leah, 46; cotton hand

358—Sally, 9.[5]

The auction began on March 2. The opening was delayed two hours by the downpour. The weeping began. If slaves thought a buyer had a kind look, they presented their best selves, marketing their worth and skill. Elisha, number 5 in the catalog, kowtowed to keep his family intact:

> Look at me, Mas'r; am prime rice planter; sho' you won't find a better man den me; no better on de whole plantation; not a bit old yet; do mo' work den ever; do carpenter work, too, little; better buy me, Mas'r; I'se be good sarvant, Mas'r. Molly, too, my wife, Sa, fus'rate rice hand; mos as good as me. Stan' out yer, Molly, and let the gen'lm'n see. Show mas'r yer arm, Molly—good arm dat, Mas'r—she do a heap of work mo' with dat arm yet. Let good Mas'r see yer teeth, Molly—see dat Mas'r, teeth all reg'lar, all good—she'm young gal yet. Come out yer, Israel, walk aroun' an' let the gen'lm'n see how spry you be.

Elisha then pointed at a three-year-old girl who stood with her chubby hand to her mouth. She held on to her mother's dress, uncertain of what to make of the strange scene. Elisha then added, "Little Vardy's only a chile yet; make prime gal by-and-by. Better buy us, Mas'r, we'm fus' rate bargain. . . ."[6] Elisha's pleas failed. The speculator found where he could strike a better deal and purchased someone else.

And so it was with hundreds of Butler's slaves. It was a frantic scene of men, women, and children clinging to each other for life, saying mournful farewells to lovers, friends, and family. It rained both days of the sale.

For decades after the Civil War, families advertised in Black newspapers, seeking information on loved ones sold away. Those who could read would inform community members looking for family where loved ones were last seen, or when they ran away, or were carried away by slave traders. The voice of the auctioneer, the tears and moans of those being sold, the stares and sweaty hands of buyers, the banging of the hammer as the sale was complete: All these sounds haunted my ancestors and pain my people's collective racial memory today.

As with many people, I had heard about auction blocks, the buying and selling of individuals and families. As the curator of the Black Holocaust Exhibit at the Shrine of the Black Madonna Cultural Center in Atlanta, I had held handwritten documents describing how enslaved humans were sold, leased, swapped, or even given away as gifts.

The selling of enslaved people became personal to me about twenty-five years ago, when my mother and my grandmother, Gustavia Shelton, visited me in Atlanta. Grandmother Shelton, as we called her, noticed that I lived on Peeples Street and softly said, "That's our family name, Peeples, spelled the same way." When they returned home, my mother called and told me Grandmother Shelton had given me an assignment to research our family history. I asked her for family names as far back as she could remember. She gave me two: Shadrack and Elmira Peeples, her great-grandparents on her mother's maternal side.

A few weeks later, I took a day trip from Atlanta to the Alabama Department of Archives and History in Montgomery, where I searched microfilm for census, estate papers, wills, tax digests, deeds, and more. (Today most of this can be accessed online.) It took a while, but I found a listing for the surname Peeples in Perry County, Alabama. It was worth a look. I requested the roll of microfilm, threaded the microfilm reader—a machine that looks like a desktop arcade machine today's youth would consider archaic—and slowly advanced the film.

Soon, I found the inventory of the estate of William H. Peeples. It was dated January 15, 1855, ten years before the ratification of the Thirteenth Amendment that abolished slavery. The inventory included livestock, furniture, tools, stock in the railroad, and "slaves." I skimmed it, hoping I would find my ancestors. I did: Shadrack, appraised at nine hundred dollars, and "Elmyra" and her three children (unnamed), appraised at eighteen hundred dollars. I made photocopies of the document—to hold on to and to share.

I don't know who purchased Shadrack and Elmira. They lived as husband and wife after slavery, so perhaps the same person purchased the entire family. Through additional research I learned of Dilcey, one of the three unnamed children listed with Elmira. I discovered that family I knew growing up—Grandmother Shelton and my great-aunts Elnora and Lucinda (and "Bobby," their sister who died before I was born) were Shadrack and Elmira's great-grandchildren. I subsequently asked my sister Rosy how Grandmother Shelton responded when she first saw the photocopy of the inventory. "She responded in her typical manner," Rosy recalled. "She looked at it, maybe uttered a slow 'hmm,' but didn't say a word." Grandmother Shelton wasn't talkative. She felt things deeply. Seeing those names, knowing her great-grandparents were sold like cattle, perhaps awakened other painful memories, pushed down but not forgotten.

Remembering those who died during or those who endured the Middle Passage and slavery is becoming a ritual among many in the African American community. We pour libation and call our ancestors' names, believing that as long as we speak their names, they will come to our aid. Memorializing the Weeping Time has become a ritual. For several years, people have come together in Savannah at the grassy field that was once a section of the Ten Broeck Race Course to remember those sold. A historical marker was erected in 2008, in a small grassy triangle close to the former Ten Broeck site to remember the sale. In 2017 the community held its first commemorative event. Attendees were asked to bring black umbrellas and open them as if to catch the tears from heaven as the names of those sold were read. The commemoration has become an annual event, with programs held throughout the Savannah area. Sponsors of ceremonies want the local community and people from around the world to know what took place at Ten Broeck.

On March 3, 1859, the last day of the auction, Carr may have wept, also. If he did not see the coffles of four hundred dejected, terrified, worn-down men, women, and children led to Ten Broeck, he certainly heard of the sale and likely felt a wrenching pain. The sale meant forced migration to the unknown, just like the Middle Passage journey he endured. Looking again at Carr's signature card for the Freedman's Bank, I imagined his sorrow, as he responded to the clerk's question about his family: "Mother My Dear in Africa." Carr's pain due to the separation probably never healed. A profound emptiness was felt on both sides of the Atlantic, a mother pining for her son and a son for his mother. This and other separations that Black people have endured give deeper understanding to the Negro spiritual, "Sometimes, I feel like a motherless child, a long way from home."

CHAPTER 9

Carr Among Montmollin's Slaves

On June 11, 1859, seven months after the landing of the *Wanderer*, Savannah's *Daily Morning News* reported that John S. Montmollin was among those missing following an explosion aboard the *Lawton*, a local steamer. On June 17, the *Georgia Citizen* (Macon) reported authorities had found Montmollin's body. He was embedded in the marsh, head downward and buried to the hips. The body was seventy or eighty yards from the site of the explosion, indicating he must have been blown high in the air. The handkerchief Montmollin held in his hand at the time of the explosion was still tightly in his grasp. The family buried his remains in Savannah's Laurel Grove Cemetery North.

Finding the newspaper article gave insight into information I had found much earlier in my search for Carr. While surfing the Internet, I came across the Digital Library on American Slavery, which hosts the Race and Slavery Petitions Project. The latter contains information from court documents and legislative petitions of civil cases filed by enslavers, the enslaved, and free people of color.

I clicked on the section "search by name" and typed in Carr, Aiken, and Montmollin. The Montmollin name returned one result. The document included the petition by his wife, Harriet Montmollin, regarding the estate of John S. Montmollin, filed in South Carolina in 1863. Mrs. Montmollin's petition revealed that John died with a debt of thirty thousand dollars. She petitioned to sell his assets, including his slaves. I checked the 1860 slave schedule for Montmollin. He was listed in St. Peter's Parish, Beaufort, South Carolina, with eighty-eight enslaved people. In 1863, four years after Montmollin's death, his estate included and listed the names of eighty-one enslaved persons, a male named Charles being one of them.

I wrote the South Carolina Department of Archives and History and ordered the estate records for John Montmollin. A photocopy of the estate documents on paper measuring 11 x 17, longer than legal size, arrived in a large white envelope. Among the enclosed documents was a copy of the handwritten record of Harriet Montmollin's petition concerning her desire to sell her late husband's slaves, stocks, tools, and other personal effects to satisfy creditors. Included was a roster of the eighty-one slaves, who were identified by first name or description, and their appraised value. Among the slaves was a seventeen-year-old Charles, appraised at eleven hundred dollars.[1] He may have been the Charles Carr that I was seeking. Perhaps Charles had been enslaved by *both* coconspirators of the *Wanderer*, and maybe a third enslaver whose surname was Carr.

Mrs. Montmollin wanted to hold the estate sale in Charleston, but the enslaved pleaded for a different location. Yes, they spoke up! Mrs. Montmollin noted in her petition that "the negroes have numerous connections about their present neighborhood and might be unwilling to be moved to Charleston." Her request to honor the wishes of her slaves was not completely selfless. She explained to the court that Savannah also appealed to her because she believed the market for slaves was better there than in Charleston. In Savannah, she could sell the slaves at higher prices. On April 10, 1863, the Savannah *Daily Morning News* reported "a gang of eighty-one negroes belonging to the estate of the late John S. Montmollin were sold at the courthouse, the lot fetching $9400."[2] I found no record of who purchased the enslaved. Given what I knew, I worked under my belief that Carr had been enslaved by Montmollin and Captain Richard Aiken. It was a hunch, perhaps a message from Carr. It was all I could go on. When I wanted to abandon the research to reconstruct Carr's life because of too many unanswered questions, Carr would lay a source before me, as if to say, "Don't give up. It all will be revealed soon."

My next goal was finding the Montmollin plantation. It was a search I undertook several times during my years of tracing the life of Carr. Montmollin played a prominent role in the *Wanderer* affair, hiding at least two hundred of the enslaved on his South Carolina plantation after the slave ship secretly landed. I scoured the Internet for historic maps of Beaufort County, South Carolina. I finally found "DeMontmollen" plantation on an 1873 map on the Library of Congress website. Additionally, I located other plantations on the map that would grant more information in the life of Carr and his community.

deMontmollin Plantation in Hardeeville, South Carolina

SOURCE: Vignoles, Charles Blacker, and Henry Ravenel, *Beaufort County, South Carolina* (South Carolina: Publisher not identified, 1873), Library of Congress, https://www.loc.gov/item/2013593120/.

Place is reassuring. If you can point to a location on a map or from the road, if you find landmarks to reference your position, it transforms oral history into something tangible. It tells you that you are on the right track, that you didn't "make it up," or "dream a place" into existence. Looking at the map, I can now envision how small boats met the *Wanderer*, took its human cargo, and traveled up the Savannah River to Montmollin's plantation. The map provided a place—a centering.

A sense of place. It grounds you. Maybe that's why families often return to the homestead at reunions. Our family visited Perry County, Chilton County, and the small towns of Plantersville and Ridersville, in Dallas

County, Alabama, during one reunion. These are places where members of my mom's matriarchal line were enslaved, sold, and under freedom made a name for themselves. We can drive up dirt roads and tell my son's generation, "This is where your great-grandmother Gustavia Shelton lived. Here is where your great-great-aunt Ellen and your great-great-great-grandmother Elmira—sold in Alabama with her three children in 1858—lived." We can go to the church in Plantersville, Dallas County, Alabama. We can walk through the church cemetery and find a few family names. We remember when Grandmother Shelton pointed to an area by the trees and told us that's where her mother was buried.

We can do the same with my father's line. The family church, Old Storm Branch Baptist Church in Clearwater, Aiken County, South Carolina, was established in 1772 as a plantation chapel in the Edgefield District. Around 1866 the widow of Thomas G. Lamar deeded the land on which the historic church stands. A freedmen's school was also built on the site. When I saw the name Lamar, I wondered if it was the same family as that of *Wanderer* coconspirator Charles Lamar. A quick genealogical check confirmed that yes, it was the same family. Thomas Lamar was the brother of Gazaway Lamar and therefore the uncle of Charles. I marveled how my own family history had become intertwined with that of the Lamar family and the *Wanderer*.

The Storm Branch congregation added a brick veneer to the church and imported stained glass windows in the early twentieth century. Today, worship service is held in the newer edifice, up the road from the historic building. We see Garrett names—the surname of my paternal great-grandparents—in the church cemetery. My father's aunt, Nona Garrett Thomas, was the secretary of the Sunday school. To honor her, they inscribed her name in bold letters on a wall in the sanctuary of the historic church. Her daughter, Barbara Bush, still attends the family church. Cousin Barbara still speaks up for the historic building with the "no holds barred" tenacity for which the Garrett family is known.

Place. Longing. Memory. Perhaps that is why the enslaved on the Montmollin plantation asserted themselves, petitioning to be taken to Savannah to be "sold." In bad times as well as in better times, they desired to be near acquaintances, loved ones, and friends held in bondage on other plantations. Family—familial and communal—were important.

Over time, buildings crumble and landscapes change. We can easily lose our footing when "home" is gone. But with photographs and maps, newspaper clippings, and family stories, we can find our sense of place. It happens. With these you can connect with your past and that which has sustained you. With reassurance you begin the story. "Once upon a time, on land far from our ancestral homes, we were once held as slaves. . . ."

CHAPTER 10

Witnessing Quasi-Freedom

Carr may have not been confined to the Montmollin plantation in Beaufort County, South Carolina, or the White Bluff community in Chatham County, Georgia. Under a watchful guard or in possession of a pass, Carr, if trusted by Montmollin or Aiken, may have been allowed to walk through the city of Savannah, catching a glimpse of life beyond the daylong stretch of fields and toil. If Carr saw slave coffles in Savannah, he also saw free Black people.

Free Negroes, or free people of color as the city would later label them, had intermingled with Savannah's population as early as the late 1700s. Savannah's 1790 census listed 112 free Blacks, compared to 8,201 enslaved persons.[1] In 1860 the Savannah census listed 705 free people of color out of a total city population of 22,000.[2] Free people strolled along the city streets, attended Negro churches, established social and benevolent societies, hawked their wares, and benefited from their skills. They were seamstresses, butchers, boat pilots, shoemakers, servants, and more.

While free people of color belonged to no one, they lived under irritating constraints. Freedom had its price. A ten-dollar tax above that paid on property was levied against free Blacks in trades of huckster, caterer, or draymen. A five-dollar tax above the property tax was levied on every other free male sixteen to forty-five years old and free females fourteen years or older.[3] Free men of color were impressed into laboring for the city. The city provided free Negroes with rations while they worked but would not pay them for their labor.

In 1813 city leaders required free Blacks age thirteen and older entering or remaining in Savannah to register yearly with the city clerk. The city recorded their names, ages, occupations, property owned, and the name of their guardians—white people who vouched for free Blacks and handled their legal affairs. Failing to register led to arrest, trial, imprisonment, a fine of one hundred dollars, or forced labor as punishment. In 1818 a state law forbade free people of color from purchasing or acquiring real estate. Free Blacks who managed to own property often did so by relying on honorable whites to purchase real estate and hold it in trust for them, secretly circumventing the law.

And then there were the badges, crude metal tags that reminded free Blacks of their lesser status. An 1839 city ordinance required free people of color to pay $8 for a badge in order to sell small wares.[4] Failure to adhere to the ordinance resulted in either a fine not exceeding $20 (around $700 today) or punishment. Tagged and taxed, free people of color as well as the slaves bore indignities of being treated as members of the "inferior race" relying on good white people to vouch for their character and represent them in legal matters.

White guardians, trusted whites, and good white people—today some Black justice seekers refer to them as allies. Black people today, as throughout our history, need good white people. We have made gains, and those gains have been anchored by white support. That's only to be expected. White people hold the political, economic, and influential power in this nation. Their whiteness grants them privilege, which if they choose can be used for good of all.

There have been good white people. During slavery white abolitionists (Yes, there were Black abolitionists, too, and thank God for them and their voices!) fought alongside Black people to end slavery. White men and women served as conductors on the Underground Railroad, helping enslaved Blacks obtain freedom. Mind you, white abolitionists did not accomplish these feats alone. White allies worked with Black freedom fighters, conductors, and seekers, and they were valued compatriots.

Good white people joined in the civil rights movement. They marched, were beaten, and murdered along with African Americans. In recent protests, an unprecedented twenty-four million people worldwide of all races and hues took to the streets in 2020 chanting "Black lives matter" to protest police killings of unarmed Black men and women. These good whites are following a tradition dating back to abolitionism. And I welcome them. United fronts are stronger and more effective. Wrong, just as right, crosses racial and socioeconomic lines. If you know some good white people, take them by the hand and bring him or her along on our struggles. Rest assured, there still are some "good white people." We just need more of them to help get things done, today as in Carr's time.

As a slave, Carr could only watch free people of color and dream of freedom. He knew more about the chains on the slaves than he did the restrictions on free people of color. Neither John Montmollin nor Richard Aiken left a known diary of plantation or farm operations; however, we can get a glimpse of what Carr saw or knew from records left by neighboring enslavers.

George Kollock, a prominent lawyer and wealthy cotton grower, forced seventy-two men, women, and children to work as slaves on his plantations in White Bluff and nearby Coffee Bluff in 1860. Between 1837 and 1861, Kollock chronicled work on three plantations: Retreat, Rosedew, and Ossabaw Island. His journal for Rosedew Plantation for years 1840 to 1849 gave detailed account of work by the enslaved. Labor included plowing, picking and ginning cotton, burning brush and trash, planting peas, planting and shucking corn, clearing the grounds and building bridges, dams, and fences, thrashing and beating rice. Enslaved Black men hauled bricks and lumber and worked on the public road. Kollock noted the number of slaves reported as ill and the number of women nursing their young, and he recorded births and deaths of his enslaved. In 1842 five women gave birth: Beck, Kate, Minty, and two women named Hannah. By October 9, 1843, death had taken four of the five babies.[5] This information would become important as I researched Carr's family life and learned that several of his children were stillborn or died in infancy.

Kollock recorded that the slaves planted eight acres of cotton and bale after bale of corn and rice in 1843.[6] He also documents that not every bondsman toed the line. The journal included notes on runaways. Billy fled in early February 1840, returning in February the following year.[7] A slave named July ran away on March 25, 1841.[8] There is no mention of the punishment meted out for absconding.

Savannah River rice planter Louis Manigault also was plagued by runaways. Enslaved field hands Charles Lucas and Jack Savage ran. Savage returned after about a year on his own accord, "looking half starved and wretched in the extreme," having lived in the dense Carolina swamp. Manigault wrote of Savage and Lucas, "We always considered him [Savage] a most dangerous character and a bad example to the others. . . . Charles Lucas fled with Savage and was caught August 7, 1863. Savage was sold in Savannah (Sept'r 1863) for $1800 & left with his new enslaver for Columbus Georgia."[9] Manigault noted that Lucas had been in charge of stock. After allowing eight of the choicest hogs to depart from the plantation in some "unaccountable manner, he received his due punishment." How Lucas was punished for the loss of the hogs or for fleeing remains unknown.

During the summer of 1862, the fourth summer Carr would have been in bondage, several slaves died on Savannah River plantations. Sickness and death were constants. Manigault wrote the slaves would "swell in every part of their body and within five or six days the case would invariably prove fatal." He continued, "We lost two prime hands from the disease but it was more fatal on other plantations."[10] Nevertheless, business continued. Manigault chronicled: "42 prime hands. For the crop of 1863 we planted on Argyle Island . . . in rice 347 acres, in corn 40 acres, in peas 20 acres. At camp we planted 12 acres in corn, five acres in potatoes and 10 acres in peas."[11]

Likely, Carr's life was as structured and physically dangerous as the lives of slaves on large plantations. Enslavers demanded hard labor, obedience to rules, and acquiescence to the enslaver or overseer. Head down, back bent, dreams unspoken. That was how the enslaved survived a system that defined them as property.

CHAPTER II

Freedom Coming

Enslavers tried to keep silent the rumblings of the Civil War. Yet the enslaved knew about it. They overheard talk at the dinner table while serving up the best food to the enslaver and his family as their own stomachs growled with hunger. The enslaved heard talk at the docks from white stevedores who predicted a quick, Yankee defeat. The cotton fields whispered news of the war; winnowed rice released it. Bondsmen dared not speak out loud of the rebellion, but they knew. Certainly Carr did, whether he was among the enslaved community in Savannah, or across the Savannah River, in South Carolina. The enslaved waited and prayed for a Union victory, akin to the day prophesied in the Book of Revelation when the sun will refuse to shine and the moon will become like blood. The enslaved waited for what Nat Turner and John Brown, their martyred heroes, foresaw—armed battle, good against evil. They waited, holding a merciful, liberating God to the Exodus promise of deliverance, and hung their last hopes on a Union victory that would "let my people go."

Former slave Lido Brown related years later that he turned to the Scriptures for the outcome of the war: "I used to read the 11th chapter of Daniel and believe[d] that would come true."[1] Perhaps Brown leaned on Daniel 11:15: "So the king of the north shall come and cast up a mount, and take the most fenced cities: and the arms of the south shall not withstand, neither his chosen people, neither shall there be any strength to withstand."[2]

The issue of slavery had divided the nation since its founding. Slaveholders were troubled in 1860 by the election of President Abraham Lincoln, who was morally opposed to slavery, and of a Republican-led Congress that opposed allowing the westward expansion of the domestic slave trade. On January 19, 1861, in a defense of slavery and a rejection of the federal government's interference in state issues, delegates at the Georgia

Secession Convention followed South Carolina's earlier lead and voted to break away from the Union. It was what "fire-eaters" like Charles Lamar, who contrived and executed the nefarious *Wanderer* scheme, had hoped would happen.

In February 1861 Georgia and five other states met in Montgomery, Alabama, to form the Confederate States of America. Before the war's end, eleven states would secede from the Union. On April 15, 1861, three days after the Confederates fired upon Union-held Fort Sumter in South Carolina, Lincoln called state militias to raise seventy-five thousand troops to suppress the Confederate rebellion. The nation was at war with itself. (With the current growing, seething divide, it feels that way today.)

Congress met in session from July 4 to August 6, 1861, devising ways to punish the Confederacy. During the session, Congress passed the Confiscation Act of 1861, which allowed the federal government to seize property, including human "property" used by Confederates to support the rebellion. Meanwhile, the enslaved could be used by the Union as needed. The human property was dubbed "contraband of war." Black people's status was unclear. As neither legally free nor legally enslaved, where did they fit into the emerging social order? It was an early version of the question of "What to do with the Negro?"

Throughout the early years of the Civil War, President Lincoln was hesitant to free the slaves or to accept Black men into the military as armed soldiers. General David Hunter, commander of the Department of the South, was willing to do both. When the combined Union army and navy forces landed on Port Royal Sound in November 1861, Sea Islands enslavers fled, leaving land and the enslaved behind. From where Hunter stood, the hundreds of Black men on the Sea Islands were soldiers-in-waiting. As a military move and perhaps reflecting his abolitionist conviction, Hunter issued a unilateral edict. On May 9, 1862, he proclaimed free those enslaved in Georgia, South Carolina, and Florida.[3] He then took the bold step of raising a regiment of Black men.

Hunter was among the first to raise Black troops in service to the Union. In the fall of 1862 there were at least three Union regiments of Black soldiers raised in New Orleans. Regiments of the 1st Kansas Colored Infantry participated in action at Island Mound, Missouri, in October 1862. These early unofficial regiments received little federal support, but they showed the strength of Black men's desire to fight for freedom.[4]

Hunter believed Sea Islands freedmen would be eager to go to war against the Southerners who had enslaved them. Now free, those formerly enslaved thought first about securing food, shelter, and land for themselves. They were slow to trust white men, even those who represented the Union. In slavery, they heard tales from enslavers that Yankees would put Black men at the front of the line of battle to be used as shields to protect white soldiers. Some freedmen residing on the Sea Islands and other coastal plantations under Northern supervision focused on raising crops and feeding their families. When men were slow to volunteer for military duty, Hunter ordered plantation superintendents to send all able-bodied Black men capable of bearing arms to recruitment posts. White officers swarmed plantations, rounding up Black men, some under the threat of injury or death. Not knowing where they were going, some men hid in the woods while others took cover fearing they were to be sold to Cuba where they would labor on harsh sugar and coffee plantations. Women wailed at the sight of their men being torn from the family. It was a wrenching away of family and friends that many had witnessed too often in slavery.

However, once the men understood they would be trained as soldiers, many freedmen willingly stepped forward. At Hunter's request, Abraham Murchison, a local Black minister, held a meeting where he explained to his fellow freedmen the importance of supporting the government and fighting the "Secests." When Murchison asked who wanted to join the Union Army, every man at the meeting rose. Within one week 150 men had enrolled. Many corralled under Hunter's orders affixed their mark in agreement. Laura Towne, a Northern missionary and teacher at Penn Center on St. Helena Island where I taught my class on African American history, witnessed and disapproved of the rounding up of Black men for service. After Murchison's appeal Towne noted that nearly all were eager to go and that they wanted to learn to fight. By June 1862 Hunter had his regiment, known as the 1st South Carolina Volunteers (African Descent).

Not all in the Lincoln administration shared Hunter's zeal for training these former slaves as soldiers. Edwin McMasters Stanton, who served as secretary of war throughout much of the Civil War, asked Hunter if he were indeed raising Negro troops. Hunter wrote back that "no regiment of 'fugitive slaves' has been or is being raised. . . . There is however, a fine regiment of persons whose late masters are 'fugitive rebels'—men who everywhere fly before the appearance of the National flag, leaving their servants behind them, to shift, as best they can, for themselves."

President Lincoln was vexed. Hunter's acts were renegade moves. Neither declaring the enslaved free nor impressing Black men into military service had the president's approval. Lincoln was still wrestling with freeing and arming former slaves or free Black men. The president quickly annulled Hunter's proclamation and issued a statement detailing that only he, the nation's commander in chief, could grant freedom to those enslaved in any state or states. While the president did not immediately order Hunter to cease recruiting Black men as soldiers, he gave no support to his effort. Lacking presidential advocacy, Hunter was forced to disband the 1st South Carolina Volunteers in August 1862, leaving only one colored company intact. He was relieved of his duty.

Still, abolitionists continued pressuring the president to arm Black men. In July 1862 Congress passed the Second Confiscation Act and the Militia Act of 1862. The Second Confiscation Act allowed the Union to seize all enslaved in areas occupied by the Union, whether or not they had been used in the rebellion. The slaves would be forever free and not returned to their enslavers. The Militia Act authorized the president to accept males of African descent into the service of the Union as laborers or for military or naval services for which they may be deemed competent.

Hunter would be vindicated. In August 1862 Lincoln quietly granted permission to the secretary of war to recruit a limited number of Black soldiers. The Union Army expanded its recruiting activities at Camp Saxton at Port Royal, South Carolina—this time under official guidance. On September 22, 1862, bowing to pressure from abolitionists and bolstered by the September 17 Union victory at Antietam, Lincoln issued the Preliminary Emancipation Proclamation. In it he officially alerted those in rebellion that if they did not rejoin the Union by January 1, 1863, he would declare their slaves free.

Seeing that freedom was imminent, many men in the region saw military service as an opportunity to earn wages, prove themselves as men, and to strike a blow at the power that had oppressed them for 250 years. By

November, the number of volunteers had swelled into the hundreds. With this surge in men, the 1st South Carolina Volunteers was reorganized. Colonel Thomas Wentworth Higginson, a prominent white Massachusetts abolitionist, took command. As one of the first Black regiments, the 1st South Carolina Volunteers trained under harsh scrutiny, with some whites—yes, Northern whites—just waiting for them to fail. Some white soldiers voiced contempt for Black soldiers, arguing that Blacks in the Union blue degraded the uniform and white men. Questions arose of whether Black men would fight or cower in fear. Some believed that the former slaves were too ignorant and childlike to become soldiers.

Men of the 1st South Carolina Volunteers knew where to turn when the weight of proving themselves worthy began to wear on them. In the midst of their camp life, they called on their African ancestors and asked them to fortify their spirits. Their African cultures emerged, breaking the men free from a lifetime of enslavement. Around the fire, out of the commanding sight of white officers, Black men of the 1st South Carolina Volunteers returned in ritual to the world of their forefathers. Higginson, white commander of the 1st South Carolina Volunteers, wrote in his diary of a ritual among the Black soldiers. To set a scene close to the Africa they remembered, the men built a fire and enclosed a booth with palm leaves and covered it to resemble an African hut. Higginson wrote:

> December 3, 1862.—7 p.m.
> This hut is now crammed with men, singing at the top of their voices, in one of their quaint, monotonous, endless, negro-Methodist chants, with obscure syllables recurring constantly, and slight variations interwoven, all accompanied with a regular drumming of the feet and clapping of the hands, like castanets. Then the excitement spreads: inside and outside the enclosure men begin to quiver and dance, others join, a circle forms, winding monotonously round some one in the centre; some "heel and toe" tumultuously, others merely tremble and stagger on, others stoop and rise, others whirl, others caper sideways, all keep steadily circling like dervishes; spectators applaud special strokes of skill; my approach only enlivens the scene; the circle enlarges, louder grows the singing, rousing shouts of encouragement come in, half bacchanalian, half devout, "Wake 'em, brudder!" "Stan' up to 'em,

> brudder!"—and still the ceaseless drumming and clapping, in perfect cadence, goes steadily on. Suddenly there comes a sort of snap, and the spell breaks, amid general sighing and laughter. And this not rarely and occasionally, but night after night, while in other parts of the camp the soberest prayers and exhortations are proceeding sedately.[5]

I wish I could have been at the campsite at night. I wish I could have peered through the darkness to see Black soldiers bringing to life their African past. Of course, the white officer could not relate. Africa was as foreign to him as America was to us. What was that time-keeping clapping? What did the men see with vision-set eyes? What caused the tremble, the trance, the whirling? What did it feel like to leave this world and enter the spirit realm?

Perhaps the soldiers' ritual was akin to the ring shout. Foreign to white men, the shout was known to Black men and women of the Sea Islands. It had survived the Middle Passage and brutal attempts to separate the African from his culture. Its roots lay in West Africa and in the Congo where Carr was born.[6]

I have witnessed the ring shout performed by twentieth- and twenty-first-century Sea Islanders. The shouters form a circle and move counterclockwise in a shuffle of sorts, being sure not to let their feet cross or leave the ground. A rhythm-keeper pounds on the ground or floor with a staff to keep the pace. Those moving with the shout keep time with their hands. They sing out in "call and response," the lead sings a line, the rest answer. The ring shout is a beautiful ritual and keeps this aspect of African culture alive. Older shouters teach it to the youth so the ritual will not die.

The ring shout differs from what we witness today in some churches. It is not the case of a person crying out, running or praising in the aisle and being slain in the spirit. It is a steady ritual performed by a group that connects family, ancestors, and community. It is a steady build that reaches a zenith and slowly winds down. It is united energy, experienced after a formal religious service that says we are African, we are one.

Members of 1st South Carolina Volunteers created and engaged in their ritual space. Their communication was with their God and their ancestors. They encouraged each other to go deeper in the spirit. "Wake 'em brudder," "Stan' up 'em brudder," came the reminder and the challenge. Caught up in the spirit, the participants went beyond the rational—until the trance was broken, and then came laughter and a sigh of relief.

For a short time, the soldiers were in a world where they could be free, sharing an experience that only they understood. With the memories of loved ones sold, with hope of finally being treated like men, they gathered in a circle and moved to the rhythm of Africa. Their ancestral spirit gave them hope, energy, and confidence.

When the Confederacy refused to comply with the demands of the Preliminary Emancipation Declaration, Lincoln followed through with his declaration to free the enslaved in states and territories in rebellion. On January 1, 1863, President Abraham Lincoln signed the Emancipation Proclamation, a military action declaring those held in bondage in states and territories in rebellion henceforth and forever free. The proclamation also officially welcomed Black men into the Union army and navy as freedom fighters. The 1st South Carolina Volunteers stood guard and gave testimony at Camp Saxton as the Emancipation Proclamation was read, in an elaborate ceremony attended by former slaves and white teachers, missionaries, and land superintendents.

Free Blacks and abolitionists in the North also celebrated the signing of the Emancipation Proclamation. On the night of the eve of January 1, 1863, thousands of people gathered at Tremont Temple in Boston, awaiting word of the president's actions. Messengers were stationed in the city near the telegraph office ready to bring word of President Lincoln's decision as it came over the wire. People rejoiced as reports reached that the president had issued the edict. The celebration at Tremont ended around midnight. The jubilant throngs then marched to the Black community of Beacon Hill and entered Twelfth Baptist Church, where the celebration continued until near dawn.

In Savannah, free and enslaved Black men and women gathered at First African Baptist Church, awaiting word of the signing of the Emancipation Proclamation. They too knew of President Lincoln's promise to free the slaves. Most likely they heard the news from Union soldiers stationed at Fort Pulaski and Tybee Island just eighteen miles from Savannah. Waterways and docks were mingling places where Union soldiers, Black riverboat pilots, spies, and scouts secretly shared military information from the North and funneled it to the Black community.

On December 31, 1862, worshippers at First African Baptist Church in Savannah held their annual watch night service, gathering to thank God for their blessings and praying for the safety of the Black community. On plantations, the enslaved gathered to pray that none of them would be sold to settle the enslavers' year-end debt. Watch Night is observed on New Year's Eve in many Black churches today. It is honored as a time for reflecting on the past and asking God's blessing on the new year.

As 1863 dawned, Black worshippers in the Savannah church also prayed that the president would hold true to his promise to declare the slaves free. Their prayers were answered. No one recorded who brought the news of the signing to First African Baptist Church, but it reached the ears of the Black minister and congregants, who departed with the news of freedom in their hearts. Unlike those celebrating at churches in the North, congregants at First African had to hold their excitement so as not to draw attention from city officials.[7] It was a quiet shout of hallelujah and a whispered, heartfelt "Amen."

I wonder where Charles was when the news of freedom arrived. If one Black person in Savannah heard that the president declared slaves free, it would be only a matter of time before word spread throughout the city and to neighboring plantations. The enslaved would quietly plot their next move. Some would wait for the Union to arrive; others would strike out for freedom. Freedom rested behind Union lines. It was up to the enslaved to get there. Some took the risk that many of the enslaved had since the first Africans in chains were brought here—they claimed their freedom and fled.

In past years, Lincoln scholars have debated whether the Emancipation Proclamation actually freed any of the enslaved. Growing up, I was taught the proclamation freed the slaves and thus, Black people were beholden for generations to President Lincoln and his Republican Party. It was quite common, at least in the 1960s, to see copies of photographs of Abraham Lincoln, John F. Kennedy, and Dr. Martin Luther King Jr. displayed with pride in the homes of some Black people. Lincoln's reputation as the Great Liberator began to fade as many in the African American community looked at his political life and realized that he considered preserving the Union as his primary responsibility, which outweighed his personal support for abolishing slavery. Lincoln stated in August 1862, one month before the preliminary emancipation, "If I could save the union without freeing any slaves I would do it; and if I could save it by freeing all the slaves I would do it; and if I could save it by freeing some and leaving others alone, I would also do that."

In truth, the Emancipation Proclamation did not immediately change the status of the enslaved. Confederate states ignored the proclamation. Those enslaved in border states where enslavers were still loyal to the Union were unaffected by the proclamation. As federal troops secured slaveholding states, they read the proclamation to the enslaved, who began to test freedom. On June 19, 1865, two and a half years after the signing of the Emancipation Proclamation, federal troops in Texas informed the enslaved that they were free. June 19th, celebrated as Juneteenth for generations in the Black community, became a federal holiday in 2021. As white reporters and commentators heralded the day of Black liberation, a young African American colleague of mine gave me the side eye and asked, "So, why do white people get Juneteenth off?" I had no answer. I could only join her and marvel at the irony.

Looking at the Emancipation Proclamation through today's eyes, one may see only its shortcomings. But for the enslaved and the abolitionists, the Emancipation Proclamation was a godsend. It set the stage for freedom that was to come; for Black men like Carr who wanted to join the fight, it allowed them to be recognized as soldiers.

CHAPTER 12

Raising Black Regiments

In January 1863, following the signing of the Emancipation Proclamation, the 1st South Carolina Volunteers was officially recognized by the War Department. Later that month, recruitment began for the 2nd South Carolina Volunteers. In May 1863 the War Department established the Bureau of United States Colored Troops (USCT) to aid in recruiting Black soldiers.

For the first time during the war, Black men were allowed to don the Union blue. Members of the USCT received a lukewarm reception. Black enlisted men were paid ten dollars a month but only received seven dollars, as three were withheld for clothing. White enlisted men were paid thirteen dollars a month—of which three was for clothing but could be used at the soldier's discretion. To rectify the situation, Congress mandated equal pay for Black soldiers in 1864 and made the action retroactive. Black regiments were led by white officers, some who resented their assignments or believed Black men could never perform as soldiers. If Black soldiers were captured by the Confederates, they usually were treated more harshly than white prisoners of war or even killed.

Nonetheless, Black men fought, asserting their own agency and self-worth. Frederick Douglass, a former slave and leading statesman, observed, "Once let a black man get upon his person the brass letter U.S.; let him get an eagle on his button; a musket on his shoulder and bullets in his pocket and there is no power on earth which can deny that he has earned the right to citizenship in the United States."[1] Black men stood proud, ready to fight for their freedom. Carr's answers on his Freedman's Bank signature card revealed that he had served in the USCT, choosing to fight against those who held him and others in chains.

For the formerly enslaved men in Florida, Georgia, and South Carolina who awaited the opportunity to join Union forces, Hilton Head Island, South Carolina, was hallowed ground. Here, the 1st South Carolina Volunteers (redesignated the 33rd) and the 2nd South Carolina Volunteers (redesignated the 34th) were mustered into service. The 1st and 2nd South Carolina Volunteer regiments consisted primarily of contrabands—former slaves and property of Confederates, now a prize of war to be used by the Union. Their color ranged from deeply Black, confirming their African lineage, to nearly white—revealing heartless miscegenation. They were natural-born leaders, followers, servants, and field hands. They bore the scars of the whip and burden of bondage. They were men who, if given the chance, would also prove they were soldiers. These pioneer Black soldiers recruited from the South paved the way for the men of the 33rd and 34th and others to come.

The opportunity came for the 1st South Carolina Volunteers to prove they were fighters. The regiment engaged the rebels at more than a dozen points along the rivers of Georgia and northeast Florida, going ashore and destroying salt works or seizing Confederate supplies. In March 1863 the regiment was dispatched to Jacksonville, Florida, where the men were charged to "carry the proclamation of freedom to the slave." The regiment held the city until March 31, when it was abruptly recalled to Beaufort, South Carolina. Some speculated the order was given to dampen the spirit and deny a victory to the Black regiment.

One of the proudest moments for the 1st South Carolina Volunteers came in July 1863, when the regiment made an expedition to the Edisto River, in an area known as the Pon Pon. The 1st rescued enslaved men, women, and children who rushed to the Union boats for freedom. The men also would remember a special woman, Susie Baker King (Taylor), who found freedom at age fourteen and secretly learned to read. She supported the regiment, serving first as a cook and laundress, then as a nurse and teacher. Baker married Sgt. Edward King of the 1st South Carolina Volunteers and remained with the regiment until it mustered out.[2] After the war, she became a widow and later moved to Boston where she remarried, penned her wartime experiences, and became the first woman to publish a memoir of life in the army regiment.

Men of the 2nd South Carolina Volunteers, the predecessor of the 34th to which Carr was assigned, and the woman who assisted the regiment would also leave their mark on history. On June 1 and 2, 1863, Harriet

Tubman, famed Underground Railroad conductor, again demonstrated her leadership skills in a raid on rice plantations at the Combahee River. Throughout the Civil War, Tubman had worked as a spy for the Union Army. Illiterate, she committed the intelligence she gathered to memory. The 2nd, under the military leadership of Col. James Montgomery and blessed with Tubman's wisdom, eluded torpedoes as they traveled the Combahee River where the Confederate property could be destroyed. When the enslaved saw the vessel the *John Adams* and 150 men of the 2nd, they fled the plantation and ran toward the ship. The 2nd fought skirmishes most of the day, reigning victorious. The regiment destroyed at least a million dollars' worth of Confederate supplies and freed more than seven hundred enslaved people.

Perhaps fewer words were spoken of the role of the 2nd in the raid on Darien, a coastal Georgia town deserted by all but a few citizens, free Blacks and the enslaved. The regiment, under Col. James Montgomery and the Massachusetts 54th led by Col. Robert Gould Shaw, invaded the town on June 11, 1863. They looted homes and carried off fine furniture, books, tools, cotton, lumber, and livestock. During the raid, regiments transported any of the slaves who wanted to leave. If Carr heard the report, it is likely that he understood the hesitancy of one aged African called Nancy. When asked if she wanted to board the Union vessel, she refused. Perhaps recalling the traumatizing Middle Passage aboard a slave ship, she told them she would "not go again on the Big Water."[3] At Montgomery's command, the 2nd and 54th set fire to Darien, reducing homes and stores to smoldering ashes. The order troubled Shaw and no doubt many of the regiment. Black men longed to prove their bravery against rebel soldiers, not defenseless civilians.

During the Civil War, more than 2,198,000 men enlisted in the Union Army. Nearly 180,000 were Black men. An estimated 19,000 Black men enlisted in the United States Navy. Black soldiers fought in more than forty major battles and many times were sent in the heat of the battle, often on near suicide missions. Through it all, 25 Black enlisted men (army and navy) were awarded the Congressional Medal of Honor. Nearly 40,000 Black soldiers died over the course of the war—10,000 in battle and 30,000 of infection or disease. I find it disturbing that their worth was measured by the number of Black bodies left to rot on the battlefields.

In every war in which this nation has been engaged, Black soldiers returned fighting for freedoms they secured for others. We continue to fight for the ideals on which America was founded. The spirit we called on during the Civil War, the civil rights struggles, and all righteous rebellions is the same spirit we summoned in the early twenty-first-century protests against the killing of unarmed Black men and women by persons in authority. When we feel we can't go on, that the odds are stacked against us, we call on the unseen, as did Black soldiers in their whirling, circular ritual, to strengthen us and help us to stand for freedom.

CHAPTER 13

General Sherman—Warrior, not Liberator

The Atlanta campaign of 1864 was the turning point in the Civil War. On September 2, Union Gen. William Tecumseh Sherman took Atlanta, a major manufacturing city and railroad hub of the Confederacy. He ordered federal troops to cut supply routes, destroy rail lines, and torch homes, hospitals, and schools. Sherman's aim in Georgia was psychological warfare, making civilians in rebellion suffer and abandon support for the war. The Union victory in Atlanta went a long way in convincing the Northern public that the war had turned in its favor. On November 15, 1864, with some sixty thousand Union soldiers, Sherman led his march to the sea, a 285-mile trek of terror and plunder from Atlanta to Savannah. His men raided farms, carried off livestock, and ignored cries for mercy. Sherman would make the South pay for starting the war. He aimed "to whip the rebels, to humble their pride, to follow them to their innermost recesses."[1]

Now Southern whites stood in horror, fear, and deprivation—like the enslaved they fought to keep. Blacks and whites saw the Union blue coming. The enslaved told how they hoped for a rebel defeat. Recalled Alfred Barnard, "Yes sir, I had a love for the Yankee. I did that. I ever will as long as I live. When the war broke out we were glad . . . the white people used to treat us very ridiculous—sell us families from each other. . . . In the field at work we used to say that we hope the Yankee would whip the rebels and the white people used to curse us and say that we wished to be free but before we should be free they would put us in the barn and burn us up. They said if they didn't come on water, they never could come on land. But finally they did come on land and these small brave men ran away and left the city."[2]

Slaves had witnessed Union forces raiding farms, leaving Blacks and whites to scratch out subsistence. Sambo Jefferson had been freed in 1861 and had worked the land of his former enslaver, the *Wanderer's* John S. Montmollin. He recalled how Montmollin had been "blown up in a boat some years before the war." Jefferson recalled his own confusion and disappointment when Northern men took his property, attesting that he "held to the Union cause all the time." Despite his loyalty, he suffered at the hands of Union soldiers. Said Jefferson, "I saw soldiers as far as I could see as thick as black birds. I can't say how many.... They didn't say anything when they took this property.... They fed their mules and horses with my corn. I don't know what they did with the rice. They took the property to the camp."[3] In all, Jefferson claimed the Union army took $1,478.00 worth in livestock and crops, more than $30,000 in today's dollars, a fortune for a newly freed Black man. The U.S. government only compensated Jefferson $70.00 for his losses.

Still, those in bondage rejoiced at the sound of war. "I sympathized with the Union cause," remembered Diana Cummings, who left Bryan County for Savannah after Sherman's men came. "We all felt joyous when we heard the war was going on because we thought it would bring some good to us. We used to pray for it to come through. We prayed for it all the time. I cast my influence on the Yankee side, and on God's side, too."[4] The enslaved were threatened and beaten for siding with the Union. In my research on this period, I soon discovered a mention of Charles Lamar, who made known his hatred for the Union. Recalled Rachel Bromfield, "I was threatened with the bayonet by Charlie LaMar—a rebel, for carrying bread and milk to Union soldiers. He kicked it all over and threatened to run the bayonet through me."[5]

On December 21 Sherman and Union soldiers approached Savannah. He spared the city, choosing not to burn it as he did the industrial district of Atlanta. On December 22 Sherman wrote President Lincoln a note, to be transmitted via the telegraph office at Fortress Monroe, Virginia: "I beg to present to you as a Christmas gift the city of Savannah, with one hundred fifty heavy guns and plenty of ammunition, also about 25,000 bales of cotton."

The presence of Union troops shook many Savannah locals to their core. While grateful for being spared, many of the townspeople and former residents resented Sherman and all he stood for. From Columbia, South Carolina, young Emma Florence LeConte entered in her diary

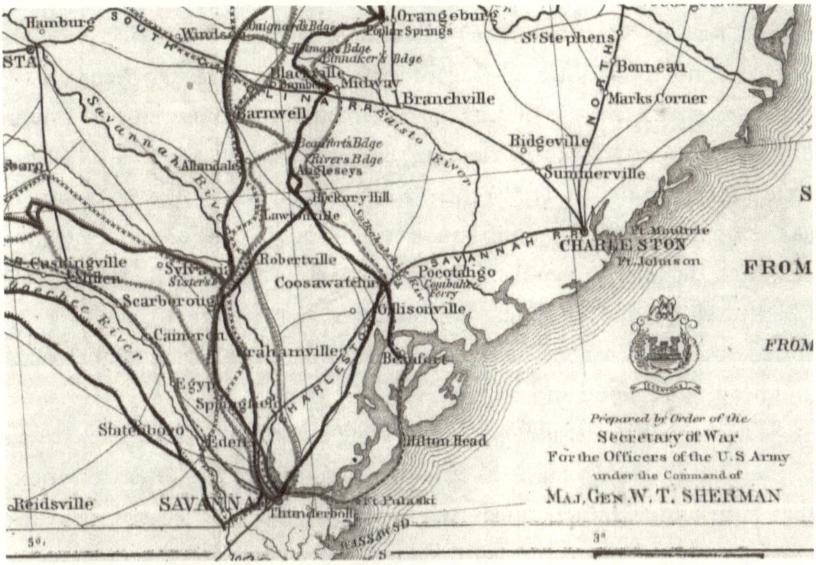

General Sherman's march through Savannah

Source: United States War Department, Corps of Engineers, and William T. Sherman, *Map Showing Route of Marches of the Army of Genl. W. T. Sherman, from Atlanta, Ga. to Goldsboro, N.C.: To Accompany the Report of Operations from Savannah, Ga. to Goldsboro, N.C.* (Washington, D.C.: United States War Dept., Corps of Engineers, 1865), Library of Congress, https://www.loc.gov/item/99447077/.

January 12, 1865: "Savannah has gone down on her knees, and humbly begged pardon of Father Abraham, gratefully acknowledging Sherman's clemency in burning and laying waste their State! Oh it is a crying shame, such poltronnery [*sic*]!"[6]

While white Savannah natives wrung their hands, Black men, women, and children praised Sherman as a liberator. Major Henry Hitchcock recorded in his journal that "a constant stream of them, old and young, men, women, and children, Black, yellow and cream-colored, uncouth and well-bred, bashful and talkative—but always respectful and well-behaved" came to see the Union general. Sherman greeted them with "Well, boys—come to see Mr. Sherman have you? Well, I'm Mr. Sherman—glad to meet you."[7] Delia Rivers, a former slave, exuded gratitude: "It was such a happy day to us when the army came. I went on the Bay and I screeched and screamed until I hadn't any voice. I had no handkerchief with me when General Sherman came and I took my apron off and waved that."[8]

For the enslaved, Sherman personified hope. Yet, he held no special affinity for the Black race. The general held on to his prejudices. He was a warrior, not an abolitionist. He aimed to win, not free. Northern newspapers and others close to Lincoln commented on Sherman's treatment of Blacks. Sherman seemed aloof, perhaps irritated by former slaves. They were ragged, hungry men, women, and children who followed Sherman as the oppressed would a messiah. The able-bodied were useful as laborers, ditch diggers, and cooks. But the aged, children, and the infirm were weight. All needed to be fed and Sherman came to treat them as a despised asset—thousands of persons trailing behind, clogging the roads, and begging for food and protection.

Secretary Stanton and Gen. Henry Halleck, chief of staff of the Armies of the United States, called Sherman to account for the negative rumors that surrounded him. Halleck wrote to Sherman, "They say you have manifested an almost 'criminal' dislike of the Negro, and that you are not willing to carry out the wishes of the Government in regard to him, but repulse him with contempt. They say you might have brought with you to Savannah more than fifty thousand, thus stripping Georgia of that number of laborers, and opening a road by which as many more could have escaped from their masters; but that, instead of this, you drove them from your rank."[9]

In response, Sherman remarked, "Because I had not loaded down my army by the hundreds of thousands of poor negroes, I was construed by others to be hostile to the Black race."[10] He admitted he opposed using the Negro as a soldier, writing, "If Negroes became soldiers, they would demand a voice in government; it was better to use them as laborers."[11]

Secretary Stanton moved to quiet the sharp criticism leveled at Sherman for his treatment of liberated slaves seeking shelter behind his army. He asked Sherman to arrange an interview for him with Black leaders. Sherman invited individuals whom he deemed the most intelligent, primarily Baptist and Methodist ministers. Twenty responded. They elected Reverend Garrison Frazier, a former slave, who had purchased his and his wife's freedom, as their spokesperson. On January 12, 1865, Stanton and Sherman met with the Black leaders, who answered questions about the condition and hopes of freedmen. When asked how former slaves could best take care of themselves, Reverend Frazier responded, "The way we can best take care of ourselves is to have land, and turn it and till it by our own labor . . . and we can soon maintain ourselves and have something to spare. . . . We want to be placed on land until we are able to buy it and make it our own."

When asked how freed slaves would prefer to live, with white people or by themselves, Frazier offered, "I would prefer to live by ourselves, for there is a prejudice against us in the South that will take years to get over." All but one of the pastors agreed. To the question of which was the best way to enlist colored men into the army, Frazier responded, "I think, sir, that all compulsory operations should be put a stop to. The ministers would talk to them, and the young men would enlist. It is my opinion that it would be far better for the State agents to stay at home, and the enlistments to be made for the United States under the direction of General Sherman."[12]

Sherman understood their desire. On January 16, 1865, he issued his Special Field Order no. 15, granting forty acres of land to each family residing on the Sea Islands. Later came word that freedmen and women would receive a mule from the government. This was the forty acres and a mule Black people still speak about. The land gift totaled more than four hundred thousand acres along the Atlantic coast and extending thirty miles inland. It stretched from Charleston, South Carolina, to the St. Johns River in Florida and included the Sea Islands of South Carolina and Georgia. The promised acreage was good, tillable land confiscated by the federal government when Confederate enslavers fled the plantations at the start of the war. It was land hundreds of enslaved Africans had worked by planting and harvesting rice that made the enslavers rich. The federal government would distribute lots to families and Congress would grant clear titles to the freedmen. No white individuals, with the exception of military personnel, could preside on any portion of the land. Federal soldiers would protect the freedmen. With the Emancipation Proclamation granting freedom and Special Field Order no.15 setting aside land, those formerly enslaved began to see a future.

I reflected on the minister's comment "to live by ourselves for there is great prejudice against us." It sounded reasonable to me. I wondered if I too prefer to live alongside Black people instead of white ones. In all honesty, yes. And now I'm thinking, "Wait! Does that make me as bad as they? Am I guilty of being like those whom I criticize?" I recall one

Sunday when I was on my way to church in the neighborhood I love and used to live in. The area is "changing." That's a nice way of saying it's going from Black to white. A fortyish white woman saw me and chirped, "Good morning!" loud enough for me to hear her as I drove by. I was livid! How dare she speak to me as if nothing was new! Was her greeting forewarning of what was to come? More white people? Or was she truly being neighborly?

During altar call at church, I came forward. I repented (sort of) for the horrible things I thought and wanted to say to that white woman. I explained to God that I was upset, that they get to live where they want, and nobody questions them. But let Black people move into a white neighborhood and all hell breaks loose. I told God if He didn't believe me, then let *me* make the telephone call that they make. You know the one: "Officer. There's someone in the neighborhood who doesn't look like she belongs here." It's a non-accusatory statement, with just enough concern to convince the officer to "check it out." If I had called, would the police have come to question the white girl?

Maybe my attitude is wrong. Perhaps I am a baby boomer reacting out of anger and fear. Anger that the flavor and feel of the neighbor is changing. There will be white people walking pedigree dogs of breeds you only see on television. There will be moms and dads jogging while pushing their child in a three-wheel stroller. Windows lacking curtains, blinds, or shades will show off the dark walls and Ikea and antique furnishing. They'll complain about our music and the smoke and smell of our food on the grill and ask a million questions, like "You bake your macaroni and cheese?" I was responding out of fear . . . that more will come, that property values will rise, that they will outnumber us and take over neighborhood meetings and the city council seat. That once again, Black people will be moved out or left powerless in our communities.

Yes, I prefer to live with Black people—sensible, caring Black people. If I can't have us, I'll take sensible white people. (No thoughtless people of any color, please!) But I can understand the concern of freedmen and women. They are the same concerns Black people have today. Whites had privilege, power, and plans. And none of these would benefit the former slaves whom they despised.

Sherman left Savannah soon after issuing the field order, heading across the Savannah River with his army to South Carolina. He advanced on Hardeeville, South Carolina, a town that would factor substantially in Carr's life in freedom.

Carr may not have been among those celebrating the arrival of Sherman's army. He may not have fed the Union troops or stood dumbfounded as Yankees took from Black people as well as white residents. He later would hear of the promise of forty acres. But he had undoubtedly learned of newly freed slaves escaping behind Union lines on the Sea Islands. He heard, maybe only in his spirit, the sound of Black men marching. He saw, in his mind's eye, Black men in blue uniforms, Black men bearing arms, Black men fighting for their own freedom. He saw an opening and slipped through it. Hilton Head, South Carolina, was twenty miles away. There, Union agents were recruiting Black men into service.

In early January 1865, as Sherman counted Savannah a victory, Carr fled Savannah and chanced the land and water journey to Hilton Head, where he stood with other Black men to take up arms for freedom.

CHAPTER 14

Private Carr Injured

Carr did not reveal how he made it safely behind Union lines. Some, like Private Cato Wareing, fled and hid in the woods. During his harrowing experience, Wareing dodged Confederate pickets, ate what he could find, and at times went days without food. He begged shelter from sympathetic slaves and faced betrayal of slaves who feared white reprisal. He trudged through the swamp, outrunning dogs trained to tear Black flesh. He thought quickly when he approached a white woman, showing her deference lest she spew accusations and sound an alarm. Wareing wandered for two weeks, lost, tired, and weary. When he came upon a Yankee gunboat, he exclaimed, "Wen I git on de boat, I thought I was in hebben."[1]

Carr was among the hundreds of freedom fighters accepted to help Northern states fill their requirement for enlistments. The war was losing support within the Union, as white Northerners began showing less enthusiasm for risking their lives to free those in bondage or to reunite the Union. The Enrollment Act of 1863 required male citizens and applicants for citizenship ages twenty to thirty-five and unmarried men ages thirty-five to forty-five to enlist. Many in the North balked. They argued that it was time for the Black man to fight for his own freedom. Riots broke out in New York. The wealthy and privileged bought their way out of conscription, paying three hundred dollars or more to a substitute who would go to war in their place. Unscrupulous recruits signed up in several places and collected their bounty, then never showed up to serve. When an amendment to the act allowed agents to recruit in the rebellion states, agents moved quickly to the South. They targeted Black men, promising them the bounty from the Northern state if they enlisted. The promise was often broken. Colonel M. S. Littlefield, an Illinois lawyer who was counted as a friend of President Lincoln, oversaw recruitment of Blacks in the South. Even Littlefield's recruiting practices came under investigation following the war.[2]

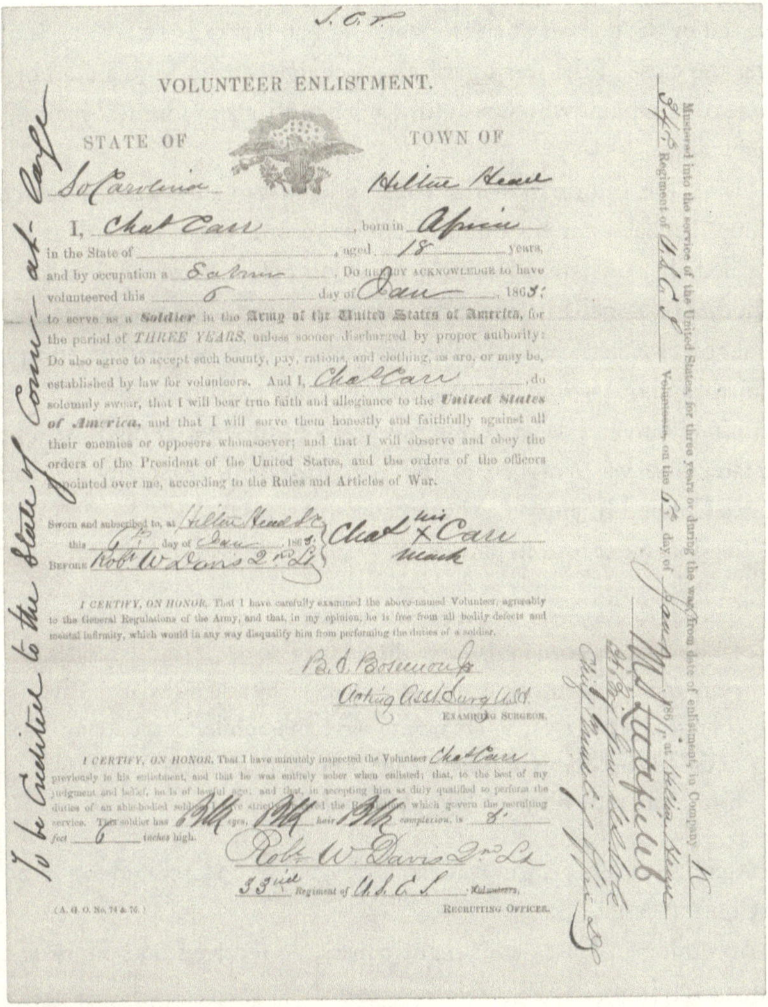
S. C. T.

VOLUNTEER ENLISTMENT.

STATE OF So Carolina TOWN OF Hilton Head

I, Chat Carr, born in Africa in the State of ______, aged 18 years, and by occupation a Sailor, Do hereby acknowledge to have volunteered this 6 day of Jan, 1865, to serve as a Soldier in the Army of the United States of America, for the period of THREE YEARS, unless sooner discharged by proper authority: Do also agree to accept such bounty, pay, rations, and clothing, as are, or may be, established by law for volunteers. And I, Chat Carr, do solemnly swear, that I will bear true faith and allegiance to the United States of America, and that I will serve them honestly and faithfully against all their enemies or opposers whomsoever; and that I will observe and obey the orders of the President of the United States, and the orders of the officers appointed over me, according to the Rules and Articles of War.

Sworn and subscribed to, at Hilton Head S.C. this 6th day of Jan 1865. Before Robt W Davis 2d Lt

Chat his X mark Carr

I CERTIFY, ON HONOR, That I have carefully examined the above-named Volunteer, agreeably to the General Regulations of the Army, and that, in my opinion, he is free from all bodily defects and mental infirmity, which would in any way disqualify him from performing the duties of a soldier.

B. A. Boseman Jr
Acting Asst Surg USA
EXAMINING SURGEON.

I CERTIFY, ON HONOR, That I have minutely inspected the Volunteer Chat Carr previously to his enlistment, and that he was entirely sober when enlisted; that, to the best of my judgment and belief, he is of lawful age; and that, in accepting him as duly qualified to perform the duties of an able-bodied soldier, I have strictly observed the Regulations which govern the recruiting service. This soldier has Blk eyes, Blk hair, Blk complexion, is 5 feet 6 inches high.

Robt W Davis 2d Lt
33rd Regiment of U.S.C.T. Volunteers,
RECRUITING OFFICER.

(A. G. O. No. 74 & 76.)

To be Credited to the State of Conn at large

Mustered into the service of the United States, for three years or during the war, from date of enlistment, in Company K 34th Regiment of U.S.C.T. Volunteers, on the 6th day of Jany 1865, at Hilton Head

M. S. Littlefield
Brig Gen Vols
Chief Comm. Col. Troops

Carr enlists at Hilton Head

SOURCE: The National Archives at Washington, D.C., *Compiled Military Service Records of Volunteer Union Soldiers Who Served with the United States Colored Troops: Infantry Organizations, 31st Through 35th*, Microfilm Serial: M1992, Microfilm Roll: 51.

Under protection of Union troops, recruits were transported safely to Hilton Head. Marcus Maxwell of Edisto Island enlisted at Hilton Head in 1862. Although Maxwell mustered in as a private, he soon was promoted to sergeant. Nonetheless, the recruitment and discharge experience held painful and disappointing memories. He recalled, "I was about 25 years of age. General Littlefield enlisted me. I was stripped naked and examined by the doctors at enlistment. I had no marks as a slave. . . . Shortly after the close of the war I gave my discharge certificate to a man by the name of Tompkins who was getting my bounty claim for me. I have never seen it since."[3]

Using the information from Carr's bank signature card, I searched online databases for his military service record. Carr's enlistment paper revealed that on January 6, 1865, he stood before commanding officers, including Colonel Littlefield. It was determined Carr was sober and of legal age to enlist. Carr told the recruiters his age, occupation, and place of birth, and they wrote the information on his enlistment papers. Officers examined him and deemed him physically fit to serve. Perhaps with little fanfare, Carr was assigned to the 34th Regiment, Company K, United States Colored Infantry. Carr then affixed his mark.

The document read in part:

> State of *So Carolina* Town of *Hilton Head*
> I, *Charles Carr*, born in *Africa* in the State of ______________, aged *18* years and by occupation of a *Laborer*, Do hereby acknowledge to have volunteered this *6* day of *Jan* 1865 to serve as a **Soldier** in the **Army of the United States of America** for the period of THREE Years . . . Sworn and subscribed. . . . Signed (his mark).

Written in the left margin was the message, "To be Credited to the State of Conn-at-large."

According to Carr's enlistment papers, he received no bounty at the time of signing.

Carr was among the many liberated slaves in Savannah enlisting in the war in early 1865. He may have gotten to know several men who also were assigned to the 34th, Company K. Isaiah Henderson joined January 3, 1865, a free man. His brothers Isaac and Virgil also served in the USCT.[4] Isaac died in service in Jacksonville. One can only wonder if Isaiah reached Isaac on the battlefield in time to cradle him as he took his dying breath. Joseph Richards also enlisted January 3. Demonstrating leadership skills, he was promoted to corporal in March 1865 and to sergeant in October of that year. Gabriel Davis enlisted January 5, 1865. He was held enslaved by George Wiley, one of Savannah's leading slave traders and an associate of the *Wanderer*'s Charles Lamar. Davis' military career did not go well. He was absent from duty November 1865 through January 1866. Davis had been arrested and was awaiting court trial for breaking into a store in Fernandina, Florida, while on duty with the 34th in Jacksonville.

By chance Robert Stephens, 34th Regiment, Company D, may have crossed paths with Carr and shared time and painful memories. Stephens was also born in Africa and, like Carr, was believed to be eighteen years old when he enlisted. It is possible that Stephens and Carr were countrymen brought over on the *Wanderer*. There is no way to know, as no written account of Stephens' life has been found. He, like Davis, was absent in November and December 1865. He had served time in prison in Jacksonville, January 1 to January 20, 1865, whereupon he returned to duty. Charges were never specified in the records. These were among the men who, like Carr, took their freedom and enlisted with the Union to ensure freedom for those still enslaved. Perhaps they formed a brotherhood, having enlisted within days of each other and having escaped seeking safety behind Union lines at Hilton Head, South Carolina.

Once in uniform Carr and his comrades settled into camp life. The men spent the early months learning to drill and to serve picket or guard duty. Training Black troops could prove challenging, as they could not read the tactics manuals. Forbidden to learn to read and write under slavery, the men relied on their officers to teach them tactics. If the officers were dedicated, if they believed in their men, they found Black troops learned and executed maneuvers as well as white soldiers. The 34th Regiment proved its mettle at an expedition along the St. John's River along the coast of Florida. In March 1865 the regiment joined with the 3rd United States Colored Infantry and seven Black civilians, and led a raid up St. John's River. In addition to burning a sawmill and distillery, the regiments captured four whites and freed more than ninety slaves.[5] From August to November 1864, the 34th was involved in expeditions between Jacksonville and Gainesville.

While Carr was in service with the 34th, Congress was identifying ways to assist former slaves now in territories under Union control. In March 1865 Congress established the Bureau of Refugees, Freedmen and Abandoned Lands, commonly referred to as the Freedmen's Bureau. The bureau aimed to assist freedmen and displaced whites in rebel and border states rebuild their lives after the devastation of the war. Also in March of 1865, Congress enacted legislation to establish the Freedman's Savings and Trust Company to provide a place for freedmen to safely deposit their savings. It seemed that the government was finally going to aid those whose forced labor had built this nation. Although Carr signed up for three years, his active military duty was short. Three months after Carr enlisted, the war ended. On April 9, 1865, at Appomattox, Virginia, Confederate Gen. Robert E. Lee surrendered his twenty-eight thousand troops to Union Gen. Ulysses Grant. Black soldiers mustered out and were greeted by the newly freed. Black men, women, and children envisioned a brighter day. And it did seem brighter . . . for a while.

On April 14, 1865, five days after the Confederate surrender, news shook the nation. Confederate sympathizer John Wilkes Booth had fired a bullet into President Lincoln while he attended a play with his wife at Ford's Theatre. The bullet entered the left back side of the president's head, passing through his brain and lodging behind his right eye. On April 15, the president succumbed to the wound. Black people who looked upon Lincoln as a long-awaited answered prayer wept and mourned. The Great Liberator was dead. An eerie, uncertain future awaited freedmen.

Carr remained in the service following the war, his company stationed in Jacksonville and Fernandina to keep the peace. White residents were openly hostile to Black troops and resented their presence. In Jacksonville, a white officer recounted that a Black soldier informed him that a resident "owned" one of his daughters. The soldier took the officer to the home where his child was enslaved. They were met by a white woman who cursed them and sneered she had sent the child to Confederate lines because she knew the father would come for her. The officer reminded the woman that President Lincoln had signed the Emancipation Proclamation, freeing the slaves, but the woman would not yield. The officer then ordered the Black soldier to seize the white woman's child, which he did, and they returned to camp with the boy. A few days later the woman arrived at the camp with the Black child. The exchange was made. It was a sweet victory for the Black father.

Not every relationship between Black soldiers and white officers was one of mutual respect. Despite laying down their lives and fighting next to white soldiers, Black soldiers still faced discrimination within the military.

While stationed in Jacksonville, Carr must have heard about the Jacksonville mutiny. The incident turned violent when Black soldiers challenged the actions of their white officers. In the eyes of the military, a revolt against authority was considered mutiny—an act punishable by death. On October 29, 1865, while the 34th and 3rd USCT regiments were stationed in the Jacksonville area, a Black soldier from the 3rd witnessed a disturbing sight. On the parade ground two white officers decided to punish a Black soldier accused of stealing a jar of molasses from the commissary. The officers stripped the Black soldier of his shirt and had him tied up by his thumbs. The soldier's toes barely touched the ground, the weight of his body caused his thumbs to be pulled from their sockets. It was one of several forms of gruesome punishment issued by the military.

Black soldiers surrounded their tortured comrade and objected loudly to his punishment. Perhaps the sight was a reminder of the whippings, mutilation, and other forms of punishment they had witnessed and maybe suffered while enslaved on plantations. Slaves were beaten for "stealing" food for self or for family. A runaway was strung up in front of all the slaves as a lesson on what happened when one dared to be free. Jaws were broken for talking back. A slave woman was physically and emotionally scarred for fighting the advances of the enslaver. No, these Black soldiers could not stand by and watch one of their own brutalized for a minor offense. They took a united stand.

One officer, angered at seeing Black soldiers challenge white and military authority, took out his revolver and fired, hitting one of the Black soldiers. The Black men hurried back to their tents and emerged with weapons. A melee broke out—hand-to-hand fighting and then gunfire. No lives were lost. Men of the 34th were called in to calm the situation. Two days later, fifteen Black soldiers were arrested and charged with various crimes. All but one were convicted of serious crimes. Nine received prison sentences up to fifteen years. Six men were sentenced to death by firing squad. On December 1, 1865, the convicted soldiers were blindfolded and lined up in front of their own caskets. Carr must have winced when he learned the execution was carried out by thirty-six men of the 34th Regiment, Company O and of Company K, men with whom he served.

Carr knew how powerful white people tortured powerless Blacks. He had seen the crew of the slave ship *Wanderer* pitch Black bodies over the side of the vessel and cram the living into the rancid death trap of the hold. He heard of and saw slaves whipped and punished for offenses to the "master-slave order." This may have been the first time that Carr heard of Black men being forced to riddle other Black men with bullets.

Black soldiers executing fellow Black soldiers for defending a Black soldier. I am sure men of the 34th who carried out the order carried the memory to their graves. I do not fault the Black men who were ordered to execute their brothers. I fault the system that teaches that Black people are worthless and metes out the harshest penalties. It is a lesson especially detrimental to the Black community, one that we must push back against and challenge others to do the same.

The Jacksonville mutiny was not the last time Black men would be punished by the military for refusing orders that seemed racist. On December 11, 1917, during World War I, thirteen African American soldiers of the 3rd Battalion, 24th Infantry Regiment, were hanged just outside San Antonio, Texas, for alleged participation in the Camp Logan Mutiny (or Houston Riot) in August of that year. Nine others were hanged in 1918. The mutiny, which ended in the deaths of fifteen whites and four Blacks and the arrest of more than one hundred others, was sparked when a Black soldier was pistol-whipped for coming to the defense of a Black woman falsely accused, arrested, and dragged into the street by two white police officers.

During World War II, a deadly explosion on July 17, 1944, at the Port Chicago Naval Magazine in California killed 320 sailors and civilians and injured 390 others. Most of the casualties were Black sailors, as they were relegated to the manual, dangerous labor of loading munitions. Ultimately, 250 sailors refused to work until safety measures were implemented. Of these, 50 Black men were charged with mutiny. They were defended by Thurgood Marshall, who would become the first African American to sit on the United States Supreme Court. Marshall told the press, "This is not 50 men on trial for mutiny. This is the Navy on trial for its whole vicious policy toward Negroes." The 50 sailors were sentenced to eight to fifteen years in prison, reduced in rank, and discharged "under dishonorable conditions."[6] On July 17, 2024, the Port Chicago 50, along with 208 men who initially refused to work and were subsequently court-martialed, were officially exonerated by the secretary of the navy.

I wonder how Black servicemen and women feel they are treated today. A 2017 Department of Defense survey, released in 2020, showed servicemen and women who reported racial discrimination were dissatisfied with the military's response to their complaints. In 2020 Congress passed the National Defense Authorization Act (2019–2020) mandating the removal of Confederate names from Department of Defense–owned property. I questioned if that will be enough to erase the racism Blacks in the military experience today.

The company's muster roll lists Carr as present from April 1865 to December 1865. He was last paid on June 30, 1865. His pay was halted temporarily in November and December 1865 for one capital letter ("K" for Company K), two numbers, and one bugle stitched on his uniform cap. Carr must have lost his cap during the war and was charged to replace it.

During his last months of service, while on picket duty in the darkness of the evening, Carr heard a noise. His commanding officer ordered him to shoot. Carr did, and the musket "kicked back," hitting him in his arm. The pain haunted him later in life. Carr's recollection of the incident was later recorded by a physician: "While at Jacksonville florida in August the last year of his service, he thinks, and while on picket duty at night, he was told to shoot at anyone who came in front of him. So when he fired the gun, the [musket] kicked him upon the [?] side of the left wrist."

The pain would grow worse with time, as would his general health. I found that his comrades would attest that Carr lost time from the rice fields and complained of stiffness in his arms and legs, shortness of breath, and headaches. The war injury and labor in the rice fields in sweltering heat would weigh heavily on him. . . . Carr would look to the government that promised freedom for help.

In February 1866 the 34th was mustered out. Carr owed the government sixty-four dollars for his uniform. The U.S. government owed him one hundred dollars.[7] If the government subtracted the difference, Carr received thirty-six dollars when discharged.

On December 6, 1865, two months before Carr was discharged, Congress ratified the Thirteenth Amendment. It read, "Neither slavery or involuntary servitude, except as a punishment for crime whereof the party shall have been duly convicted, shall exist within the United States or any place subject to its jurisdiction." It seemed what Carr and other freedom seekers had fought for had become a reality. The formerly enslaved, abolitionists, and free Black men and women rejoiced. Little did they know that the exception in the amendment would be used to justify a new kind of slavery inflicted disproportionally on people of African descent.

Discharged from duty, Carr set out to make a new life remembering the father and sister aboard the *Wanderer*, who also were sold into slavery. The proud USCT volunteer who had survived the harrowing Middle Passage, who escaped slavery to enlist, who mustered out with less than thirty dollars pay for his service in the Civil War, who during his service sustained what became a nagging chronic injury, was now a civilian, and finally free!

CHAPTER 15

Freedman's Bank Signature Card

On April 21, 1866, one month after being mustered out of the USCT, Charles Carr stood at the entrance of the Savannah branch of the Freedman's Savings and Trust Company. Each step along the way to the bank resurrected a heavy memory. Carr had traversed these streets before—perhaps in shackles as part of a slave coffle of men, women, and youth marched through Savannah, or while carrying a pass as a trusted slave who fully understood the penalty of daring to flee. Chartered by Congress in 1865 and established to help Black soldiers and civilians save their money, the Freedman's Bank, as it became known, opened the Savannah branch in 1866 with modest fanfare. With thirty-seven branch offices in seventeen states and the nation's capital, the Freedman's Bank held promise for the race.

It must have seemed strange to Carr, a bank for Black people—most former slaves—housed in such an impressive edifice in Savannah's established banking center. The two-story structure was located on East Bryan Street near the corner of Drayton Street and Johnson Square, in the heart of Savannah's financial center. Hotels, saloons, and taverns where successful slave dealers once gathered dotted the roads to the bank. Businessmen had mingled here to boast of their profits and discuss how best to house, handle, and sell the Negro. George Wiley and John S. Montmollin, both associated with the *Wanderer*, once operated large slave markets in the area. Those days were gone. But the spirits of those prodded and bargained on auction blocks no doubt still lingered. So each step Carr took told a story—of those Africans who survived and those who withered under slavery.

From the bank's opening day, Black men and women came, carrying baggage, bundles, broken hearts, and hope. They trusted the Freedman's Bank with their savings. With the help of a bank agent, these former slaves completed the signature card.

Carr was among the first to fill out an application that day, the 203rd depositor since the bank branch was established. The agent took out an application and asked the usual questions, writing down Carr's answers:

Name of Master, Capt. Aiken

If the agent knew anything about the people in Savannah, he may have looked up from his desk upon hearing a well-noted name.

Name of Mistress, [no answer]

Plantation, Savannah

Height and complexion, 5ft, 5¼, Black

Father or mother? Married? Sallie in Savannah

Name of Children, John 6 yrs

Regiment and Company, K, 34 USCT

Place of Birth, Congo, Africa

Perhaps the agent listened more intently. Those born in Africa were always a novelty.

Residence, [no answer]

Occupation, [no answer]

Remarks, Father Mingo (Dead), Sister Rose, Mother My Dear

Carr added,

Brought over in Slave Ship *Wanderer*. Mother in Africa, others in Savannah

Carr then affixed his mark.

The survivor of the infamous *Wanderer*, one of the last documented slave ships to illegally bring Africans to the United States, had created a primary document that would chronicle his story. While Carr revealed on his USCT enlistment card that he was born in Africa, the bank registration card was the first document that told of Carr's birth in Congo, Africa, and connected him to the *Wanderer*. It was the card that kindled my research journey. Perhaps Carr heard from his comrades of the relative ease in completing the application. He needed a secure place for the bounty—less than one hundred dollars—he received upon discharge from the USCT.

The Freedman's Bank was the pride of freedmen and women. Images of President Abraham Lincoln, the Freedmen's Bureau's Oliver O. Howard, Union Gens. William Tecumseh Sherman and Ulysses Grant—men believed sympathetic to the Negro—graced the covers of deposit "pass" books. In Savannah, the women came first. They sat before bank agents opening day and completed the register of signatures of deposits. Depositors were asked about family and former "master and mistress," places where they lived, military service, occupation, and physical scars. Such personal inquiries were necessary, bank officials reasoned, to help identify individuals should they lose their deposit books. Their answers gave a glimpse of life under slavery. Some freedpeople knew the whereabouts of loved ones. Others, swallowing anger or holding back tears, could only respond, "Don't know father," "Sister, sold away," or "Brother sold away as a child."

Henrietta Saxton, the first depositor, opened an account on January 10, 1866. She told the agent she was born in Savannah and gave the names of her former master and mistress, John and Mary Stoddard. Described as "yellow" in complexion, 4 feet 6¼ inches tall, she lived at Stoddard's place at the corner of Perry and Whittaker in Savannah. Her mother, Philis Lucurgres, opened an account the same day. Saxton affixed her mark, an "X." Mack Williams, a former slave, arrived. Now a physician, he opened his account and signed his own name. Reverend Anthony L. Stanford, a free man born in Greenwich, New Jersey, stood in line. He was the pastor of a local Methodist church.

Members of the USCT came soon after being mustered out of service. Dennis Inman of the 135th, Company K, was the first Black veteran to deposit his funds in the Savannah branch. He also opened an account in February 1866 and gave the names of his wife, their two children, and his former master. Like Carr, George Stober, 34th, Company E, completed his registration. Stober answered that he was eight years old when his father was sold. Isaiah Henderson, also of the 34th, Company K, whose brother Isaac had died in Jacksonville, completed his registration on April 9, 1866. Over the next eight years, hundreds of washerwomen, teamsters, cooks, housekeepers, farmers, carpenters, and others deposited their meager savings and earnings. They trusted the Freedman's Bank. With their money in a safe place, freedmen saved to build schools and churches, support benevolent societies, and finance Black cooperatives.

Then, in 1874, Carr and others heard the terrible news. The Freedman's Bank was in financial trouble. Murmurs ensued of mismanagement, changes in the bank's charter, risky investment, and fraud. Trustees tried to assure depositors that their funds were safe, but there was little use in pretending. The financial institution collapsed on June 29, 1874. On July 2 the Savannah branch of Freedman's Bank closed its doors. The failure affected the community of freedmen. Churches, fraternal organizations, burial societies, and individuals lost money. Looking back, the *Savannah Morning News* printed this brief remark on September 27, 1876: "The Republican party boasts of 'freeing the negro.' They certainly managed to free seventy thousand families of their only means of support by their gigantic Freedman's Bank Swindle."[1]

Throughout this journey, I remind myself to stand where my foreparents stood. I searched for Black responses to the closing of the Freedman's Bank. The *Savannah Morning News* reported on July 9, 1874, that freedpeople gathered at St. Philip AME Church to discuss establishing their own bank or depositing future funds in a different city bank.[2] The grandmother of USCT nurse and teacher Susie King Taylor had invested her life's savings—some three thousand dollars—in the bank. When it collapsed, she was too old to start an economic enterprise anew. Without scorn or self-pity, she said, "I will leave it all in God's hand. If the Yankees did take all our money, they freed my race; God will take care of us."[3]

No doubt the bank's failure bred mistrust of the government and banking institutions among freedmen, who felt betrayed by a promise of freedom and a better life. The hard-earned dollars of Black people and other depositors were gone, but they made peace with that. If there was an uproar, the white press did not print it. One voice of protest has become part of the historical narrative, however. Frederick Douglass was brought aboard as the bank was failing, a Black face to calm the Black masses. When he saw the impressive three-story bank in Washington, D.C., he remarked that he felt "like the Queen of Sheba when she saw the riches of Solomon, that 'half had not been told me'." He later realized that the bank was in deep trouble. Trying to save it and Black people's faith in the new freedom, Douglass poured ten thousand dollars of his own money into the bank. He was too late. The bank had become "the Black man's cow and the white man's milk. Black people fed it, white industrialists drained it."[4] Carr and other freedmen and women, saddled with one more disappointment, gathered strength and faith and pressed onward.

CHAPTER 16

Hope and Dark Days Ahead

The formerly enslaved found a new world at the end of the Civil War. It held promise and hardships. A bitter, defeated South backed by the Union's sympathetic new president geared up to restrict gains and negate promises to freedmen. President Andrew Johnson, a former enslaver and a supporter of states' rights, warred against Congress throughout his presidency over how to reunite the nation and protect newly earned rights of freedmen. It was the era known as Reconstruction, lasting from 1865 to 1877. It was a turbulent era, in which Congress sought to redress the political, social, and economic inequities of slavery while wrestling with a president sympathetic to the South.

Freedmen saw a glimmer of hope in 1867, when Congress passed two Reconstruction Acts. The first divided Confederate states into five military districts under control of federal troops. The second required the military to register eligible male voters and to hold state conventions to draft new constitutions. In 1868 Congress ratified the Fourteenth Amendment granting citizenship to all born in the United States and guaranteeing equal protection under the laws. Congress ratified the Fifteenth Amendment in 1870, prohibiting states from denying the vote based on race, color, or previous condition of servitude (slavery). Laws and amendments could change men's actions, but not their hearts. Angry whites held fast to their feelings of superiority, and Black men and women continued to fight for rights that were legally theirs.

Care of freedmen and impoverished whites fell to the Freedmen's Bureau. Established by Congress in March 1865 and extended in 1866 over President Johnson's veto, the bureau provided freedmen transportation to rejoin family or to search for better opportunities. It distributed food, supervised work contracts, built schools, provided medical aid, and legalized those marriages forged in slavery. Bureau supervisors and agents often were overwhelmed by the needs and wants of freedmen. White landowners withheld pay due Black laborers and ignored the bureau's orders. Agents counseled freedmen to sign contracts, leaving freedmen to wonder if the federal government was truly a friend. With all its imperfections, the bureau was the freedmen's best hope for survival in an angry South.

Transition to freedom was difficult. Hatred stirred deeply in conquered whites. Wrote Gen. A. P. Ketchum, assistant commissioner of the Freedmen's Bureau:

> [F]rom all sections, come freedmen and poor whites, driven to the city by starvation and cruelty of guerrilla bands that spared neither friend nor foe, and besought the government for food and shelter. Thus a vast multitude of paupers were thrown upon us for support. The municipal authorities assisted to the extent of their ability with the help of relief establishments, but confined their efforts to the city poor.
>
> The authorities of Savannah having relinquished charge of the city's poor, which includes about 1500 families, their supply of provisions being exhausted, such of these as are refugees and freedmen, apply for assistance to the Freedmen's Bureau. Unless we help them, hundreds must die from starvation, and I have, therefore, felt it is my duty to issue rations to the really destitute, who have no means of attaining employment.
>
> Amid the most annoying provocation they are calm and reasonable. Insult, assault and persecution they receive not only from Secessionists and their former masters, but from United States soldiers, and the manly forbearance they display, is the result not of cowardice, but of a Christian spirit.

Of work and contracts between freedmen and whites, the commissioner reported:

> Complaints crowd upon us from the Interior negroes who have worked upon the crop until it is "laid by," and are entitled to a share of it for their services are suddenly driven from the plantation, and thrown upon Government for support. Just enough hands are retained to harvest the crop. The proprietor is insulting and defiant, and living as he does, perhaps, in some back county of the state, not within a hundred miles of United States troops, is in no fear of punishment.

> A boy of twelve years old came to my office a few days since, battered and bruised, his flesh lacerated by the cruel blows of his former master, who had driven him off, helpless and hungry, to find food and shelter as best he could. In view of facts like these it is difficult to convince the negro that under any circumstances he will be fairly treated by his former master, and that the rights which that master never before regarded he will now accord to him.[1]

More disappointment and hardship arrived. The Freedmen's Bureau broke the news to freedmen that land promised in Sherman's Field Order no. 15 would not be theirs. In summer 1865 President Johnson rescinded the order that gave them forty acres and gave the land back to former enslavers. It was a promise of land that was not only for civilian freedmen but for Black men like Carr who fought on the Union side during the Civil War. I reread Special Field Order no. 15. There usually isn't much talk about section IV. It read in part, "Whenever a negro has enlisted in the military service of the United States, he may locate his family in any one of the settlements at pleasure, and acquire a homestead, and all other rights and privileges of a settler, as though present in person."[2] Like their civilian counterparts, soldiers too were disappointed. Any hope for Carr and other men of the USCT to receive Sea Island land once they mustered out was gone.

With nowhere to go, no land on which to plant, no compensation or provisions, thousands of freedmen had no choice but to return to the former enslaver. Freedmen and women signed contracts with former owners to work for cents per task. Contracts limited when workers could come or go and who could visit them during work hours. Formerly enslaved Black men and women labored as sharecroppers, with ole massa and his descendants taking the proceeds from one half to three-fourths of the crop. The one-sided arrangement left sharecroppers with a minimal share and in debt to the landowner for essentials bought on credit. Carr found work where he could, toiling on rice and cotton plantations on the Georgia and South Carolina sides of the Savannah River. Being landless, enduring insults, and suffering debilitating pain in the arm he injured on the battlefield took a toll on Carr. On May 27, 1870, authorities arrested him for being disorderly, drunk, and lying on the sidewalk. Carr pled guilty and was assessed a one-dollar fine, an amount equal to twenty-four dollars in the year 2025.

Some freedmen under work contracts took matters into their own hands, demanding fair treatment. White residents of Savannah panicked in October 1871 over reports of an armed confrontation on the plantation of the late John S. Montmollin. Perhaps these freedmen were among Africans on the *Wanderer* dropped off at Montmollin's plantation in 1858 as the crew hurriedly off-loaded Carr and others. Carr likely heard news of the uprising and may have known some of the sharecroppers involved.

Reports were sketchy, but they read that Montmollin's son, Louis DeMontmollin, ejected Zettler, his white foreman, and drove off several freedmen when he learned Zettler sublet a portion of the plantation to freedmen at a rate of twelve bushels of rice per acre.[3] Montmollin forcibly seized all the rice planted by freedmen, using hired hands to harvest the crop. He then held the crop as collateral for rent.

The freedmen complained and a warrant was issued for Montmollin, which he rebuffed. Zettler and the freedmen returned and were met by Montmollin and two of his associates. Shots were fired. Rumors spread that Montmollin and his companions were killed and that freedmen had loaded their bodies in a boat and headed for Bluffton to bury the dead. The *Edgefield Advertiser* reported, "Savannah is even now in a high state of excitement over this bloody and high-handed outrage."[4] One editorial writer of the *Savannah Morning News* commented that Montmollin "most assuredly had the right to eject negroes from his premises for non-payment of his just dues."[5]

Montmollin and his two associates survived the attack. While in Bluffton, they were treated for their wounds and held there for trial by "Radical negro authorities." The law sided with the freedmen, and a few days later Trial Justice J. D. Robertson, who was described in the news article as a "carpet bagger," submitted an account of the incident. Justice Robertson wrote that Montmollin's "first mistake was taking armed possession of the place and the crops; second in resisting the officers sent to arrest him."[6] I believe Montmollin's first mistake was assuming Black workers would accept less than what was due them. These were freedmen, no longer slaves. They exerted their newfound rights, demanding to be treated and paid fairly for their labor.

Some freedmen branched out on their own, churning a plot of land with makeshift tools or human-drawn plows. They prayed the land would produce. Land. The denial or loss of land has plagued African Americans for generations. Black families left land in the troubled South and moved west and north seeking "a better life." Some could not afford the taxes, others were swindled out of their land. Too often African Americans speak of land in the past tense. It's what we used to have. In 1910 African Americans constituted approximately 14 percent of all U.S. farmers. By 2012 we represented just 16 percent of the farming community, owning 3.6 million acres. In 1999 Black farmers successfully sued the federal government in the class action suit *Pigford v. Glickman*. Congress eventually appropriated approximately $1.6 billion to Black farmers who were unfairly turned down for loans by the United States Department of Agriculture.

Despite loss and discrimination, some African American farmers and organizations hold land. The Nation of Islam farms fifteen hundred acres in Michigan and Georgia. The Pan African Orthodox Christian Church owns three thousand acres in South Carolina. In 2020 Black families pooled their resources and purchased ninety-seven acres south of Macon, Georgia. They call their budding city "Freedom."

Freedmen understood the value of land. A former slave asked what good is it to be free if you don't own enough land to be buried on? Black farmers today ask when will they be justly compensated for farmland lost or stolen. Millions of African Americans ask when will we receive Reparations—restitution to the descendants of the enslaved for unpaid labor and suffering under slavery. The nation seems silent on both questions, slowed by studies of these issues that never go anywhere and white backlash.

In Savannah and elsewhere, freedmen also witnessed political gains. From 1865 to 1872, Savannah was a hotbed of political activities with Black men holding rallies, pushing for their rights, and winning elections to local and state offices. Aaron Bradley was one such man. Born enslaved in South Carolina, he fled to Massachusetts, a free state, where he earned a law degree. Bradley returned south to Savannah—outspoken and fearless. Carr may have watched in amazement at this Black man—fair skinned and nattily dressed—whose appearance and speeches on a Savannah square drew hundreds of freedmen and women.[7] Carr may have witnessed the boldness of other freedmen, laborers like himself, who formed militias to secure safety and sustain liberty.

If Carr took advantage of the Fifteenth Amendment enabling Black men to vote, it cost him. Carr was listed in the Chatham County tax digest in 1871, 1872, 1875, and 1880, paying a poll tax of one dollar each year. Prior to 1877, the poll tax raised funds for education. From 1877 to 1945 the poll tax in Georgia served as a prerequisite to voting. The tax would be used to suppress the Black vote in state and local elections for one hundred years, ending with the passage of the 1965 Voting Rights Act. (The most important provisions of the 1965 act were struck down in 2009 and again in 2013 by the Supreme Court after the election of Barack Obama, the nation's first African American president.) Carr, like thousands of newly franchised Black men, stood in line and paid the poll tax. It was a sacrifice for men such as Carr and his Black male neighbors, who were field hands more often paid in crops than in cash.

Some free Blacks and those formerly enslaved sought freedom outside the United States. After unmerciful treatment before, during, and after slavery, they concluded that people of African lineage would never be treated fairly in this nation. In South Carolina and Georgia, some freedmen joined with others emigrating from the United States to Africa. They cast their lots with the American Colonization Society (ACS), founded in 1816 by white Americans to send free Black men and women to Africa. Many abolitionists opposed the ACS, supporting emancipation of the enslaved rather than the removal of free Blacks who may otherwise inspire enslaved Black men and women to aspire for freedom. Still, the ACS continued its mission and in 1822 established a colony in West Africa. In 1847 the colony became the independent nation of Liberia. By 1867 the ACS had sent more than thirteen thousand emigrants to Liberia.[8]

In May 1867 the ACS's *Golconda* sailed from Baltimore to Charleston, where it departed for Liberia. On board were 320 freedmen, ready to start life anew in the land of their forefathers. The freedmen were farmers, bricklayers, blacksmiths, cabinet makers, engineers, and more. According to the *Weekly Constitutionalist*, on June 5, 1867, three of the passengers were Africans (their names not given) returning to their home country. One of the three was brought into Savannah aboard the *Wanderer*.[9] Carr had the opportunity to return to the land of his birth. Liberia was not the Congo, but perhaps it was close enough to home for one kidnapped in his youth and brought to these shores. Maybe he could not afford the voyage or had no desire to return to Africa. After being in the United States since 1858 and fighting for his freedom in the Civil War, Carr may have viewed this country as his home.

Since arriving here on death-trap slave ships, Black people in America have waffled between staying in the United States or returning to ancestral Africa. I'm still making up my mind as to which course I will take—remain in America or leave. Some mornings I wake up, take a deep breath, and tell myself, "Come on girl, you can hang in here!" Other mornings, when the news blares of unarmed Blacks being shot down by law enforcement, of health disparities in which Black women—regardless of social class—have the highest rate of infant and maternal mortality, of groups that have configured yet another way to suppress the vote, I look at my passport, and tell myself, "Start packing." Perhaps I will do as others and divide my time between the United States and an African country. Sometimes, I just need a break, a minute of sanity, time to replenish and regroup.

For every step freedmen took forward, they were shoved two steps back. Reconstruction that promised so much was doomed to fail. Racism would not let it succeed. Carr may have succumbed to liquor that led to his arrest in 1870 to erase haunting memories of the capture, Middle Passage, chattel slavery, war, and his present reality. He may have looked around and realized that he wasn't really free, at least not like white men—rich or poor—who had privileges because they were white. For Black men and women of the reconstructed South, true freedom was a long way off.

CHAPTER 17

Wife Dianah and Help for Veterans

Despite the hardships he endured, Carr began building his life as a free man in Savannah. I wanted to locate his wife Sallie and his six-year-old son, John, listed on the signature card. Newly freed Blacks often made it a priority to find loved ones and reunite their families broken by the selling away of the enslaved. Checking for Sallie with the last name Aiken and Carr in the 1870 census, the first federal census to list all African Americans by first and last name, yielded no results.

It is not unusual that a host of freedmen cannot be found in the 1870 census. They were moving about, they were choosing their own last names. Without Sallie's last name, however, finding her in the 1870 census would also be an arduous undertaking. I also began to wonder if Sallie and Carr met in Savannah after he had been mustered out of the USCT and if John may have been Sallie's child, but not Carr's.

In my research I found that Carr spoke of a woman in Savannah to a friend, Chrismas Graham, who recalled, "He [Carr] told me he had a woman in Savannah whom he had lived with, but I do not recall her name."[1] Carr never again mentioned Sallie or John, unusual for a husband and a father. I found no record of a marriage between the two. I accepted the fact that I may never understand Carr's and Sallie's relationship and that I may never find Sallie and John.

I searched census records, continuing to look for Carr. The enumerator in the 1880 federal census recorded Carr in Yamassee, South Carolina, in the household of Dick and Beck Bythewood. Carr was noted as thirty-five years of age and was listed as their son. To my surprise, Carr also had a new wife, Di, age twenty-two. All were farmhands. The enumerator reported that all had been born in South Carolina. No one could read or write.[2]

This information was profoundly different from what Carr related nearly fifteen years earlier on his register for the Freedman's Bank. Enumerators often relied on information from neighbors if individuals were not home. It may be that Carr and others considered the Bythewood as extended family, if not blood kinship. While the enumerator recorded Carr's birthplace as South Carolina, Carr always claimed Africa as his birthplace and that of his mother and father.

After finding Carr enumerated in 1880, I was disappointed to discover he would not appear in the census again. Likely, Carr traveled between Savannah, Georgia, for work and Yemassee, South Carolina, for home and community. The assistant marshal who conducted the 1870 Agriculture Census for Beaufort County commented, "The small product realized from the quantity of land planted by the colored people is attributable to the extreme drought that prevailed during the summer of 1869 beside the fact additional of the cultivation of crops being neglected owing to a want of subsistence, by which they are compelled to desert their farms and work day labor. A number of the farmers who crop in Carolina claim residence and citizenship across the Savannah River, in Georgia."[3]

Carr's life may have continued as one of strain and backbreaking farming with little hope of better days, had it not been for another government promise. In 1890 Congress passed the Dependent Pension Act. It was a sweeping act that expanded pension eligibility to Union veterans who had served for at least ninety days, had an honorable discharge, and who were unable to work regardless of when and how injuries were sustained. It also provided for widows of veterans and their dependent children, ages sixteen years or younger. In the eyes of veterans, the act gave life to words spoken by President Lincoln twenty-five years earlier on March 4, 1865, during his second inaugural address: "With malice toward none, charity for all . . . let us strive on to finish the work we are in; to bind up the nation's wounds; to care for him who shall have borne the battle, and for his widow, and his orphan." Those who had served the Union breathed a sigh of relief.

Word that the government would help take care of its disabled loyal veterans and their families through a pension was welcomed news. I took the chance to see if Carr had applied for a pension. He injured his arm while on garrison duty in Jacksonville. If it had troubled him or prevented him from working, Carr may have been eligible for an invalid soldier's pension. According to the Dependent and Disability Pension Act of 1890,

Carr could receive between six and twelve dollars a month, depending on the degree of his inability to work. This would be guaranteed money—something of which most freedmen could only dream. If Dianah continued to work, with their combined income, life could look a little brighter. Over time, with a pension Carr could save to buy a patch of land, seed, or an ox, work horse, or mule, gaining greater financial security and independence. Surely his military service, the injury he sustained while firing his musket, and his waning health merited government support. And indeed, Carr applied for the invalid soldier's pension. The documents in his file revealed more about his harrowing experience aboard the *Wanderer*, his life, and that of his family and the community he called home.

CHAPTER 18

Pension Application and the Terrible Voyage

Carr applied for an invalid pension September 13, 1890. He attested that he was "duly unable to earn support by reason of rheumatism in my legs sometimes I can't walk all so [*sic*] getting headaches and pain in arm." Serving as witnesses were W. R. Hubbard and Marcus Maxwell, who twenty-five years later still held in his mind the humiliating experience of being stripped naked and examined upon joining the USCT. Hubbard signed the document; Maxwell affixed his mark.

The bureau received the application April 25, 1891, and assigned Carr's pension application the number 912191. His hardship claim was rheumatism. Carr was to report to Dr. Arthur Prioleau, in Beaufort. Carr requested to see a physician in Savannah, as that city was more convenient to his home. Delays plagued the process early. Carr again wrote to the bureau. In a letter dated June 20, 1892, he stated that he had not received orders to be examined and that he was willing to go at any time.

At some point Edward S. Bailey, an attorney based in Washington, D.C., was hired or assigned to Carr's case. Carr paid Bailey ten dollars, the standard fee the federal government allowed an attorney to charge when assisting a veteran complete an invalid pension application. That would be more than $370.00 in 2025! I can't imagine how he found the money to pay the attorney. Bailey also petitioned the bureau to promptly comply with Carr's request to be examined by a physician in Savannah. Hearing nothing from the Pensions Bureau, Carr sought someone in Hardeeville who could help. On the letterhead of C. A. Williams, a dealer in general merchandise, Williams penned a letter to the bureau on behalf of Carr, dated February 20, 1893.

> Dear sir
> I made a claim for pension under the new law and I can not hear any thing from it. I am not able to do any work. Please bring it up for me and let me know when I can get it.

Yours truly
Charles Car [*sic*] [his mark]
Late private Co K 34 U.S.C.T.[1]
P.O. Hardeeville, S.C.

The bureau responded July 31, 1894. It directed Carr to Savannah to the office of E. H. Nichols, MD, the bureau's examining physician. Carr was to report any Wednesday within three months of the order.

On August 20 Carr met with Dr. Nichols at his office at 84 South Broad Street, near Savannah's Old Cemetery. Approaching Broad Street, Carr was within walking distance of ventures once associated with slavery and the *Wanderer*: the Custom House where the *Wanderer* trial was held; Johnson Square, the heart of Savannah's slave trading center where bordering streets held slave brokerage operations of *Wanderer* coconspirator John Montmollin and other men in the trade; and Wright Square, across from the old courthouse where on the first Tuesday of each month, slaves were hammered off to the highest bidder.

Dr. Nichols examined Carr and jotted his notes. Cause of disability: injury to left arm and rheumatism. He made the following statement upon which Carr based his claim:

> While at Jacksonville florida [*sic*] in August the last year of his service, he thinks, and while on picket duty at night, he was told to shoot at anyone who came in front of him. So when he fired the gun, the [musket] kicked him upon the [?] side of the left wrist. His rheumatism comes on in winter. In damp weather also.

Upon examination, Dr. Nichols noted the following: pulse rate 72; respiration 18; temperature 98 ½; height 5 feet 4 inches; weight 135 pounds; age 55 years.

The interview continued, with Dr. Nichols reporting:

> This applicant's history is a queer one; he is probably the only one of the original gulla negroes who were brought over to this country from the Congo in or about 1859 or 1860 in the "Slaver WANDERER" by Charlie Lamar of this state. He was about 20 years of age at the time, and remembers the voyage well and tells how many died upon that terrible trip. Sometimes 15 were picked up dead in the morning and

> thrown overboard. He is a squarely built negro of 55, sound in mind and limb. Heart, lung and all internal organs perfect. The area to which he directs affliction shows no evidence of ever having been hurt; at all. I questioned him if he showed it at the time to the "DOCTOR". He said no, nor did he ever lay up or ever go to the hospital. So much for the arm it is all bosh, and does not deserve any consideration as he is perfect in all movement and strength. I fail to see any evidence of any rheumatism. He is undoubtedly left handed. And the hand, (arm), he says was hurt is much more muscular and hard [?] than the good one. He is in my opinion, entitled to a non rating for the disability caused by injury to the left arm—nil
>
> Signed E. H. Nichols, M.D.[2]

Nichols wrote of Carr, "And he remembers the voyage well. . . ." There was no diagnosis for Carr's feelings. Today, people troubled by a past horror may be diagnosed with post-traumatic stress disorder. For descendants of those herded on slave ships, the capture in Africa and the horrid Middle Passage were the beginnings of a succession of traumatizing events. What African Americans live with today are traumas experienced by each generation, resulting in what social scientist and clinical psychologist Dr. Joy DeGruy calls post-traumatic slave syndrome.

I was surprised that Dr. Nichols did not believe Carr. I guess I should not have been. African American cries of pain often go unheard by white medical professionals. Surely our pain cannot be significant or worth more than noting. A prevailing view was that Black people were built to endure pain. That's why the enslaved were worked from sunup to sundown. That's why Dr. J. Marion Sims, a nineteenth-century physician often heralded as the "father of gynecology," experimented on enslaved women, without administering anesthesia.

Belief that Black people have a higher tolerance for pain than their white counterparts still influences how some in the medical profession treat African American patients. An April 2016 report titled "Racial Bias in Pain Assessment and Treatment Recommendations, and False Beliefs About Biological Differences Between Blacks and Whites," published in *Proceedings of the National Academy of Sciences*, found nearly 60 percent of the 222 white medical students and residents in the study held beliefs that African Americans had thicker skins and 12 percent thought their

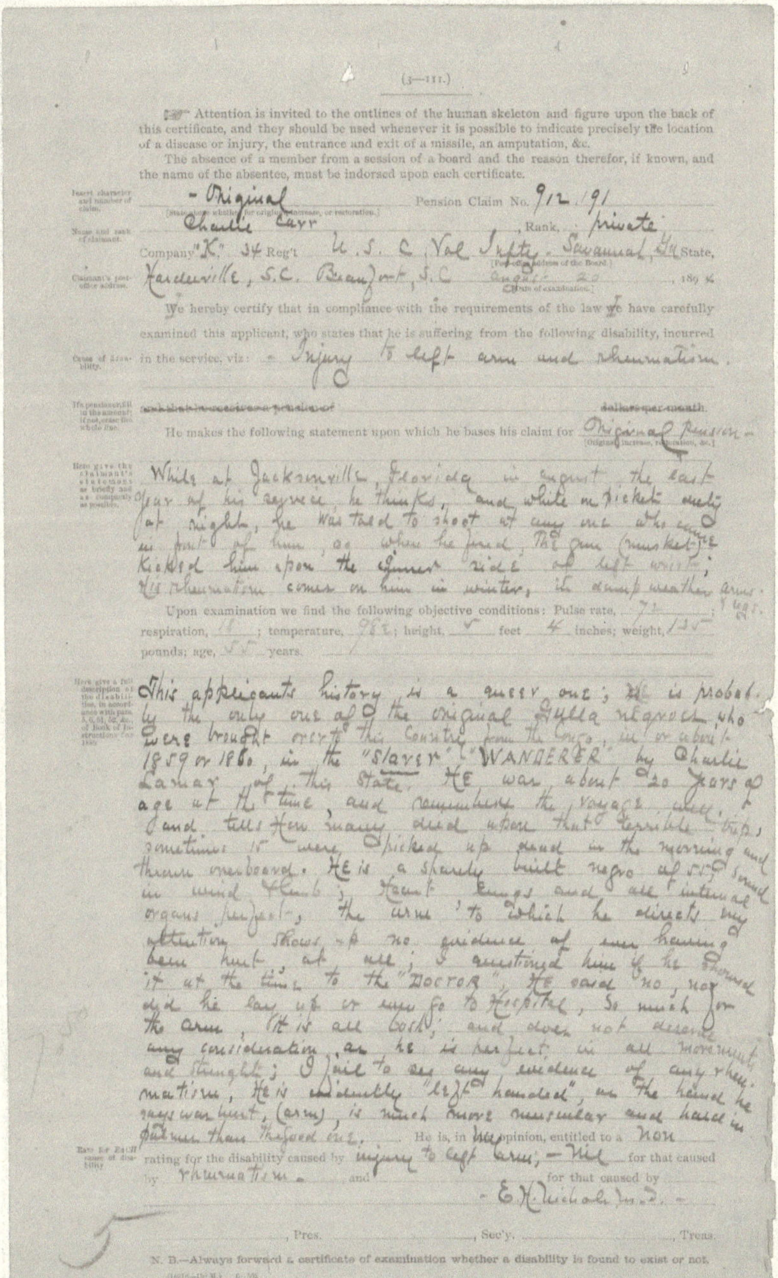
(3—111.)

Attention is invited to the outlines of the human skeleton and figure upon the back of this certificate, and they should be used whenever it is possible to indicate precisely the location of a disease or injury, the entrance and exit of a missile, an amputation, &c.

The absence of a member from a session of a board and the reason therefor, if known, and the name of the absentee, must be indorsed upon each certificate.

Insert character and number of claim. — Original — Pension Claim No. 912,191

Name and rank of claimant. Charlie Carr, Rank, private

Company "K." 34 Reg't U. S. C. Vol Infty. Savannah, Ga State,

Claimant's post-office address. Hardeeville, S.C. Beaufort, S.C. August 20, 189[illegible]

We hereby certify that in compliance with the requirements of the law I have carefully examined this applicant, who states that he is suffering from the following disability, incurred

Cause of disability. in the service, viz: Injury to left arm and rheumatism.

If pensioner, fill in the amount; if not, erase the whole line. ~~and that he is receiving a pension of~~ ~~dollars per month.~~

He makes the following statement upon which he bases his claim for Original Pension —

Here give the claimant's statements as briefly and as compactly as possible. While at Jacksonville, Florida in August the last year of his service he thinks, and while on picket duty at night, he was told to shoot at any one who came in front of him, so when he fired, the gun (musket) kicked him upon the inner side of left wrist; His rheumatism comes on him in winter, in damp weather arms & legs.

Upon examination we find the following objective conditions: Pulse rate, 72; respiration, 18; temperature, 98½; height, 5 feet 4 inches; weight, 135 pounds; age, 55 years.

Here give a full description of the disabilities, in accordance with pars. 5, 6, 51, 52, &c., of Book of Instructions for 1889. This applicants history is a queer one; He is probably the only one of the original Gulla negroes who were brought over to this country from the Congo, in or about 1859 or 1860, in the "slaver" "WANDERER" by Charlie Lamar of this State. He was about 20 years of age at the time, and remembers the voyage well, and tells how many died upon that terrible trip, sometimes 15 were picked up dead in the morning and thrown overboard. He is a sparely built negro of 55; sound in wind & limb; Heart, lungs and all internal organs perfect; the arm to which he directs my attention shows up no evidence of ever having been hurt, at all; I questioned him if he showed it at the time to the "DOCTOR", He said "no", nor did he lay up or ever go to Hospital, So much for the arm, It is all bosh; and does not deserve any consideration, as he is perfect in all movements and strength; I fail to see any evidence of any rheumatism, He is evidently "left handed", as the hand he says was hurt, (arm), is much more muscular and harder in palm than the good one. He is, in my opinion, entitled to a Non

Rate for each cause of disability. rating for the disability caused by injury to left arm, — Nil for that caused by rheumatism, and for that caused by

— E. H. Nichols M.D. —

, Pres. , Sec'y. , Treas.

N. B.—Always forward a certificate of examination whether a disability is found to exist or not.

(16218—15 M.) 6—[illegible]

No other disabilities found to exist.

Carr tells of the dead thrown overboard

SOURCE: National Archives in Washington, D.C., Charley Carr (Pvt. Co. K USCT, Union, Civil War), Invalid pension application no. 912191 (Rejected) Department of Veteran Affairs, RG 15. Also in WO no. 638231 (Rejected).

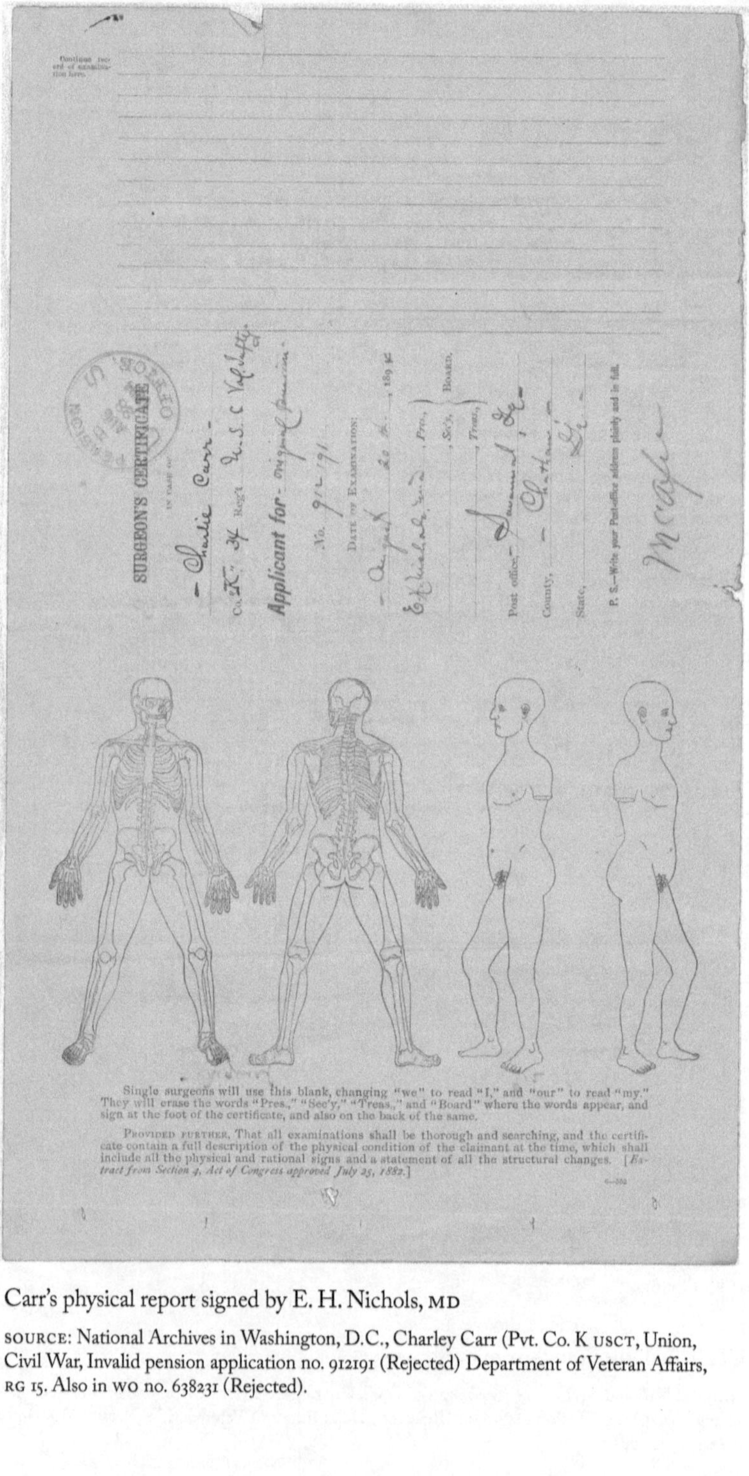
Single surgeons will use this blank, changing "we" to read "I," and "our" to read "my." They will erase the words "Pres.," "Sec'y," "Treas.," and "Board" where the words appear, and sign at the foot of the certificate, and also on the back of the same.

PROVIDED FURTHER, That all examinations shall be thorough and searching, and the certificate contain a full description of the physical condition of the claimant at the time, which shall include all the physical and rational signs and a statement of all the structural changes. [*Extract from Section 4, Act of Congress approved July 25, 1882.*]

Carr's physical report signed by E. H. Nichols, MD

SOURCE: National Archives in Washington, D.C., Charley Carr (Pvt. Co. K USCT, Union, Civil War, Invalid pension application no. 912191 (Rejected) Department of Veteran Affairs, RG 15. Also in WO no. 638231 (Rejected).

nerve endings were less sensitive than those of white people. Medical students and residents who endorsed false beliefs like these were more likely to rate the pain of a Black patient as less severe than that of an otherwise identical white patient and less likely to recommend treating Black patients' pain.[3]

Carr's inability to convince Dr. Nichols that he was in pain reflected the struggle of Black Civil War veterans to be awarded an invalid pension. The Pensions Bureau did not grant them the same leniency it gave to white soldiers. When white and Black veterans claimed disabilities that were easily verifiable, outcomes were similar.[4] But when verification required a degree of trust, Black veterans fared worse than whites. Sadly, Black veterans face the same discrimination in the twenty-first century. In July 2023 the Government Accountability Office released a report, titled "VA Disability Benefits," that found between the years 2010 and 2020, Black veterans had the lowest approval rate for disability claims among all racial and ethnic groups. According to the report, Black veterans' approval rate for disability claims was 61 percent compared to 75 percent for white veterans.[5] It is a sad continuing story of Black pain not being taken seriously, even if the pain is felt by those who have put their lives on the line for this nation.

Carr undoubtedly kept his memories of the Middle Passage in a secret place in his soul. When asked, he probably shared more of what he recollected of the gruesome journey than what he told the white Bureau of Pension physician or what was noted in the Freedman's Bank register. Carr remembered the daily heaving of bodies overboard on the slave ship, which to him represented the tragic loss of comrades. If not for this record of his hellish, forced journey across the Atlantic, Carr's firsthand experience would be lost to history. Corrie, the captain, and Charles Lamar, the mastermind of the *Wanderer*'s illegal expedition, would go down in history. To them, those deaths of the Africans on board equated to a loss of money. To Carr it was a loss of community and a message sent that African people were less than human. Black people, when no longer of value, could be thrown out like garbage. Killing a Black person meant nothing. Black lives did not and, to some today, do not matter.

Discovering Carr was a turning point in my understanding of the slave trade. I had read the journals kept by slave ship captains and other whites who were party to the business of human cargo, but in Carr's succinct account I felt the African's pain. Enslavers have recorded the number of deaths, but never had I read a primary account of one who witnessed death and who undoubtedly winced at the retelling of the traumatic voyage. Carr remembered it well. In my mind's eye, I could see the bodies heaved over the side of the ship. His haunting memory stirs something deep inside me whenever I think of Carr.

I wish Carr had said more, or that Dr. Nichols had recorded more, if Carr spoke of the voyage. "Sometimes 15 were picked up dead in the morning and thrown overboard." What else did Carr remember? The cries of the terrified or despondent? The stench of the slave ship? The cockroaches that crawled on the captives or in their noses, mouths, or private parts? Did he remember sharks, which upon smelling blood and awaiting the next corpse, swam close by? Did he remember the sickening smell of the salt water, or the rough sway of the ship in the midst of the storm? Did he recall the *Wanderer* racing to outrun slave ship patrollers? Or its slow departure from the Congo River, heavy-laden with captives? The Middle Passage was an approximate forty-five-day undertaking. Did the pain of hunger stir his memory? How about waking up perhaps chained to the dead—someone he knew, someone from his village, someone with whom he shared hopes of taking over the vessel and returning home?

Carr left Dr. Nichols' office, perhaps without knowing that the physician ruled his claim foolishness. What appeared to impress the physician most was that Carr was a survivor of the *Wanderer*. By the time Carr was examined by Dr. Nichols, more than thirty-five years had passed since the *Wanderer* landed, and the event still reverberated with at least one Savannah resident. In his medical report, Dr. Nichols described Carr as one of the original gulla (Gullah) negroes who came over on the *Wanderer*. *Gullah*, like *Gullah Geechee*, is a term heard more and more often today referencing descendants of enslaved Africans forced to work on Lowcountry coastal plantations. Isolated from the mainland for generations, these descendants retained speech patterns, foodways, crafts, and more that mirror those of West and Central Africa.

For many who know of revolts by the enslaved, the name Gullah Jack comes to mind. He conspired with Denmark Vesey in 1822 to spark a rebellion in Charleston, South Carolina. A number of scholars believe

Gullah is a variation of the word *Gola*, which names a people of Sierra Leone and Liberia. Other scholars suggest the word describes one from Angola, or BaKongo—a spelling that some contemporary scholars prefer rather than dwelling on the area's subjugation to the Belgium Congo—the region adjacent to the Congo from where Carr and his countrymen were taken and sold.

Dr. Nichols closed his book on Carr, seeing other veterans who needed his attention. No doubt Carr's story was one Dr. Nichols would remember, or at least one that caused him to ponder and shake his head.

CHAPTER 19

Carr's African American Physician

I took note that the Bureau of Pension did not seek information from Carr's family physician, Benjamin James, MD, who had been born enslaved in Baltimore. His grandmother purchased his freedom and that of his mother when he was an infant, and he received his medical education at two historically Black educational institutions. He attended the medical department of Lincoln University in Pennsylvania, founded in 1854 as Ashmun Institute, and earned his medical degree in 1876 from the medical department of Howard University, in Washington, D.C., founded in 1867 by Gen. Oliver O. Howard with financial support from the Freedmen's Bureau. Well respected, Dr. James practiced medicine in Savannah and in the Beaufort County, South Carolina, city of Beaufort, as well as the towns of Sheldon and Jonesville, close to where Carr spent his adult life.[1] Dr. James began treating Carr in 1890 for rheumatism, which caused Carr to lose at least a third of his working time, and later for heart trouble and dropsy.[2]

In addition to being a physician, Dr. James was a missionary and a revered member of the American Missionary Association (AMA), a Protestant abolitionist organization founded in 1846, and a primary educator of freedmen in spite of open hostility from angry whites. In the late 1870s Dr. James joined a corps of Black missionaries and their families and traveled with the AMA to West Africa to serve at the Mendi Mission in Sierra Leone. Dr. James, his family, and other missionaries and their families sailed from New York on the barque *Jasper* on September 24, 1877, arriving in Sierra Leone nearly two months later. Mr. A. E. White, an AMA missionary, wrote of their travels: "As you know we had fifty seven days on our voyage. The sea is a bad road to ride. All of us were sick some, and Mr. and Mrs. Snelson, Mrs. James, and Mrs. Pardoe's little boy we thought would not be able to make the voyage."[3]

As he was Carr's family physician, Dr. James and Carr grew to know each other and likely shared stories of their different lives. Dr. James and Carr had journeyed across the Atlantic, but under vastly different circumstances. Dr. James was born in the North and enslaved. Carr lived his life in America enslaved until he struck out for freedom. Dr. James crossed the Atlantic to Africa on his own free will. Carr was carried across the ocean in the other direction in shackles. While America brought slavery to Carr, Africa brought death to Dr. James' family. In the midst of all his medical and missionary work, Dr. James lost his first wife to sickness in Sierra Leone. The AMA sent word of her passing to their colleagues in this statement in 1878:

> With painful regret I must inform you that Death has entered our ranks and has taken away one of our missionaries—our sister, Mrs. James. I wrote you in my last that she and her little daughter were unwell. I learned by letter May 20th from Dr. James (who is stationed at Avery), that his wife was seized with a convulsion on the morning of Sunday the 19th, while engaged in her domestic business, was taken to her room, and that one convulsion succeeded another rapidly, and with such violence that she could not speak until two o'clock in the night when she could speak.[4]

A shared sorrow bonded Carr and Dr. James, but so too did smiles and laughter. Perhaps, while attending to Carr, Dr. James spoke of the great number of Africans who willingly assisted in decorating the chapel in the Mendi Mission for Christmas. Dr. James reminisced of dinner for the holy day: the festivities, fruit, poultry, vegetables, cakes, pies, candies, raisins, and music. He talked of the challenge of bringing Western culture to West Africa and the laughter of the Africans as they discovered using cutlery as they ate. Recalled Dr. James:

> I sat opposite a boat's crew, and they began to laugh; as they would use the knife, then the spoon (large), after that the fork, such laughing after each use of these pieces of cutlery I have never witnessed before. I began to inquire of the waiter, an interpreter, what they were so amused at, and he informed me that they were laughing at their use of knives, forks, and spoons. The spoons did not hold enough, they said;

> the food rolled off the knife in their unsteady hands, and the fork was like putting water in a fish-net instead of a calabash. Every day since that, when they eat dinner, they laugh about those pieces of cutlery.[5]

Dr. James also witnessed a secret rite of passage, one that he may have recounted to Carr. It was a woman's ceremony, the Bundu (Bundoo) ritual, held in the bush away from men, whether Black or white. Following the sound of drums, Dr. James and his guide came upon the town of Debia, governed by a female chief, a descendant of interracial marriage between the Anglo Caulker family and families of Sierra Leone. She acknowledged him and set food before him. For reasons untold, the chieftainess allowed Dr. James to view the dance, and he gave an account of what he witnessed:

> In a grove near this town within which no male was allowed to enter, proceeded those sounds of mystic drums which attracted us to this place. Madame Caulker gave me a very cordial welcome; indeed her dignified manners made me almost forget that she was the representative of a heathen clan.[6] . . . Soon after eating, the drumming ceased from the forest; then came out a large number of women. . . . When they saw me they were amazed and appeared timid. But this perplexed condition of the organization was soon removed by the head woman. . . . Soon the drums, which had attracted me, began to rumble out their peculiar sounds to dancing thumps, beaten by female drummers, arranged in dancing orders with their backs toward us, coming from where they were placed in this array. These same women who appeared timid, bashful and reserved a little while before, sung, beat and stepped to time slowly, motioned with their hands to something apparently to me in the sky, and moved towards a place where they were soon to stand.

As the ceremony proceeded, three "well-formed and comely" girls of about nineteen years old danced side by side, tossing their bodies right and left, to-and-fro in a graceful manner. They danced for about fifteen minutes. The three, became two, then one. Soon others stepped in to fill their places. "Many feats of skills were performed by the first three," Dr. James wrote. "I noticed that when they danced, their supple limbs were tossed in many enigmatic postures which drew forth applause and great laughter from the bystanders who understood them. After dancing for an hour before us, the leader of the mystic sisterhood ordered it discontinued and they retired to a capacious bamboo-covered hut to partake of refreshments."[7]

Pleased by the performance, Dr. James asked the chieftainess about the women. She replied that they were Bundoo women who were moving further into the interior because they were "molested or hindered by the advancement of Christianity."[8] Dr. James and other missionaries counted the advancement of Christianity a victory. However, to the indigenous people, this religion from across the water was a danger and an encroachment upon their culture and centuries-old way of life.

Dr. James brought to America tales of Africa, ceremonial drumming, dancing, and a secret society, all of which stirred memories. Surely these brought peace to Carr's ailing body and wistful soul. Benjamin James, MD, was a Christian missionary who taught the gospel of Jesus. Yet he looked upon Africans as backward, uncivilized people who needed to be saved. He saw them as the white man saw them. Perhaps he showed more compassion, but still his stance was from a position of superiority, and that troubled me.

I understand why Dr. James viewed Africans the way he did. He had been indoctrinated, much like we are today. The images Western media show of Africa are those of war-torn lands and starving babies. Rarely are the continent's modern advancements and beauty highlighted. Africa, we are told, is the place you help. Some of us don't see the continent as the place that has blessed and continues to nourish the world.

I am a Christian, and I cringe at what I know about the religion. I'm not a religious scholar, but I do know that the Bible has been translated and reworded, that sacred books (apocrypha) were dropped, that slaveholders used scriptural injunctions, like "slaves obey your masters," to keep the enslaved focused on heaven rather than freedom on earth. I concur with the statement often attributed to freedom fighter Jomo Kenyatta, Kenya's first president: "When the [white] missionaries arrived, the Africans had the land and the missionaries had the Bible. They taught us how to pray with our eyes closed. When we opened them, they had the land and we had the Bible."

The Christianity that Dr. James and other missionaries brought disrupted traditional African religions and cultures. Africans could see little value in some of the foreigners' ways. A knife? Why, so food could roll off it? A spoon? Why, when a calabash could hold so much more? What Dr. James witnessed as the women took part in their ritual was African spirituality—a oneness with the creator and creation.

The experience touched him deeply. He commented on the beauty of the women's movements—yes, their bodies—the sensuous Black female body that in America had been demeaned, raped, whipped, and sold. There, in Africa, in the bush, he saw only its beauty. He beheld their joy and community, and confidence. He saw women laughing, dancing their best, surprising their own selves, not caring what "the men" thought. In a cluster of women, men can change the energy field, confuse it, cloud it, often force themselves into it. This was the women's ritual—the creative, life-giving, mysterious female energy.

I believe Dr. James intuitively knew this, and he humbled himself before them. Maybe for a few minutes, Dr. James saw the women as worthy as he. Perhaps he let his guard down long enough to see the beauty in their way of life. He may have said to himself, there in that ritual is God, is spirit, is unity, more so than in the ways of the white man who in the name of God had enslaved even him.

Dr. James remained faithful to the American Missionary Association, and I respect him for that. Surely the exchange between him and the men and women of Sierra Leone had positive moments. I would not dare question his love for African people. He dedicated his life as a physician and a minister to healing his people in Africa and America. I do hope he left Africa wiser, more accepting, and with more answers than questions about life, God, and community. When the ritual ended, Dr. James walked away rejoicing that Christianity had made an inroad. But his account of the ceremony showed that the Africans who shared their lives and rituals left an uplifting, unforgettable impression on him. From deep in the bush Dr. Benjamin James heard a drumming. He could not ignore it. He could not resist it. Perhaps the sound was the heartbeat of Africa welcoming him home.

CHAPTER 20

Dianah Seeks a Widow's Pension

On November 13, 1894, the Pensions Bureau issued its findings. "Claimant Charles Carr: Rejection—no notable disability under Act June 27, 1890, from injury to the left arm." Ailing, Carr lived out his life in the Hardeeville area, where death claimed his body. No documents survived that recorded the specific day Carr died. Chrismas Graham, a member of Carr's community, remembered it was the day Ned Brisbane was shot. Other community members recalled Carr died in December, near rice-cutting time. Dr. Benjamin James gave this forthright account: "He finally died on or about the first-Sunday in December 1895, early in the morning from the dropsy then present."[1]

Carr lived thirty-seven years in the United States, never experiencing true freedom. As a youth, he was captured in Africa and transported to Georgia aboard the slave ship *Wanderer*. His African name was taken away, replaced with one given by his enslaver. He endured slavery. He escaped to join the USCT to fight for his freedom, where he was injured yet denied a pension. He embraced freedom, opening an account at the Freedman's Bank, which failed. A worker, family man, community member, like millions of poor freedmen, he died unnoticed by all but family and community. His friend Enoch Johnson recalled how he helped to carve the box Carr was buried in. Unlike the men who enslaved him who are interred in historic cemeteries in Savannah and surrounding communities, Carr was laid to rest in an unnamed place.

Lowcountry African tradition often dictated that the deceased be buried lying east-west with the head at the western point, thereby facing the Angel Gabriel when he blows his trumpet at the eastern sunrise. Others suggest the bodies were buried facing east so the deceased would see his homeland, Africa. Graves often were decorated with personal items or shells, broken plates or bottles, or plants. If the community kept with tradition, Carr was interred in the Lowcountry manner: his grave marked with items he cherished, his body facing Africa and the rising sun.

Carr's death was not the end of his story, but in a way, a beginning. Death is celebrated and ritualized in African cultures, as it was in the community of the enslaved. It marked the end of earthly toil and signaled a reuniting with ancestors and friends in the spirit world. That's why the Igbo people I mentioned earlier walked back into the waters when they arrived on these shores. Their watery graves opened doors to their spirit world, where they could exert influence when called upon. African Americans remember Ebo Landing. They speak the name so the enslaved Africans will not be forgotten.

In many African cultures, as long as the departed's name is called, he or she continues to live. Carr's community remembered him and called his name. Even today in rallies we chant, "Say their names." Perhaps unknowingly, the federal government, through pension applications, ensured that those who fought for freedom—even those formerly enslaved—would be remembered. History recorded only a few words spoken by Carr—his recollection told to the white physician about the terrible Middle Passage voyage. Carr's community filled in his life, allowing researchers like me to speak his name more than 150 years after he was shipped to this country in chains.

After Carr's death, Dianah, his wife, was now alone. At some point, Dianah learned that she may be able to receive a widow's pension. The application required Dianah to complete several documents. Because she was illiterate, she depended on others to write her sworn statements to which she would affix her mark. C. E. Boyd, a notary in Hardeeville, assisted Dianah, helping her to amass affidavits and testimonies. The widow was required to submit evidence of the veteran's death. She needed to provide proof of marriage and of whether she had remarried since her husband's death. The pension application asked the names of children, living or dead. She had to pass a "means test," revealing whether she held property or had means of support.

The widow's sworn statements were not enough to convince the bureau, which would also send an agent to speak with the widow's family and friends to verify or dispute her remarks. I found these community accounts captivating, warm, and engaging. They told the joys and disappointments in the claimant's life. Members revealed cultural norms, forgiveness, and unacceptable behavior. They shared gossip and spoke truths. It was a close-knit community where it seemed like everyone's needs were met. Today most of us don't really know our neighbors. Generations ago, your neighbors were all you had. You leaned on them as much as they leaned on you, through the good and tough times.

Dianah sat before Boyd, who wrote down her statements. She attested her maiden name was Boldin. She declared that she and Charles married in 1872. They had a child, a son named Arthur. She declared that she was never married before uniting with Carr, that he was not previously married, and that she had not remarried since his death. She affirmed that she had no means of support, stating, "I have no property whatever either or personal only my own daily labor and have no one that is legally bound to help me."

I could hear the loneliness in Dianah's voice, and my heart ached for her. As a widow with a child, her lot would be difficult. She had lost her husband, her confidant and friend. She no longer had someone to talk to or to share dreams with. There would be less laughter in the home as well as less money. She would need to work in the field more but also be home to care for her young son. It's a choice single parents—especially women—make. The COVID-19 pandemic proved that. Women lost employment at a higher rate than men. It was due to the kinds of jobs women held, in the hospitality and service industries. Many mothers had to decide whether to work or stay home with children who were learning virtually. Some mothers manage to do it all—care for a child or children at home, work as the family breadwinner, find daycare, and stay financially afloat. They put one foot in front of the other and keep going.

Dianah did not have written documentation for all her answers. When the bureau required proof that she didn't have, her neighbors' testimonies would help. Boyd, her agent, traveled to surrounding communities to take and notarize statements from Carr and Dianah's acquaintances. John Howard, Chester Chislom, USCT veteran Marcus Maxwell, Bettie Fields, and Beaufort County auditor H. C. Pollitzer signed affidavits supporting Dianah's testimony.

On July 24, 1896, Dianah submitted her application to the Pensions Bureau. Her file was designated as Widow's Original or WO number 638231.

Months later, Dianah realized that she made a mistake when giving the date of her marriage. Dianah filed another affidavit, stating in part:

> I am the wife of Chas Carr deceased and was married to him in 1883. He has told me repeatedly that he served in the war of rebellion and no other and only the one time in the said war. I am unable to find any of his comrads that served with him. I am poor and have no means of finding them from what he has told me. . . . I am unable to find any one that knew him before he enlisted. I further sware that at the time I filed my application and gave the date of my marriage to Chas Carr I could not remember correct date as I am ignorant and cannot wright or read and I maid a mistake in the year saying it was in 1872 when it should have been in September 1883 instead of 1872.[2]

In 1898 Boyd and Dianah submitted the second affidavit, giving the correct date of her marriage. Fortunately, the bureau accepted her sworn statement. From Dianah's statements and depositions given by those who knew her and Carr, I learned what the Black community of their time was like.

CHAPTER 21

The Church Where They Married

Many acquainted with Dianah recalled her marriage to Charles Carr, although their accounts of when and where the couple were wedded differed. Just reading their remarks reminded me of family and community members coming together to discuss the same event, each recalling it differently and each person adamant that his recollection is the *right* one! I, along with my husband Ahdwele, who has since made his transition, were fortunate enough to visit the church where they exchanged their vows. It's a memory I hold dear.

"Dianah Carr and Charles Carr were married in the Colored Methodist Church in the vicinity by Rev. F. D. Jones," believed Mrs. Graham. "I was not present. I heard of the marriage soon after it occurred. I was then living on the same plantation with Dianah." "I can't give the date," Mrs. Graham added. "I have no idea of such things."[1]

Chrismas Graham recalled the wedding and why the couple made their union legal. "Charles and Dianah had staid together two or three years before they got married," Chrismas Graham said. "The rules of the church made them marry. I was not present."

Although the community recognized common-law marriages, the church did not. In the early Black community, the church was the center of community life. Staying in the fellowship with the congregation was important. To be separated from the church was to be separated from the lifeline of the community. Charles and Dianah were living together outside of marriage. It was known in this close-knit community that children were born to this union. Someone in the church reminded leaders that Dianah and Charles were not legally joined and therefore were "living in sin." Charles and Dianah were given a choice. They chose to abide by the church rule and agreed to make their relationship legal.

"I was living on the same plantation and saw them go off on Saturday to the church and they said they were going to get married," Mr. Graham continued. "I saw them the next day and they said they had gotten married at the St. Matthews Methodist Church. They lived together as husband and wife to the death of Chars Carr." Of the courtship, Graham recalled Charles came over to South Carolina after working a while across the Savannah River in Chatham, Georgia. "He saw Dianah and went to courting her and they began to live together."[2]

John Howard gave a different account of the place of the wedding. "The marriage occurred at the Jonesville Baptist Church. . . . Preacher Johnson married them on Sunday morning after preaching his sermon."[3]

And in yet a third account, Enoch Johnson stated, "A minister named Johnson performed the ceremony at the Branch Methodist. . . . It took place on Sunday in the presence of a crowd." Johnson added, "Charles and Dianah never separated permanently. They had quarrels like everybody else and he would go away for a week and maybe a month. But he always came back. They lived together as man and wife at the date of his death."[4]

Fortunately, a copy of the marriage certificate was included in Dianah's pension file. It gave additional clues as to where Carr and Dianah exchanged their wedding vows. The church record certified that "Mr. Charles Carr of Beaufort C. and Misses Diana Boldin of Beaufort C. have this day been joined in MATRIMONY, covenanting to live together as husband and wife, after God's holy ordinance of MARRIAGE until separated by death. Dated September 15, 1883, South Carolina."

Witness: John Howard

Rev. J. H. Johnson, Officiating Minister

R. O. Bright

A. W. Bright

Church Clerk[5]

In a communication accompanying the marriage certificate, Reverend J. W. Coles, pastor of First African Baptist Church, attested that the certificate "is a true copy of marriage of Dianna [*sic*] Boldin and Charles Carr as it appears in church books." Reverend Coles' deposition was dated January 1900.[6] I had to stop and think. Each person remembered a dif-

For this cause shall a man leave Father and Mother, and shall cleave to his Wife; and they twain shall be one flesh.

MARRIAGE CERTIFICATE

THIS CERTIFIES

That Mr Charles Carr

of [illegible] and Miss [illegible]

of [illegible] have this day been joined in MATRIMONY, covenanting to live together as husband and wife, after God's holy ordinance of MARRIAGE, until separated by death.

Dated [illegible] South Carolina.

Rev J H Johnson

Officiating Minister.

Witnesses:

John Howard

R C Bright

A W Bright

Church Clerk

Wherefore they are no more twain but one flesh. What therefore God hath joined together, let no man put asunder.—*Matt. xix, 5, 6.*

Page 32, Ex "K".

Marriage certificate found in church records

SOURCE: National Archives in Washington, D.C., Dianah Carr, wo no. 638231 (Rejected).

ferent name for the church and at times a different pastor who performed the ceremony: Chrismas Graham, St. Matthews Methodist Church; John Howard, Jonesville Baptist Church; Enoch Johnson, Branch Methodist. According to Reverend Coles, the marriage took place at First African Baptist Church, where it was recorded in the church's books.

I searched the Internet for a First African Baptist Church near the Yemassee and Hardeeville areas. From the beginning of my research, I hoped to find something that I could point to or lay hands on that confirmed where Carr lived, walked, or spent time. If there is one institution in the African American community that has withstood the test of time, it is the Black church. I found First African Missionary Baptist

Church near Hardeeville. I made several calls to the church, choosing Sunday around 10:00 a.m., hoping to catch someone in the office between Sunday School and the morning worship service. After several attempts, I reached someone who may have been the church secretary. I explained I was a writer and was conducting research. I quickly asked, "Was this once Jonesville Baptist Church?" "Yes," she answered.

John Howard, who witnessed the marriage, was correct. Charles and Dianah married at Jonesville Baptist, in a ceremony officiated by Reverend J. H. Johnson. The congregation had changed the church's name. Jonesville was now First African Missionary Baptist Church.

Not wanting to hold her longer, I asked for the address and when homecoming or anniversary service was scheduled. Usually past and current members attend those services, and perhaps I could find someone with the family names of those who knew Charles and Dianah. The church secretary told me the church's anniversary was in May. This was the time that most longtime members returned. I made up my mind to be there.

Sunday, May 18, 2014, marked the 142nd anniversary of First African Missionary Baptist Church. This time Ahdwele must have sensed, as husbands do, that this was a special venture. He always left the research trips to me. Not his thing. I was too adventurous. That's part of conducting research. You have to get out of the chair, check the microfilm back in at the library desk, or leave the Internet behind and when possible, get a firsthand sense of place. I would walk up to strangers and ask for directions, stop at a nondescript structure where folks were congregating, and ask if they knew of certain families, and the like. Ahdwele was super protective. "You need to be careful!" he admonished, "You don't know those people!" "You went where?!" And the big fuss: "Oh! So you finally decided to call! You've been there for what, a half hour now?" It was best that he stayed home. But this trip was different. He wanted to go to Savannah, Hardeeville, and to Jekyll Island, for reasons that made sense years later.

Upon arriving at the church, I realized I had seen it before. On one of my vacations to Savannah with my sister Rosy—long before I had discovered Carr—we passed the church. I remembered the name—First African. It reminded me that after slavery, many Black people still identified with our mother continent. This time the church was enclosed within a chain link fence. I was told later that there had been some "concerns" but was not given details.

An usher gave Ahdwele and me each a church program as we entered. It was a small church, perhaps room for two hundred people. It was well attended but not full. I had grown up in a traditional Black Baptist church that size. I knew every hymn the congregation sang, knew when to stand in reverence of the Lord, when to be seated and quiet. Ahdwele took his cues from me. I was surprised a woman served as assistant pastor of this church. During my growing up, it was news when a woman was appointed to the trustee board.

Then came time to acknowledge visitors. I knew what to expect. My husband and I stood. I spoke first. "I am Velma Maia Thomas Fann, and I bring you greetings from the Shrines of the Black Madonna of the Pan African Orthodox Christian Church in Atlanta." The pastor nodded. Earlier I had sent the church a signed copy of my book, *Lest We Forget: The Passage from Africa to Slavery and Emancipation*, as a thank you for their once having retained a church record, a historical document probably unknown to them, certifying the marriage of Charles and Dianah Carr.

My husband spoke next. "I am Reverend Milton Ahdwele Fann," he began. He may have said more, but what he had said was enough. In true Baptist fashion, the pastor invited him to join other ministers on the pulpit. My husband was a bit stunned; this was not his religious tradition. But I was tickled. Someone just coming along for the ride was now front and center. He joined the other ministers and assisted in serving the Communion.

I remained in the congregation throughout service, although I, too, am an ordained minister. But I don't introduce myself that way. I want people to relax and be themselves around me. I am an observer and a bit of an introvert. I could be in a room for twenty minutes before anyone knew I was there. My husband, on the other hand, owned the room when he entered. His deportment was a way of saying, "Be honest. Don't bring any stuff!" He was street-smart, outgoing, and would cut to the chase. Our church loved him for that.

After the formality of church introductions, I began reading the church bulletin. It included the history and growth of the church, and the changes in the name since its founding. According to church history, in 1872, faithful members of May River Baptist Church in nearby Pritchardville, South Carolina, branched off from the mother church, establishing Jonesville Baptist. Reverend J. H. Johnson was selected as the pastor and leader. It was this Reverend Johnson who officiated the marriage of Charles and Dianah. Members worshipped in a bush tent, out of doors under the trees, until the building was erected.

Reverend I. W. (J. W.) Coles served as second pastor, leading until his passing in 1927. It was he who attested in 1900 that the marriage was in the church's books. He was followed by Reverend J. J. Jenkins of Bluffton, who served from 1928 to 1961. According to church history, the first building was erected, and the church renamed under Reverend Jenkins' leadership. This information was a bit different from the affidavit Reverend Coles submitted in 1900 as part of Dianah's application for the widow's pension. The affidavit relates that the church was called First African Baptist while he shepherded the congregation. It sometimes happens that oral history and written histories recall events differently.

The church documented other familiar names. Christmas (Chrismas) Graham, who told he had known Dianah since she was a little girl, was listed as an early officer of the church. R. O. Bright, clerk on the marriage certificate, appeared in the bulletin as Richard Bright and was remembered among other church clerks. At the time of our visit, members of the Bright family still were active in the congregation. I wished I had planned the time to speak with them. Who knows what they may have revealed?

I wondered if the sense of community was still there. It was. I was deeply moved by a member who stood before the congregation and apologized for something said that offended another congregant. A public apology and an ask for forgiveness is something I rarely see in churches or anywhere else these days.

In true Black church tradition, fellowship hour followed the service with great food. We could not stay long; my husband needed to rest.

Finding this church, seeing those names from Carr's life have been highlights of this research. The Black church often holds a key to our stories. Because First African Missionary Baptist knew its history, because Charles and Dianah chose to abide by "church rules," today we can touch a part of their lives.

CHAPTER 22

Their Community Speaks

In 1901, three years after Dianah submitted the corrected date of her marriage, the Freedmen's Bureau began the next phase of determining whether her claim would be approved. It dispatched special examiner W. H. Stovall to interview her community. He scoured the Hardeeville countryside in search of those who knew Dianah and Charles and to take depositions from their neighbors and acquaintances of her character and the couple's private lives. Dianah was a lifelong member of the Yemassee and Levy communities, both near Hardeeville. Those who vouched for Dianah knew her in her youth and through her, came to know Charles Carr, his ties to Africa, and his struggles to work despite pain in his arm and rheumatism. I wanted to learn about these members of the turn-of-the-century Lowcountry community. I turned to the 1900 census and to their depositions to find more of those who would testify on Dianah's behalf. What emerged were snapshots of these once-enslaved Black men and women, forging a community in freedom.

Enoch Johnson, a fifty-seven-year-old farmer living in Levy, knew Dianah and her family. According to the 1900 census, he had been married twenty-five years and had a daughter living in his home. Johnson could read but could not write. He owned his home, mortgage-free. Johnson reported that he had known Dianah since she was a little child, noting that her mother brought her into the county soon after she was born. Johnson remembered Dianah, while still young, had a girl named Cinda and that the child's father was a married man. "Dianah just caught up Cinda while she was running with the wind," Johnson told.[1]

"Running with the wind." It was such a beautiful phrase I thought, a declaration of innocence and freedom. From the 1900 census, Dianah had Cinda when she was twelve or thirteen years of age. One can imagine an adolescent Dianah, a free spirit, testing her boundaries. How much she knew about sexual intimacy and the possible outcome—pregnancy—will never be known. It is known that the man the community identified as the father of the child was married and was years older than Dianah. He was a neighbor who watched a budding Dianah and acted upon his urges, and forced himself onto her.

Johnson added more information about Carr's past. "Charles told me he was born in Africa and came to this country shortly before the war began. His master settled him on a place near Savannah, Georgia. After his freedom he staid over in Georgia a long time and finally came over here. I got acquainted with him soon after he came over here."[2]

John Howard, the witness to Dianah and Carr's marriage, had known Dianah since he was young. "We grew up together in this part of Beaufort County, S.C. and have always been neighbors," Howard remembered. "She had a child by some colored fellow, but she just picked it up, so we all thought." According to Howard, Dianah's father reportedly owned land and left it to her. "She soon lost it in some way. She lost it before Charles died."[3]

Enoch Johnson added, "She staid up here awhile then went to live in Hardeeville. . . . Charles Carr left no real estate to Dianah Carr at his death and very little if any personal property. They were poor people and rented places to live."[4]

Chrismas Graham, a Yamassee farmer who could read and write, reported, "I have known Dianah Carr since she was a little child. We grew up together in this part of the Beaufort, S.C., and generally on the same plantation." Graham remembered, "She had a child by some fellow . . . when she was a young girl, but they were not married. He was already a married man with a house full of children."[5] His wife, Josephine Graham, was Dianah's cousin. Mrs. Graham echoed his story. "She got the child when she was on the run," said Mrs. Graham. "The child is named Cinda Brown and she lives near here."[6]

Frank Brown, a forty-six-year-old farm laborer, had known Dianah for more than twenty years. Brown and Dianah stayed on the farm of H. Lynah. He recalled, "The child was named Cinda or Lucinda and was very young when I first saw her mother. I knew Charles Carr while he lived over in Georgia. He was working on the Winkler Plantation near Monteith, Georgia. I went there and staid a short time. It was before Charles took up with Dianah. It was several years before they took up together," Brown continued. "He was living with old man Tom Simmons near Monteith, Georgia. No sir, I heard nothing of any previous marriage on his part. If he had a wife over there she was not in sight when I was around. I think Dianah was his first wife."[7]

No one spoke disparagingly of Dianah as a young, unwed mother. They accepted her and her child as part of the community. They expressed disgust for the man who took advantage of her. Their testimonies drew me closer to this community. Members knew one another's secrets, joys, and sorrows. Few people lived alone, most resided with family. Black communities like the one in Yamassee were filled with people who had toiled together, had watched each other mature, had given funds to the impoverished, built churches, attended weddings, and buried their dead.

Even today, when the Black community often looks broken, there are still good people, individuals who will rally for a good cause, folks who will give to those in need. Surrogate fathers and mothers and mentoring groups step in to give guidance. Churches still feed and clothe those in need. Community is where we are reaffirmed, where we share our lives. Community is where we laugh until the pain of being Black in America subsides . . . at least for a moment. It's where we gather strength and strategize for justice.

Cinda was Dianah's firstborn, but Cinda and Arthur (Carr's son) were not her only children. Dianah had given birth to several children and had wept over small graves.

Josephine Graham, wife of Chrismas Graham, remembered the other children. "They had about six children. Only one is living, Arthur Carr." Mrs. Graham added, "He and Dianah were married after they had two children."[8] Josephine Graham remembered Carr's relationships differently. "I made the acquaintance of Charles Carr just a short time before he married to Dianah Carr," Mrs. Graham recalled. "Before Charles Carr came up here to stay, he had lived in Georgia so they said. He had a wife over in that state, so I once heard my husband say. I have no personal knowledge on this point."

Samuel Bennett saw Dianah and Carr's other children. Born during slavery around 1850, Bennett had done well for himself. In 1900 he and his wife, Malinda, lived in Yemassee. Bennett was head of household. Residing with him were his wife, their children, sons-in-law, and grandchildren—a total of thirteen people. Bennett worked for the railroad and was a farmer. He and most members of his household could read and write. He owned his home free and clear. He had known the Carr family, which lived five or six miles from him, since 1880.

Bennett remembered that Charles introduced Dianah as his wife, although Bennett was not sure if they were legally married. "I saw several of their children, but never knew their names or ages," recalled Bennett. He knew of someone named Arthur but confessed to the special examiner taking depositions, "I do not know the age of Arthur Carr. Do not know whether they have a child by that name or not."[9]

Enoch Johnson had more to share. "Charles and Dianah had three children to my personal knowledge though they may have had more. All of the child(ren) died before Charles died, except a boy named Arthur. I saw him last week."[10]

Fellow USCT veteran Marcus Maxwell gave his testimony. Maxwell applied for a pension in 1890. He declared he suffered from rheumatism and was wholly unable to work. Maxwell owned land, was an officer in his church, and was well-known and respected. Despite some delays, Maxwell's application was approved, sparing him the disappointment Carr experienced. He spoke of Dianah as follows: "She was very poor after his [Charles'] death. She begged me for help year before last and I gave her some money, gave her $7.00 altogether at different times." He continued, "I saw Charles Carr who formerly lived in this section of Beaufort County. I got acquainted with him about 22 years ago when we worked together on the farm of a man named McMullin six miles from this town. We worked there two years and then separated and after that I saw him only occasionally. . . . He came to the McMullin place every morning and after working all day would go over to the pinelands to stay all night."[11]

John Howard relayed what he recalled of Carr. "He came over from Georgia about the time he took up with Dianah. I don't know where he lived when in Georgia. He belonged to a Mcmullin so he once said when he was a slave."[12]

No one with the surname McMullin is recorded in the Lowcountry in the federal population censuses of 1860, 1870, or 1880. My hunch was that the pronunciation of Montmollin caused the spelling of the last name to differ, and when Maxwell and Howard spoke of McMullin they were referring to John S. Montmollin, one of the *Wanderer* coconspirators who owned a plantation on the South Carolina side of the Savannah River.

Each bit of information, each new person interviewed by the special examiner, added a new stroke to the painting of the members of Carr's community. They were hard-working, self-assured men and women. They knew their community. Some could read and write. They farmed, took in family and boarders. One person joined the USCT as did Carr, to fight for freedom. Community sustained Carr and Dianah during Reconstruction and the Jim Crow era, when laws and Black Codes limited the freedom, labor, and civil rights of freedmen—periods many historians consider the cruelest of the American South.

CHAPTER 23

Arthur's Birth

Dianah and Charles possibly buried six children, according to the testimonies of those in their community. There could be several reasons why their children died. Dianah had been through a lot and may have been in poor health. She may not have eaten well during her pregnancies; she may have worked too long and too hard. Maybe her body was weakened by having Cinda, her daughter, so early in her life. If Dianah did carry the children full-term, they may have died soon after, their chances of survival weakened by a mother who had no or little prenatal care.

Childbirth was a strain on women, both slave and free. Fanny Kimble, the English-born wife of Pierce Butler, owner of the four hundred enslaved men, women, and children sold during the great Weeping Time, wrote in her diary dreadful accounts of miscarriages among slave women on her husband's plantation. Here are some of her entries:

> Fanny has had six children, all dead but one. She came to beg to have her work in the field lightened.
>
> Nanny has had three children, two of them are dead; she came to implore that the rule of sending them into the field three weeks after their confinement might be altered.
>
> Leah, Caesar's wife, has had six children, three are dead.
>
> Sophy, Lewis' wife, came to beg for some old linen; she is suffering fearfully, has had ten children, five of them are dead. The principal favour she asked was a piece of meat, which I gave her.
>
> Sally, Scipio's wife, has had two miscarriages and three children born, one of whom is dead. She came complaining of incessant pain and weakness in her back. This woman was a mulatto daughter of a slave called Sophy, by a white man of the name of Walker, who visited the plantation.

> Charlotte, Renty's wife, had had two miscarriages, and was with child again. She was almost crippled with rheumatism, and showed me a pair of poor swollen knees that made my heart ache. I have promised her a pair of flannel trousers, which I must forthwith set about making.
>
> Sarah, Stephen's wife—this woman's case and history were, alike, deplorable, she had had four miscarriages, had brought seven children into the world, five of whom were dead, and was again with child. She complained of dreadful pains in the back, and an internal tumour which swells with the exertion of working in the fields; probably, I think, she is ruptured.

Fannie Kemble recorded one enslaved family's reaction to the death of another one of their children: "But the father and mother, and old Rose, the nurse, who was their little baby's grandmother, all seemed apathetic, and apparently indifferent to the event. The mother merely repeated over and over again, 'I've lost a many, they all goes so;' and the father, without word or comment, went out to his enforced labour."[1]

Perhaps similarly, after burying so many of their babies, Dianah and Charles may have resigned themselves to the probability that few if any of their children would survive.

But one did. Arthur, the only documented child of the African Charles Carr, was born around the time of the "Big Shake." That is how the community referred to the 1886 Charleston earthquake and aftershocks felt as late as 1887. Frank Brown told special examiner Stovall he had known Dianah when they both lived on the farm of H. Lynah and that he was with the Carr family shortly after Arthur's birth. "Dianah Carr was still sick in the bed when the quake came and Arthur was one or two weeks old," said Brown. "I was at her house the day after the big shake occurred and saw her still in the bed and saw her child."[2] Josephine Graham also recalled the child. "I don't know the age of Arthur Carr," said Mrs. Graham. "I know he was over the age of 13 years. He was born soon after the big earthquake."[3]

The big shake would long be remembered. On August 31, 1886, at 9:50 p.m. Charleston, South Carolina, buckled under shifting ground. The magnitude of the earthquake claimed lives, struck terror, leveled buildings, and sparked flames and flooding. On September 8, 1886, the

Yorkville Enquirer newspaper reprinted the following dispatch from Charleston:

> The principle business portion of the city was destroyed, and hundreds of persons were rendered homeless. Men were frantic and women were beseeching the Almighty. . . . Broad Street presented a spectacle of the utmost horror. Even women with hatchets fought valiantly to rescue imprisoned unfortunates. Meeting Street, from Broad to Hazel, is a wreck and lined with unfortunates. To add to the horror of the scene, many fires broke out and were ineffectually fought by the fire department. The night was hideous with groans of the dying, the screams of the wounded and the prayers of the uninjured.

The *Yorkville Enquirer* added that "nearly every town felt the shock. . . . Beaufort feeling it at 9:50."[4]

Certainly, Carr and Dianah were anxious. They had buried more of their children than had lived. Carr had been snatched from Africa, had been shackled on the *Wanderer*, had been enslaved, had escaped, had been injured as a soldier in the Civil War, and led a life of poverty. After losing several children Dianah was ready to give birth again, but this time as the earth shook in a manner that none but God could control.

In her affidavit of June 1897, midwife Bettie Fields, age seventy, of the Bruton (Brewton) Plantation in Beaufort County, identified the year of Carr's birth as 1887, not 1886. As with the date of Carr and Dianah's marriage, the community remembered special events, even if they remembered different dates. Stated Fields:

> I was called on to attend Dianah Carr the wife of Chas Carr in her confinement on or a bought August 30 day, this part in A.D. 1887 and she gave birth to a boy child and it was named Arthur Carr and I do further declair that the said Arthur Carr is still living at this time with his mother Dianah Carr the wife of the deceased Charley Carr. I further declair that I have been following midwifery for over 40 years and attended the said Dianah Carr. Arthur Carr was born on the 30 day of August A.D. 1887.[5]

Midwives were valued members of the community. They visited pregnant women, brought forth life, and used herbs to soothe pains of childbirth. Young women learned standing alongside experienced midwives, who upon retiring would pass on the trade to their apprentices. With more than forty years of experience, Fields undoubtedly knew the Lowcountry folklore surrounding the birth of a child that I discovered over my years of research. A child born in a caul—a thin membrane covering the face—was said to have visionary powers or ability to see spirits. A breech birth signaled that the child would travel. A child born with a square head was destined to be smart; one born with a flat head would be a hard worker.[6] Fields revealed nothing more of the birth of Arthur Carr.

The 1900 federal population census for Yemassee supported what acquaintances told the examiner. That year, Dianah (Deanah) and her son Arthur (Artha) resided with Dianah's daughter Cinda (Linda) Brown and Cinda's husband, William Brown. Dianah was age thirty-six; Cinda was twenty-five years old, Arthur was twelve years of age. Also in the household were Ame Blight, age sixty, and Stella Grant, age six, family of William Brown. William and Dianah worked as rice hands. When asked by the census taker, "Mother of how many children?" Dianah replied, "Nine." To the question, "How many children living," Dianah, remembering her loss, may have dropped her head and quietly answered, "Two."

CHAPTER 24

Carr's African People

I returned to Dianah's claim to read more about Carr and Dianah's community, which directed special examiner Stovall to people who lived in Monteith about ten miles north of Savannah. The names of people there who knew Carr proved a treasure, giving answers to questions about his family and introducing others born in Africa who created community near Savannah. Frank Brown had told Stovall that Carr had a friend in Monteith named Tom Simmons. Enoch Johnson told Stovall that Carr "had a friend named Jack Gadaden [*sic*] in Georgia near Monteith and he would know about any previous marriage. Alice Godfrey and Silvey Simmons also would."[1]

Seeking more information for the widow's claim, the Pensions Bureau followed up on October 13, 1901, with a form letter to the postmaster in Monteith, Georgia, seeking persons who knew Charles Carr. The bureau assigned A. B. Parkey to speak to persons in communities near Savannah.

> Sir:
> Please state, on the back of this letter, whether Thomas Simmons, Silvey Simmons, John Wiley, Jack Gadsden and Alice Godfrey, resides within your mail delivery, and if so, at what distance from the post-office and in what direction. If they do not receive mail at your office, any assistance you may be able to give in locating them, will be appreciated.
>
> This information is desired for use in a claim for pension, No. 638,231, and it is requested that your reply, in the envelope herewith, be forwarded as soon as possible.
>
> A. B. Parkey
> Special Examiner

Parkey added in his own handwriting, "I think these are all negroes."

Days later, on October 17, the reply came that Thomas Simmons and John Wiley were dead, but that Silvey Simmons, Jack Gadson and Alice

Golphin (Godfrey) lived nearby. To me they were more than "negroes." They were Africans related to Carr by blood or the shared Middle Passage horror. The 1880 federal census was the first to ask individuals their place of birth and to ask the birthplaces of parents. Tom (Thos.) Simmons, his wife Selvra (Silvey), and John W[h]iley gave Africa as their place of birth and the birthplace of their parents. I discovered that Alice was Carr's niece, the daughter of his sister Rose, who had been brought over with him on the *Wanderer*.

Alice Golphin related her mother's ties to Africa, giving her deposition in 1901 with her daughter, Patience Small, by her side.

> I am about 45 years of age; am the wife of John Golphin, P.O. address Meinhard, Chatham County, Georgia. I am well acquainted with the claimant, Diana Carr. I have known her since about the time she married Charles Carr, who was my uncle. I knew Charles Carr all my life. He and my mother, dead, were brother and sister. They were brought to this country from Africa when they were small. Charley Lamar, dead, of this city there, owned uncle Charles and Dr. May[s] of Florida owned my mother. . . . Soon after freedom, my mother and I came to this county where I have since resided. . . .
>
> When I came here I found my uncle Charles Carr. He was there residing on the Berrien plantation. He there had a wife named Hester. I called her aunt Hester. She was the first wife uncle Charles ever had. Do not know where he married her. He and Hester lived together as man and wife until Hester died. Hester died on the Berrien plantation in this county about twenty-five years ago. I waited on her during her last sickness, saw her die and was present at her burial. She was buried on the Berrien graveyard. She took a kind of swelling which caused her death. There was no doctor called to treat her. Her husband came to this city and bought medicine for her. She was sick about a year, lingering along. Pretty soon after the death of Hester uncle Charles and all of us moved near Hardeeville, South Carolina and there uncle Charles met this Diana Bolin [?] and they went to living together as man and wife. After a while, the church made them get married. . . .
>
> Dianah is crazy and is in the asylum. Aunt Silvey Simmons saw Hester but she is too old and idiotic to tell you anything. She was born

> in Africa herself. My husband and daughter knew about the death of first wife Hester.[2]

John Golphin, Alice's husband, told much of the same. He remembered Hester, recalling:

> I first heard of the marriage. Charley Carr visited my house a heap and told me about it. I became acquainted with Charley Carr about 20 years ago he was residing on the Berrien Plantation when I first knew him. When I first knew Charley Carr he was called a widower. When I first knew him Carr told me that he had been married to a woman named Hester and that his wife shortly before this died on the Berrien plantation. . . . She was named Hester Porshe. She was buried at the Berrien graveyard. I guess Hester had been dead about four years before he married the claimant.[3]

Patience Small was the final person interviewed. She stated she was twenty-four years of age, a servant, and the daughter of Alice Golphin. She knew of Charles' first wife. "I always spoke of her as aunt Hester. Do not know how long Charles Carr had her for his wife. Aunt Hester died before I could recall—before I was born. I knew the place where they said she was buried. She was buried at the Berrien graveyard, about 1 mile from the place."[4]

Much to my surprise, Carr had two relationships before his marriage to Dianah: Sallie in Savannah and Hester, on the Berrien plantation in Georgia. As Hester is not recorded on any legal document, we know of her only because the community remembered her. Carr also had been fortunate to reunite with family—Alice Golphin, his sister's daughter, and with friends born in Africa, John W[h]iley born in 1840, and Tom Simmons born in 1832, and Silvey born about 1830. It is possible that they too were on the *Wanderer*.

I discovered much from the depositions of Carr and Dianah's neighbors. The sharing was community chatter, as everyone seemed to know a little about everybody. Back in the day, at least one person (usually a revered, older woman) saw and knew everything that went on in the community. She watched the children and told if they did something wrong. She watched the courtships and gave approvals or warnings. She watched secret lovers creep, told the police which way an intruder ran, and knew who was "asked to leave" the neighborhood and who was moving in.

Before the advent of the Community Watch program in the 1960s, there was someone who watched the community.

It was hard to live in secret in a community. Everyone was bound by space and experience. For Black folks in the North and South, segregated housing kept us together. Everyone knew the street, road, or tracks that separated the Black from the white section of town. In the Black neighborhood, the business owner and factory worker lived on the same street. The schoolteacher was a member of a nearby church. Children attended the same schools with each other, from kindergarten to high school. You saw the same people every day, at the bus stop or on the long walk to work. And while you didn't want everybody in all your business, you were thankful when they were in some of it, like when you got laid off and needed help feeding your children, or when the rent was due and folks chipped in or held rent parties, or when you wanted to celebrate a milestone—landing a "good job," completing night school, seeing your photo and accolades in the Negro press.

Today's community is different from that of Charles' and Dianah's. It's playdates, the Nextdoor app, and connecting through social media with like-minded people who live thousands of miles away. Regardless how communities look or form, they should care about their members and have a handle on things. Community is our connectedness to people with whom we share space and experience.

Through testimonies of Alice and John Golphin and Patience Small, I now knew more about Charles' family. On the Freedman's Bank registry, Carr reported having a sister in Savannah named Rose. Alice Golphin told that Charles was her uncle, the brother of her mother, both of whom where brought over from Africa when they were small. According to Mrs. Golphin, Carr was owned by Charles Lamar, a *Wanderer* coconspirator. Mrs. Golphin said her mother was owned by a physician in Florida. Documents recording the actions of *Wanderer* coconspirators stated that several of the enslaved were taken to Florida, making Alice Golphin's claim plausible.

I considered it a win to be able to find documents to piece together

Carr's story, from his capture by slavers to the sale of his sister to Florida, to their reuniting in Monteith, Georgia. For most African Americans, finding documents that connect oral and written family history is rare. I recall when years ago I drove to Aiken County, South Carolina, to learn more about my father's people. I stopped at Old Storm Branch Baptist Church, my family's church, and parked in front of the annex where seniors were sitting and talking. I got out of the car and asked for information about my cousin, Barbara Bush. Because she has been so active in the church, I was sure they knew her. The elders knew her, but they didn't know me. I could sense their hesitation. It was then that I recited the Garrett family lineage. The elders nodded in approval and told me where I could find my cousin. Had I not known my family lineage, the elders might not have been so helpful.

People connect these days by DNA. They find long-lost relatives and people they never knew. Our ancestors didn't have that advantage. They, like Alice Golphin, became griots—keepers of family and community history. They memorized family history and told it to the next generation. I'm glad I heard and that I listened to my family's stories. If I had not, I might still be standing at the door!

CHAPTER 25

Death in an Asylum

After living with her daughter Cindy Brown in Yemassee, Dianah moved to Hardeeville, where she eked out a living taking work as she could find it. Eventually, dire circumstances overwhelmed Dianah. In late 1900 or early 1901, she had a nervous breakdown and was committed to the state psychiatric hospital. Acquaintances in Hardeeville and in Monteith remembered how Dianah suffered.

"She had hired out to work in the field for a living. She worked some with Mr. C. B. Boyd, notary public, several years ago," recalled Josephine Graham. "She is now in the State Insane Asylum in Columbia, S.C."[1]

Private Jacob Martin of the 24th USCT had known Dianah and Carr for more than twenty years. Born enslaved in Georgia, Martin fled or was taken by his enslaver to Pennsylvania, where later, as a free man, he enlisted in the Union Army. His military records showed he served as a substitute for a white man who paid five hundred dollars (more than nineteen thousand dollars in 2024) to avoid serving in the Civil War. Martin, who moved to the Hardeeville area after the war, recalled Charles and Dianah were living as man and wife when he knew them. He said of Dianah, "She has no property of any kind. She was an object of charity when she went crazy."[2]

I wrote to the South Carolina Department of Archives and History and requested records from the South Carolina State Hospital. I hoped they would give insight into Dianah's mental state, or tell who visited her. On March 7, 1901, Probate Judge Cunningham read Dianah's case. She had been placed in the Hardeeville jail for her own safety. She had been deemed a risk to herself. Dr. Pollitzer completed the form for her commitment.

The form asked a number of questions: Property owned by the patient or relatives. Answer: Nothing. Full name: Diannah Carr, colored, female age thirty. Personal property: Nothing. Questions about health, state of mind, use of alcohol or opium, whether she had children, her parents' mental health, and more, were answered "Don't know."

Some information was given. Dianah had been taken and kept in jail for "safe keeping." According to one comment, "the woman is a pauper [and as] such has by one of the magistrates on a charge of lunacy." When asked her state upon examination, the physician wrote, "She used vile and filthy language. She would not wear any clothing, struck herself against walls of cell, etc." The patient's appearance was "that of a lunatic." Other factors indicating insanity included "her language, conduct and general appearance. She was considered a danger to herself and with no means of support." After reading the report I was haunted by images of Dianah. I imagined her wandering about the roads, cursing, filthy, and in a state of delirium.

On March 15, 1901, officials loaded Dianah into a wagon or some other rough-riding vehicle and took her to the State Hospital in Columbia. Dianah was confined in the asylum, with only strangers to bid her farewell as her broken spirit embarked upon its next journey.

Dianah, what happened! I wondered out loud. Where were your daughter, Cindy, and son Arthur? You were only thirty years old, perhaps younger. What triggered your downfall into despair? Whom were you cursing, Dianah? Charles, for dying and leaving you alone? The government for tying up your widow's pension and your sanity in scores of files, questions, letters, and interviews? They said you stripped off your clothing. What were you desperately trying to get rid of? What were you peeling away, scratching at, and clawing at? Dianah, you threw yourself against cold, unyielding, jail cell walls. Whump! Whump! Whump! Maybe the sound of your body hitting the walls drowned out the voices in your head. Maybe you were trying to break free, to run with the wind once again.

Asylums (psychiatric hospitals) of the nineteenth and early twentieth centuries were dreadful institutions. Few patients were expected to return to their communities. The South Carolina Lunatic Asylum (later the South Carolina State Hospital) opened in 1828 for wealthy white patients whose fees, along with public funds, would subsidize care for middle-class and poor whites and on occasion, the few enslaved and free Black men and women it accepted. From October 1864 to February 1865, it served as a prisoner of war camp for Union officers. Following the Civil War, the

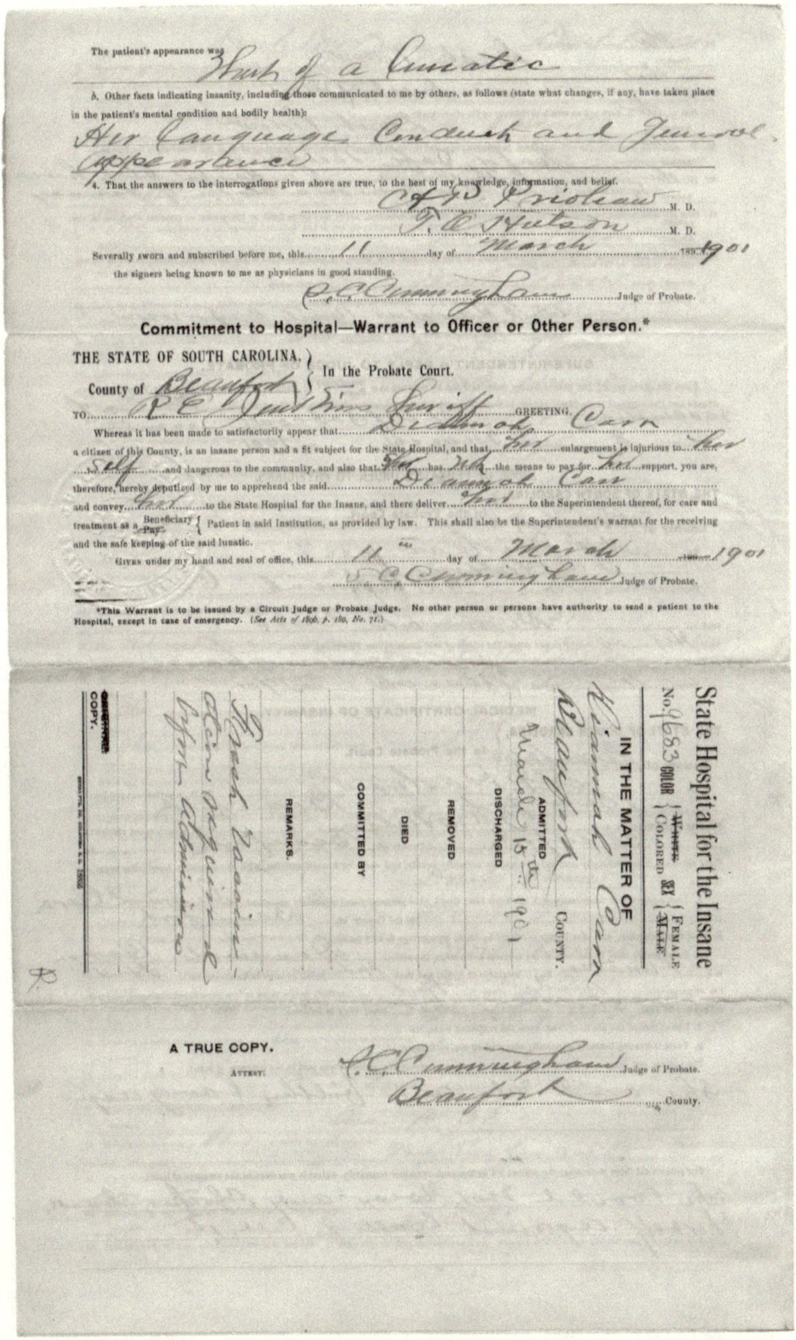

The patient's appearance was Wush of a Lunatic

5. Other facts indicating insanity, including those communicated to me by others, as follows (state what changes, if any, have taken place in the patient's mental condition and bodily health):

Her language Conduct and General appearance

4. That the answers to the interrogations given above are true, to the best of my knowledge, information, and belief.

C. F. P. Prioleau, M. D.

F. C. Hutson, M. D.

Severally sworn and subscribed before me, this 11 day of March 1901

the signers being known to me as physicians in good standing.

S. C. Cunningham, Judge of Probate.

Commitment to Hospital—Warrant to Officer or Other Person.*

THE STATE OF SOUTH CAROLINA. }
County of Beaufort } In the Probate Court.

TO R. C. Jenkins Sheriff GREETING.

Whereas it has been made to satisfactorily appear that Dianah Carr a citizen of this County, is an insane person and a fit subject for the State Hospital, and that her enlargement is injurious to her self and dangerous to the community, and also that she has no the means to pay for her support, you are, therefore, hereby deputized by me to apprehend the said Diannah Carr and convey her to the State Hospital for the Insane, and there deliver her to the Superintendent thereof, for care and treatment as a Beneficiary Patient in said Institution, as provided by law. This shall also be the Superintendent's warrant for the receiving and the safe keeping of the said lunatic.

Given under my hand and seal of office, this 11th day of March 1901

S. C. Cunningham, Judge of Probate.

*This Warrant is to be issued by a Circuit Judge or Probate Judge. No other person or persons have authority to send a patient to the Hospital, except in case of emergency. (See Acts of 1896, p. 180, No. 71.)

State Hospital for the Insane

No. 9683 COLOR { ~~White~~ Colored } SEX { Female ~~Male~~ }

IN THE MATTER OF

Diannah Carr

Beaufort COUNTY.

ADMITTED March 15th 1901

DISCHARGED

REMOVED

DIED

COMMITTED BY

REMARKS. Found [illegible] [illegible] [illegible]

COPY.

A TRUE COPY.

ATTEST: S. C. Cunningham, Judge of Probate.

Beaufort County.

Dianah committed to South Carolina State Hospital

Source: South Carolina Department of Archives and History, Columbia, S.C., State Hospital Commitment files, s190024 #9683, box 9, 376E06, Diannah Carr.

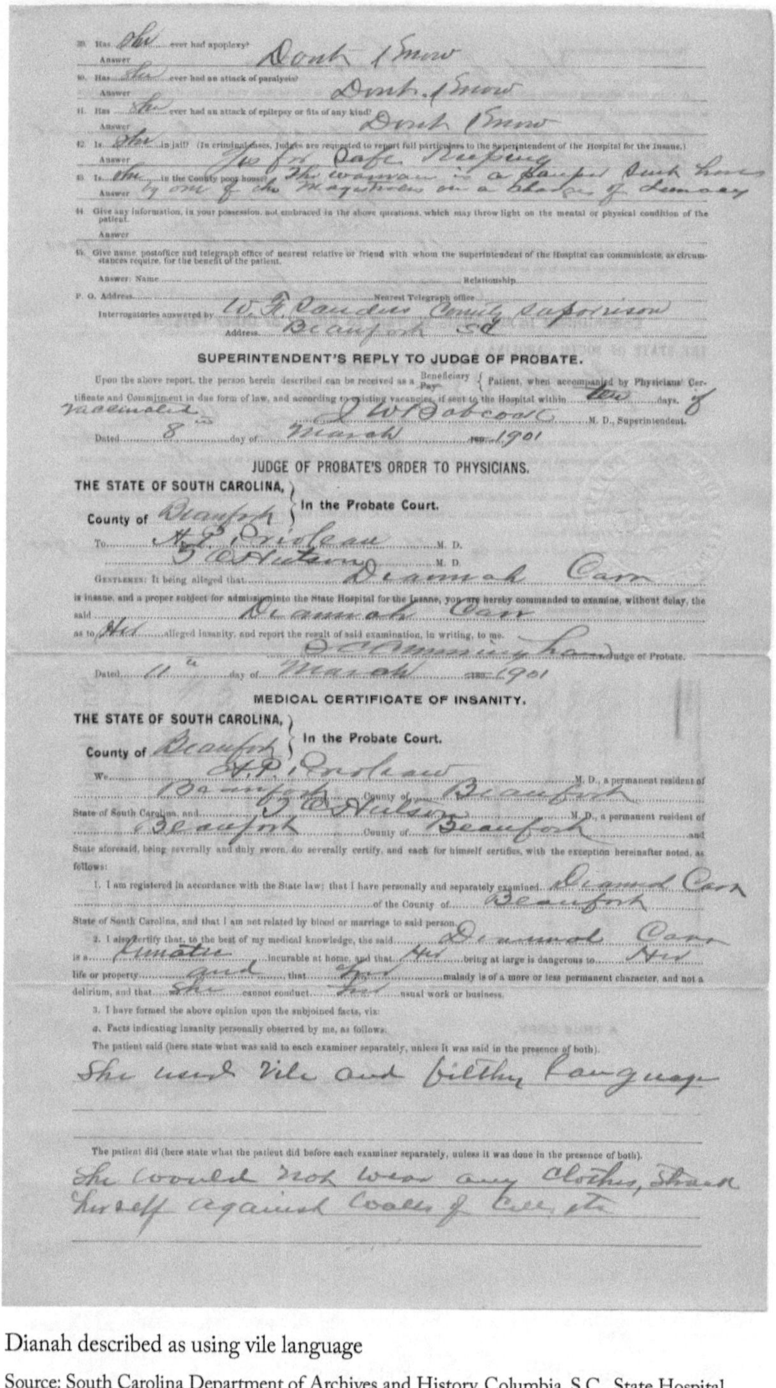

39. Has She ever had apoplexy?
Answer Dont know

40. Has She ever had an attack of paralysis?
Answer Dont know

41. Has She ever had an attack of epilepsy or fits of any kind?
Answer Dont know

42. Is She in jail? (In criminal cases, Judges are requested to report full particulars to the Superintendent of the Hospital for the Insane.)
Answer Yes for safe keeping

43. Is She in the County poor house?
Answer The woman is a pauper sent here by one of the Magistrates on a charge of lunacy

44. Give any information, in your possession, not embraced in the above questions, which may throw light on the mental or physical condition of the patient.
Answer

45. Give name, postoffice and telegraph office of nearest relative or friend with whom the superintendent of the Hospital can communicate, as circumstances require, for the benefit of the patient.
Answer: Name .... Relationship ....
P. O. Address .... Nearest Telegraph office ....
Interrogatories answered by W. F. Sanders County Supervisor
Address Beaufort SC

SUPERINTENDENT'S REPLY TO JUDGE OF PROBATE.

Upon the above report, the person herein described can be received as a Beneficiary / Pay Patient, when accompanied by Physicians' Certificate and Commitment in due form of law, and according to existing vacancies, if sent to the Hospital within two days, if vaccinated
J. W. Babcock M. D., Superintendent.
Dated 8th day of March 1901

JUDGE OF PROBATE'S ORDER TO PHYSICIANS.

THE STATE OF SOUTH CAROLINA, County of Beaufort } In the Probate Court.

To H. P. Drisleau M. D.
J. A. Hutson M. D.

GENTLEMEN: It being alleged that Dianah Carr is insane, and a proper subject for admission into the State Hospital for the Insane, you are hereby commanded to examine, without delay, the said Dianah Carr as to Her alleged insanity, and report the result of said examination, in writing, to me.
D. C. Cunningham Judge of Probate.
Dated 11th day of March 1901

MEDICAL CERTIFICATE OF INSANITY.

THE STATE OF SOUTH CAROLINA, County of Beaufort } In the Probate Court.

We H. P. Drisleau M. D., a permanent resident of Beaufort County of Beaufort State of South Carolina, and J. A. Hutson M. D., a permanent resident of Beaufort County of Beaufort and State aforesaid, being severally and duly sworn, do severally certify, and each for himself certifies, with the exception hereinafter noted, as follows:

1. I am registered in accordance with the State law; that I have personally and separately examined Dianah Carr of the County of Beaufort State of South Carolina, and that I am not related by blood or marriage to said person.

2. I also certify that, to the best of my medical knowledge, the said Dianah Carr is a lunatic incurable at home, and that Her being at large is dangerous to Her life or property and that Her malady is of a more or less permanent character, and not a delirium, and that She cannot conduct her usual work or business.

3. I have formed the above opinion upon the subjoined facts, viz:

4. Facts indicating insanity personally observed by me, as follows:

The patient said (here state what was said to each examiner separately, unless it was said in the presence of both).

She used vile and filthy language

The patient did (here state what the patient did before each examiner separately, unless it was done in the presence of both).

She would not wear any clothes, struck herself against walls of cell etc

Dianah described as using vile language

Source: South Carolina Department of Archives and History, Columbia, S.C., State Hospital Commitment files, S190024 #9683, box 9, 376E06, Diannah Carr.

hospital began accepting more Black patients, keeping white and Black patients in separate facilities.

Culturally, most families preferred to keep their loved ones at home rather than institutionalize them. This may have been true for Dianah—unless she became too unruly or despondent to be cared for by family. At the time of her confinement the asylum had 1,040 patients, with a more than 30 percent mortality rate. Poor living conditions, overcrowding, drafty rooms, and inadequate supervision contributed to patients' deaths.[3]

An investigation of the South Carolina facility by the State Board of Health in 1909, a year in which Dianah was still a patient, found violations including financial waste, excessive force used by staff, two to five patients in a room in one ward, fifteen patients bathed in the same water, no physical examination given when patients entered, and patients with tuberculosis allowed to mingle with other patients. Concerning the dead, those interred in Elmwood were buried two to three in the same plot in an area shared by hogs with cholera: "The wards, even of the white women, are overrun with vermin, and the patients are allowed to go unkept and ragged."[4] The state hospital became a house of slow death. It was so deplorable that even state officials seemed ashamed to report their findings to the public.

A ward of the state psychiatric hospital, Dianah would be absent from the Lowcountry community that watched her grow from a child running with the wind into a wife and mother. The year Dianah was committed, the Pensions Bureau had not yet made its decision on her claim. Special examiners Stovall and Parkey were still taking depositions from her acquaintances. An approval would have granted Dianah a monthly payment of twelve dollars for herself and two for Arthur. Two years had passed since she mailed her application, yet she had heard nothing. The wait on the bureau's decision had taken its toll. As she waited, poverty sapped her joy and her sanity, leaving her to waste away. Young and vibrant when she met the African who became Charles Carr, Dianah spent the remainder of her life in the state asylum, perhaps with no recollection of Charles, their child, or the life they once knew.

I came across online records of the South Carolina State Hospital Cemetery hoping to find how and when Dianah died and where she might be buried. I searched for the surname Carr and three names appeared. I came across a good match: Name: Carr, Diamale; Date of Death: 4-May-1911; Cemetery: Sligh; Grave # (no entry); County of Birth (no entry); Gender: Female; Race: Colored; Cause of death 1; Endocarditis; Age at death (no entry).

With so many fields left blank, I can only guess that no one who knew Dianah visited or even accompanied her to the hospital. It's understandable. The family was poor, and Yamassee, South Carolina, was more than 140 miles away. Dianah died either of lung or heart problems. She died alone and perhaps largely forgotten. According to records of the South Carolina Insane Asylum, Dianah was buried in the cemetery known as Sligh, where Black patients of the asylum were interred—cemeteries were also segregated, with Blacks and whites buried in different sections. Today, a golf driving range, supported by the city of Columbia, is situated over Sligh. Out of respect for the deceased, officials mounted a net to catch golf balls, keeping them from landing where graves are believed to be located.[5]

Abandoned Black cemeteries like Sligh are often desecrated, as "in the way." They are in the way of development, new housing, a "must-have" highway, or widening of a road. Being in the way, many colored cemeteries were paved over, built upon, and erased from memory and record. Some developers figured, "Hey, nobody living knows the cemetery is there." Or perhaps they thought, "Well, no one's taking care of burial ground so let's take the land for better use." Some landowners removed headstones and allowed the undergrowth to overtake burial grounds. They said nothing, sold the property (illegally, by the way), and walked away. Some entities may not have known a Black cemetery was at a particular site. Who paid attention to us? Look it up: Mississippi, Florida, Illinois, Texas, Georgia, all are guilty and the list goes on. African American cemeteries exist in towns and cities wherever there was a handful of Black people. These burial grounds have simply been forgotten or disregarded. It happens when you are "in the way."

Cemeteries hold secrets and give clues about culture. Years ago, African American graves in the Lowcountry were decorated with items of the deceased—a favorite plate, a clock whose hands marked the time of death, a chair that the deceased loved, shells from the ocean, shining objects to frighten unwanted spirits. It's a ritual that's coming back, but still not as widely practiced as in the late nineteenth and early twentieth centuries.

Early leaders and pillars of the community are buried in colored cemeteries, often forgotten as succeeding generations move from home and community historians join the ancestral realm. Our communities have changed. We moved away to find better opportunities and to escape the chokehold of Jim Crow. Black cemeteries were abandoned, fell into neglect or victim to treasure seekers who thought nothing of taking grave decorations. As the earth claimed our bodies, vines and overgrown brush covered our markers, obstructing the identities of those laid to rest. African Americans were discounted in life and in death. We were "in the way" then, just as some believe we are in the way now. We are in the way with our demands for justice, in the way of gentrification, in the way of national football games by taking a knee, in the way with "woke" protests.

The African American community's heart breaks when we learn that our cemeteries have been erased from record or built upon. Older folk shake their heads in sorrow: "My mama and daddy told me there was a colored cemetery there. People just ignored it and did what they wanted to do," they reveal. In the early years, community members may not have spoken up for fear of retribution. But now, with so much weighing on us, we are raising our voices.

In 1991 a community united to save the forgotten (but documented) eighteenth-century African Burial Ground in lower Manhattan, New York, unearthed during the construction of a federal building. The site has been designated a national historic landmark and a national monument. In December 2022 the African American Burial Grounds Preservation Act was enacted into law. This act authorizes the National Park Service to coordinate initiatives to identify, interpret, research, preserve, and record African American burial grounds that have been left unmarked, previously abandoned, or underserved. We are lobbying; someone is listening and responding in the affirmative.

After witnessing firsthand as families try to find burial plots of loved ones in cemeteries forgotten, moved, or partially destroyed, I have decided to be cremated. My family can keep my ashes in an urn on the mantel or spread them in a place that I loved. But for those who rest in our sacred grounds, I want peace for them. I would love to place flowers at Dianah's grave. Doesn't she at least deserve that? But it cannot happen. Today when we awaken too often to news of "Another Black cemetery has been found beneath a . . ." we are reminded to be watchful, be responsive, be diligent. If we want others to honor our places of rest, we must honor them, too.

I was deeply disappointed to learn of Dianah's mental decline, her lonely death in an asylum, and her burial far from her community. She had known so much disappointment in her life—being raped when an adolescent, losing the land her father had given her, witnessing the death of seven children, living in abject poverty, burying Carr, her first and only love, never marrying again. Someone should remember Dianah. For my part, from time to time, I will pour a libation and speak her name.

CHAPTER 26

Arthur Appeals for Reparations

On August 20, 1901, examiner Stovall wrote his final report to the Commission of Pensions regarding the claim of Dianah Carr. Satisfied with the sworn testimonies of Dianah and Carr's acquaintances, Stovall submitted his report. He noted that when he arrived in Hardeeville to examine Dianah, he found she was confined in the state insane asylum, having gone insane in 1900, and added "that an application for her pension through a guardian would probably be made." Special examiner Parkey who interviewed acquaintances in Monteith, Georgia, was also satisfied with what he heard and closed his report, writing, "I recommend that the papers in this claim be referred to the Chief of the Board of Review for consideration."

Because Dianah had been committed to the state asylum with no one to act as her guardian, her case lay dormant. With thousands of pension claims coming in from Civil War veterans and their widows, the understaffed bureau did not have the manpower to follow up on cases like Dianah's that needed more attention. But who was going to appoint the guardian? The bureau, already overburdened? Dianah's family—one of scores of poor, illiterate rice growers who lived in the rural part of Beaufort County? With no one taking the lead, the bureau took no further action, placing Dianah's case in abandoned files. Dianah received nothing. So did Arthur. The bureau closed Dianah's case, assuming no one would bother to challenge its decision. Years later, someone did—Arthur Carr, Dianah and Carr's son.

In 1915 Arthur Carr set out to reopen Dianah's widow's file. At the time he appealed to reopen his mother's case, Arthur was about twenty-seven years old, had a wife named Eliza (Lizer), and was living in Marianna, the capital of Jackson County, Florida. He held that as he was not yet sixteen years of age when Dianah was committed to the asylum, he was entitled to complete the widow's pension claim of twelve dollars and the minor's two-dollar monthly pension.

Realizing he would need help in seeking redress, Arthur sought the service of Armstrong Purdee, a respected African American attorney, editor, and realtor in Marianna. Born enslaved and reared in Jackson County, Purdee was secretly taught to read and write by the Milton family to whom he was hired out as a houseboy. As a young boy, Purdee witnessed Union soldiers raid Marianna's St. Luke Episcopal Church. He later gave his eyewitness account, stating that the church was "fired up by the Yankees and all of the church records were destroyed, except for the Bible."[1]

During freedom, Purdee was an apprentice under Florida State Senator William H. Milton, where he was educated in the law, becoming the first African American lawyer in Jackson County. Purdee helped all, regardless of race. He advertised in the *Times Courier* in 1888 that he would "prosecute before the Treasury and Interior Departments claims of soldiers who were disabled in the service of the United States, heirs to pensions, widows, minor children and dependent mothers for a soldier's bounty or back pay . . . with 'no fees in advance'."[2] Purdee represented Arthur, composing handwritten and typed correspondences on his behalf. Arthur placed his mark, serving as his signature, to each.

African American residents walked a cautious highly segregated line in Marianna. They took notice, as Marianna's white residents flocked to the theater to view *The Sins of the Father*. The screen production was based on Thomas Dixon's sensational novel *The Clansman*, credited with opening the way for D. W. Griffith's racially charged film *Birth of a Nation*. The *Pensacola Journal* newspaper urged theatergoers to purchase their tickets as far in advance as possible, as *The Sins of the Father* "has a 'record of thirty weeks' run in the South with theatres sold out weeks before the arrival of the play."[3]

On April 15, 1915, Purdee, in a typed letter, began handling Arthur's case writing to the Department of Interior, Pensions Bureau. It would be the first of nearly thirty correspondences between Carr and the bureau over the next twenty months. Purdee wrote:

> By the request of Arthur Carr, minor child of Charles and Dia Carr, widow of Charles Carr, who died in the line of duty in the service of the United States in the late Civil war, and the said widow file a claim for pension as the widow of the said soldier, and the same was placed in the hand of a special agent of the Bureau of pension, and on his

> report the claim was allowed to the widow, and was told by the post Master Hattiville, S.C., and he refuse to deliver the said letter suppose to contain the voucher, for the reason that the claimant was Crazy, and the same was returned to the Bureau of pension, and from the best recollection of the minor it was about 1879 or 1880. The said soldier was born in the said State, and enlisted therefrom.[4]

Purdee asked for the claim number, records, and proceedings.

Memories fade, and information handed down from one generation to the next can be inaccurate. Charles Carr did not die in the line of duty but thirty years after the Civil War. He was born in Africa, not South Carolina. Arthur was told he was born about the time of the "big shake." If he relayed that a voucher was delivered to his mother in 1879 or 1880, this was information he received secondhand. I don't know what else Arthur was told or if anyone shared the family history with him. I will always wonder if Arthur knew that his father was one of the "original Gulla negroes" brought over illegally on the slave ship *Wanderer*.

On May 3, 1915, the commission responded. It was not the answer Arthur wanted to hear. The commission wrote, "Sir: In response to your letter of the 15th . . . you are advised that it does not appear that you are entitled to the status of the above entitled claim for pension."[5]

Undaunted, on June 1, J. C. Folsom, a white merchant in Marianna, notarized Arthur's mark on a letter to the Civil War Division, Commissioner of Pensions, again seeking pension payments that had been due Dianah and Arthur. A month later the commission requested proof of Dianah's death.

Per the commission's request, Purdee and Arthur obtained a letter from the State Hospital for the Insane, stating "Diana Carr, Colored, Age Thirty, was admitted from Beaufort County, May 15, 1901, and died at this Institution, May 4, 1911, cause of death being general tuberculosis."[6] With no guardian appointed to follow through or to receive Dianah's, her claim was closed, and Arthur was denied support. Even with documentation of Dianah's death, Arthur faced an uphill battle with the bureau.

Upon receiving verification of Dianah's date of death, the commission rejected Arthur's appeal to reopen his mother's case. It argued that in 1911, when Dianah died, "she left no minor child under sixteen years of age entitled to complete the claim."[7] Rejection of the claim was a setback, but just the beginning of Arthur's fight for his mother's widow's pension.

Although the commission believed it had made its reasons clear to Arthur for rejecting his request to reopen Dianah's file, Arthur and his lawyer continued to press his claim. Arthur argued that when Dianah became a ward of the state in 1901, she was legally dead. He held fast to his claim that the year 1901 should be considered the year of her death, not 1911. He asked for the pension funds amount due effective 1901 while he was still under the age of sixteen—money neither Dianah nor he ever received.

Attorney Purdee stated Arthur's claim and referenced the case of Margaret Morman filed against the Department of the Interior. Purdee, and perhaps Folsom, the white notary, had done their research. In the case of Margaret Morman, it was ruled that "the care and support of an insane widow in a State insane asylum, or by other charity, is not such 'means of support other than her daily labor' as will bar her title to pension under the act in the contemplation thereof. It is held, therefore, that rejection of the claim for that reason was error, and such action is reversed."[8]

If Morman was still entitled to her pension even while confined in the asylum, so too, Purdee, Folsom, and Arthur argued, was Dianah.

Letters went back and forth between Arthur and the bureau. On March 16, 1916, the bureau recapped its case as follows: On November 20, 1915, Arthur was notified that his request to complete Dianah's claim to receive the dependent's pension was rejected, as he was over the age of sixteen when Dianah died. He appealed the decision on January 10, 1916; it too was rejected. The Pensions Bureau added that it is apparent from the letters of said Arthur Carr as well as his appeal that he is totally ignorant of pensions matters. Furthermore, Arthur's subsequent motion for appeal failed to arrive at the bureau within the thirty-day deadline. Therefore, the motion would not be entertained and was dismissed. Arthur's team continued to write the bureau until December 1916, when communication bearing his name or mark ceased. Each response was the same. No funds were due. The bureau's decision was final.

Arthur would not receive payments from the Pensions Bureau. His woes, however, were not over. In 1917 an Arthur Carr sat before the local

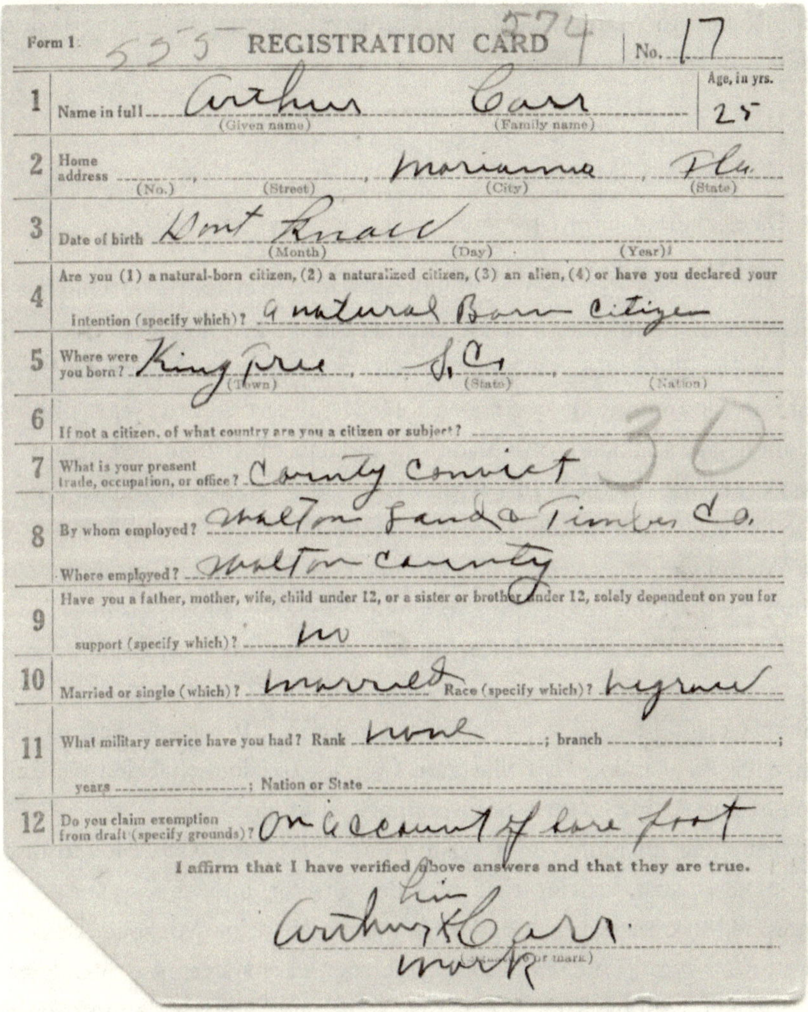
Form 1 555 REGISTRATION CARD 574 No. 17

1 Name in full Arthur Carr (Given name) (Family name) Age, in yrs. 25

2 Home address (No.) (Street) Marianna (City) Fla (State)

3 Date of birth Dont Know (Month) (Day) (Year)

4 Are you (1) a natural-born citizen, (2) a naturalized citizen, (3) an alien, (4) or have you declared your intention (specify which)? a natural Born citizen

5 Where were you born? Kingtree (Town) S.C. (State) (Nation)

6 If not a citizen, of what country are you a citizen or subject?

7 What is your present trade, occupation, or office? County Convict

8 By whom employed? Walton Land & Timber Co.
Where employed? Walton County

9 Have you a father, mother, wife, child under 12, or a sister or brother under 12, solely dependent on you for support (specify which)? no

10 Married or single (which)? married Race (specify which)? Negro

11 What military service have you had? Rank none; branch ;
years ; Nation or State

12 Do you claim exemption from draft (specify grounds)? On account of sore foot

I affirm that I have verified above answers and that they are true.

Arthur his X mark Carr
(Signature or mark)

Arthur Carr's U.S. WWI draft registration card, Jackson County, Fla.

SOURCE: Ancestry.com, *U.S., World War I Civilian Draft Registrations, 1917–1918.*

ORIGINAL DATA: United States, Selective Service System, *World War I Selective Service System Draft Registration Cards, 1917–1918*, Washington, D.C.: National Archives and Records Administration, M1509, 4,582 rolls. Imaged from Family History Library microfilm.

draft board in Marianna, Florida, and gave information for the World War I draft registration card.

Name: Arthur Carr. Age: 25.

Home Address: Marianna Fla.

Date of birth: Don't Know

Arthur declared that he was a natural-born citizen, born in King Tree (Kingstree), South Carolina. He attested that he had no parents, nor did he have a child or sister or brother twelve years or under dependent solely on him for support. He was married. He was described as a Negro of medium height and build, with black eyes and hair. He had not lost a limb or was otherwise disabled. This Arthur Carr, however, had seen hard times. He listed his trade as county convict at the Walton Land & Timber Co. in Walton County, seventy miles from Jackson County. He was exempted from the draft "on account of a sore foot."[9] He then affixed his mark.

I thought back on the Thirteenth Amendment. Long awaited by those in bondage, it ruled slavery unconstitutional. But there was an exception: Slavery could be used as punishment for a crime. It became clear to me that the very amendment that gave Carr his freedom shackled his son, sentencing Arthur to years of involuntary servitude.

Searching for more about Walton Land & Timber Co., I found historic newspaper articles that provided insight into the system that morphed into mass incarceration as written about by Michelle Alexander in *The New Jim Crow*. Florida's convict lease system was populated overwhelmingly by African Americans. In 1910 Florida's Commissioner of Agriculture B. E. McLin, who oversaw the convict lease system, commented, "As to the type of prisoners confined in Florida, we find that at least 90 percent of our convicts are negroes. Their habits of life are those of the out-door common laborer: accustomed to the saw mill, turpentine and phosphate work."[10] Two years later the *Pensacola Journal*, on December 18, 1910, reported how convicts using up-to-date machinery were grading a road four miles long in Walton County. So pleased was the County Board of Commissioners with the work that in 1916 convicts were used to construct the Gulf Beach Highway stretching to the lagoon. As the county had been unsuccessful in raising funds for the road, Mr. W. C.

Barrineau, chairman of the Board of Commissioners, stated that as far as he is "personally concerned the proposition for using the convicts is agreeable to him"; he added, however, that "the experienced county guards be employed because . . . there is a certain responsibility for the care of the convicts and the county's property, which must be safeguarded."[11]

Prisoners knew the brutality that awaited them in the camps and the convict lease system. In 1911 two white prisoners tried to escape from the turpentine camp of the Walton Land & Timber Company, where they were sentenced to a term at hard labor. Before being carried to the company, both men vowed "that they would never work in convict camps."[12] In the same time period, Charles Jones, "a negro in the lessee service of the Walton Land & Timber died at the camp." No cause of death was given. A telegram was sent to the sheriff's office and a notice published in the *Pensacola Journal*, giving instruction to the family who may desire to bring the remains for interment.[13] John Underwood Jr., "colored," sentenced to ten years of hard labor for robbery, was shot and killed as he tried to escape. Underwood had arrived at Walton Land camp just days before he was shot. The *Pensacola Journal* reported the news and also gave instructions for claiming the remains.[14]

In 1896 J. C. Powell, captain of a Florida convict camp, described the grueling labor in a turpentine camp:

> Every man went on a trot. They kept this gait up all day long, from tree to tree as the labor is exhausting in the extreme, I have frequently seen men on their way back to the camp drop of fatigue and their comrades on the squad chain drag them a dozen yards through the dirt before the pace could be checked so as to enable them to regain their feet. There would be a prodigious clamor of iron, a cloud of dust, a volley of imprecation, and a fallen man would stagger up, dash the dirt out of his eyes, and go reeling and running on.[15]

Of punishment, Powell reported:

> We discarded the old methods of punishment from the start, and adopted the strap, which has been used ever since to enforce discipline, and as of late years has been adopted by state law. It consists of a section of tough leather about a foot and a half long by three inches broad and attached to a wooden handle. The castigation is applied

> below the loins, and the convict placed on his knees with his palms on the ground. The clothing is then drawn back and the leather applied, until in the judgment of the captain, a sufficient punishment has been administered. There is no legal restriction, and never was, as to the number of blows, the frequency of punishment, or by whom it shall be applied.[16]

Walton Land & Timber Co. had a reputation for excessive beatings and cruel treatment of convicts. In a 1913 Florida state report on the convict lease system, two guards and the camp captain were singled out for beating inmates. Upon reviewing conditions at Walton, Supervisor Ferrell concluded that the beatings resulted from incompetence, not sadism, and that the captain of the camp needed to learn how to discipline his inmates. One inmate was treated so badly that he requested to be transferred to another camp. Walton also was found to have poor sanitation, as urinals and water closets were broken and no plumber had been called.[17] A visit to a Walton camp found a shortage of beds, with several men "doubling up" while they waited for more beds to arrive. Three men suffered with syphilis in one camp and at another camp one man was nearly blind in both eyes due to the communicable disease.

If a sore foot that Arthur Carr reported to the draft board in 1917 was all that he suffered while a convict at Walton Land & Timber Co., he was fortunate. As he was the only African American male named Arthur Carr born in South Carolina, living near Jackson County, Florida, during this time, this draft information merited attention. However, even this individual faded from public record. With no additional records to confirm his identity, it cannot be conclusively determined whether he was the son of Charles and Dianah Carr. The likelihood, though, is that he was.

This chapter about Arthur Carr, a convict laborer at a turpentine camp at the Walton Land & Timber Co., is by far the most difficult for me to pen. It is tougher than writing about slavery. As a slave, Charles Carr, his father, was property and thus had "value." As a freedman, Carr had options, even if he had to scratch out a living. As one caught up in the penal system and forced to work in the deep woods where towering trees muffled cries for help and blocked the light of day, Arthur, in my opinion, had a life worse than slavery. He was purchased and put to a death work.

If a convict took his last breath, temporarily halting work, guards operated under the sentiment, "One dies, get another."

They could get another because Black men were "plentiful." While some may have committed capital crimes, many were picked up for vagrancy or idleness, that is, not working. But then finding work in the early twentieth century was difficult for Black people—unless you wanted to labor for slave wages or sharecrop and never get out of debt. Sheriffs and other law enforcers arrested Black men and charged them with minor crimes—disorderly conduct, petty theft, drunkenness, and the like. These men were sentenced, and rather than pay for their "stay in jail," the penal system leased their labor to private companies, which fed and clothed them and used them as free labor for corporate gain.

The twentieth-century convict lease system was the new form of slavery. The auctioneer this time was the state or county. Industries loved the idea. Prison labor was cheaper than paying skilled laborers. No one really cared about the prisoners. Society assumed the men were getting what they deserved. No one cared about Black men, who made up the bulk of those imprisoned. This was the era of Jim Crow. To many whites, slavery had proven that strong Black backs were created for hard labor, no matter how debilitating and inhumane.

So Black men were captured (as during the slave trade) and shipped off to labor camps (i.e., new plantations). Some were sent to woodlands. That's where men leased to the turpentine producers worked. No one respected woodsmen—not whites, not Blacks. They labored long and hard under the white man's supervision. Lessees were eyed by vicious dogs and armed guards on horseback who couldn't care less if the men lived or died. Those in turpentine camps rose at 4:30 a.m. and were tethered in squads, chained to each other at the waist. They were forced to trot through the woods. They kept this gait—from tree to tree—dipping gum from daybreak to evening. Those who couldn't keep up were dragged along until the group stopped. White men died in convict camps. Black men died in convict camps. White men risked their lives to escape. Black men died trying to escape.

It gets worse, and some treatment was too inhumane to speak of. So, in this writing I am forced to "pull up," to shift my energy and thoughts to something good, so as not to sink into despair. Black lives in the early twentieth century, like Black lives today, *did not matter* to some. Today's abuse is the same as in the past, just one hundred years later. In the midst of the 2020 and 2021 protests against a sinister social, political, and policing system, I reminded myself to "pull up." "Pull up," Maia, when you see a video recording of another Black man or woman beaten by law enforcement. "Pull up" when the evening news exposes how a Black mother and her young son were denied seating at a restaurant because he, in knee-length athletic shorts, tennis shoes, and a T-shirt, did not meet the dress standard—although a white mom and youth wearing the same were seated. I've got to "pull up," when conducting research on the African American community, and I find photos of police choking a teen-aged boy—a photo from the 1960s that looks just like the photos of choke holds that lead us to plead, "I can't breathe" even today. I've got to pull up in order maintain some sanity. If I pull up, I can stand up and not give up.

Arthur Carr experienced the deadly reality of Florida's convict lease system. Even though Florida ended it in 1923, private companies continued to collude with the prison system for cheap labor. It's likely that Arthur died in the convict camp or soon thereafter if he was released. He does not appear in the 1920 census, nor in any public record. Florida recorded deaths beginning in 1892, but Arthur Carr's name is not on file. He, like his father Charles Carr, is buried in some unknown place. Unlike his father, Arthur seemed to have had no community to celebrate his life, to bury him in a coveted tradition, or to mourn his death. He may be buried in an unmarked grave in a field with others who met their death at the convict camp. If so, I can envision the warden shrugging off Arthur's death, saying cold-heartedly, "One dies, get another."

CHAPTER 27

The Women and Continuing the Fight

Another family member sought Charles Carr's pension and that of Dianah. On March 17, 1920, the Pensions Bureau received a letter with a return address from Campbellton, Florida, on stationery from the J. O. Christmas general store. Campbellton was a predominately African American community fifteen miles from Marianna. The letter was written on behalf of Eliza (Lizer) Carr, Arthur Carr's widow. It read:

> Campbellton, Fla 3-10-1920
> War Dept.
> Washington D.C.
> Gentlemen, sometime ago I wrote you concerning my claim which was due my husband from the Government—Arthur Car—for his pension to his father.
> Charles Carr Co K. 34/UNITED STATES inft. # wid org. 638,231. Please write me and let me know if I can get this claim—which has never been paid.
> The money was sent to Dinah Car at Hattieville, S.C., but she never rec'd it. This [?] is due his child's widow, I think.
> Yours truly
> H. T. Vicks
> Campbellton, Fla.
> Lizer Carr, widow of Arthur Carr[1]

A widow, Eliza had no one in the household to give her financial support. Like most Black women in Campbellton in the 1920s, she almost assuredly worked in the fields or as a servant in a white woman's house.

Eliza Carr's letter was signed by H. T. Vicks. Vicks was enumerated in the 1920 federal census of Campbellton. He was a forty-four-year-old African American farmer, married, with children. He could read and write. Perhaps Eliza worked for Vicks or lived in the community. She reached out to him, someone who could communicate with the government on her behalf.

As I read the testimonies of the women in Carr's life, I was inspired by their strength. Women were the most vulnerable under slavery. We could be taken advantage of on the enslaver's whim. We bore children for the enslaver or by whomever he decided to partner us with, and we gave birth until our wombs were dry. We worked in the fields, in the "Big House," took care of the enslaver's family and our own, nursed our sick and wounded. This is not to say that the Black man and child didn't suffer under slavery—we all did. But the women bore a special burden.

For certain, many women came out of the fields after slavery, at least for as long as they could. They took care of the home, family, and took in washing to add to the income. They wanted respect, "learnin'", and just treatment. As they straightened their backs, many freedwomen found they were alone. Their men had been killed or sold away. If found, too often their husbands had married another. Nonetheless, the women endured. We caught only glimpses of the women of Carr's life, as only segments of their lives were recorded. But even in their relative silence, the women exhibited authority and determination.

Sallie. Carr identified her on the Freedman's Bank signature card as his wife. I found nothing of her. I don't know if she was his wife during slavery or for a short period after he was discharged from service. She bore a child in slavery and was blessed that they were not separated. Carr added to her life, and he embraced her or perhaps their or her son. I think of her as an example of thousands of enslaved Black women whose stories remain unknown but who wisely navigated slavery and freedom.

Dianah. Can't you see her, vivacious and full of life? Dianah certainly caught Carr's eye. He took one look at her and began courting her. He always returned home to her even after harsh words. Carr comforted her and loved her even when she couldn't nurse their infants or children back to health. Carr thought enough of her and them as a couple to make their union legal to spare her from disapproving community looks. Dianah was a woman who found happiness even in the midst of hard times. Although illiterate, she fought to get her widow's pension so she could care for her and Charles' son, Arthur. In her final days she turned to her daughter, the child she gave birth to while herself a child. Her daughter, then a young woman, took her in. In Dianah I envision a young woman with a zest for life, who ran with the wind until her heart, lungs, and mind gave out.

Bettie Fields. She had been a midwife for forty years. She was a vital part of the community. She traveled, perhaps walked, in the August heat to be with Dianah as she gave birth to Arthur. Knowing Dianah had lost other children in childbirth, Bettie stayed with her, comforted her as the aftershocks of the Charleston earthquake troubled the earth. Bettie knew she was helping to bring innocent life into a cruel world, but she did it. Midwives prided themselves on saving babies, no matter how uncertain the future. Who knows when one would deliver a Nat Turner, a Harriet Tubman, an African warrior, or a queen diviner. She spoke forthrightly and proudly when the pensions agent inquired about Dianah. I see in Bettie a woman who knew her worth.

Hester. Carr's wife before Dianah. She too was probably enslaved. One may never know when Hester resided on the Berrien Plantation. She may have been enslaved and purchased by the plantation owner or she may have migrated there as a freedwoman seeking work. Carr's family and friends remembered her. No one spoke of Hester and Carr having children. Family and friends did remember Hester's illness. No physician attended her. Not in freedom. In slavery, ole massa would have had a doctor right there to patch her up. Hester would be good for a few more years of unpaid labor or maybe to birth a child who also by law would be his "slave." Carr, an attentive husband, brought Hester medicine from town. Lingering in sickness for a year, Hester undoubtedly knew her fate. In Hester, I sense a woman who was grateful for a taste of freedom and for the man who demonstrated his love.

Alice. She was a keeper of history. Alice confirmed that Carr and her mother, perhaps Rose, whom Carr named as his sister, were born in Africa and that Charles LaMar (Lamar) enslaved Carr. Her testimony also supported reports that some of the *Wanderer* captives were taken to Florida. Her mother was enslaved by a Florida physician named Mays. Alice and her mother left Florida soon after freedom and came to Meinhard near Savannah. The daughter of Rose, Alice was perhaps the only blood family that Carr reunited with in freedom. Because Alice felt no shame in being the daughter of a captured African, she shared her family's story of the

Wanderer with her daughter, Patience. I hold Alice as a family historian whose knowledge honored the ancestors.

Eliza. She was the daughter-in-law Carr never knew. How long were she and Arthur married before he was sentenced to convict labor? She had listened to Arthur's story of a pension denied him and his deceased mother and picked up the mantle after Arthur's death. Refusing to let the government's "no" rob her of life, Eliza moved to Jacksonville, Florida, where she worked, took in boarders, remarried, and divorced. She was a woman who knew when to "let it go." When the past no longer served her, she moved on. I recognize Eliza as a woman who would not wallow in disappointment. She managed the hand life dealt her, realizing sometimes you have to go life alone.

I finally found Rose, Carr's sister who reunited with him in the Savannah area as families scrambled after the war to find loved ones torn away during slavery. By 1900 she had died. The Savannah community recalled Silvie (Silvey) the old African, described as too idiotic (or maybe just too tired) to remember anything. Whatever their lots in life, these women weaved a tapestry from their joy and pain. That's what women do. We make the best of what's given to us and pass the promise of a better tomorrow on to those who look to us for assurance.

On behalf of Eliza, Vicks wrote the bureau again in December 1922. In the letter he respectfully complained that he had not received any response. The bureau stamped "RETURN THIS LETTER" on the correspondence.[2] On February 10, 1923, he penned a letter asking the bureau if it had received previous letters. Again, agents stamped, "RETURN THIS LETTER" on the handwritten correspondence.[3] Vicks continued to write. The bureau returned the letters, or when responding, continued to inform that Arthur's claim had been denied and no further action would be taken.

On December 1, 1923, Vicks signed a typewritten letter to Hon. Duncan U. Fletcher, United States Senate. He appealed to Florida's highest elected federal representative. He asked Senator Fletcher to investigate Arthur Carr's claim, closing with "I trust you will investigate this matter as soon as possible, and do all that you can for him in this matter."[4]

Senator Fletcher wrote the Commissioner of Pensions and Vicks, acknowledging receipt of his letter. Ten days later, the commissioner replied to Senator Fletcher, the letter bearing the same information that Arthur was over sixteen years of age when his mother died. The letter concluded that "there is nothing now pending or unadjudicated in the case and further correspondence will be useless."[5]

Letters on behalf of Eliza Carr ceased. Perhaps she finally accepted that the government would pay nothing. Perhaps others grew weary of assisting her. Maybe the day-to-day struggles of survival became more important or more difficult, needing all her time and strength. She left Marianna and began a new life.

Arthur and Eliza never had a child. In Africa, Charles Carr's family line stretched back to the beginning of mankind. In America, his future seemed to have died in one generation.

CHAPTER 28

Tennessee and the Last Word

A letter from another relative of Charles Carr arrived in 1936, more than forty years after Carr filed an application for his pension. It was placed on the desk of W. C. Black, chief clerk, the Office of the Adjutant General, Widow Division. It was a handwritten letter, scribed by one with a formal education:

> 218 15th Ave. N
> Nashville, Tenn
> August 10, 1936
> The Adjutant General Office
>
> Dear Sir—My uncle Charles Carr is the same complexion and height as the one you referred to in your letter of Hartsville, South Carolina who is said to have served in the United States Army during the Civil War.
>
> He was enrolled and mustered into service January 6, 1865, at Hilton Head, S.C. as a private of Company K 34th Regiment United States Colored Infantry, Civil War, to serve 3 years, and was mustered out honorably discharged, with the company February 28, 1866 at Jacksonville Florida as a private. He has never got any thing. I wish you would please look into it for me. He was my Uncle.
>
> Yours truly
> Charley Jones
> 218 15th Ave. N
> Nashville, Tenn[1]

I expected Carr's immediate family to pursue his pension. I never dreamed that a nephew, living in another state and forty years later, would seek what Carr was denied.

Charley Jones had followed the lives of his uncle, Charles Carr, and Carr's family. Thinking back, I remembered coming across a letter in the widow's pension file written January 2, 1912, to L. P. Padgett, U.S. Representative from Tennessee, Jones' home state. As there was no signature, envelope, or return address, I set the letter aside, unable to ascertain its importance or provenance. The letter may have been written on behalf of Jones, asking Congressman Padgett to inquire about the case of Charles Carr. The letter was written seven months after Dianah's death in 1911. Someone must have told Jones about Dianah's death and Carr's pension. In 1936 Jones resumed the family's quest for Carr's or the widow's pension.

In 1940 Jones was living in Davidson County, Tennessee, with his wife Lula and his married stepdaughter, Margaret Amos. He and his family members were born in Tennessee. Jones was seventy-nine years old; his wife was sixty-seven, and Margaret was twenty-seven. Jones lacked the benefit of a formal education, his wife had a fourth-grade education, and Margaret had completed her third year in high school. Perhaps she wrote the letter to the adjutant general, or perhaps a neighbor, one who was a teacher.

Carr stated in the Freedman's Bank register that he had one sister, Rose, of whom, besides the family's oral history, no other record has been found. In 1901 Alice Golphin attested in her deposition that her mother and Charles were sister and brother. Charley Jones was born around 1860, two years after the landing of the *Wanderer*. It was possible that Charley Jones was related to Charles Carr, even being named after him. I found Alice's and John Golphin's marriage record. Prior to her marriage to Golphin, Alice's maiden name was Jones. Perhaps she and Charley Jones were brother and sister, the children of Rose, Carr's sister.

Chief Clerk Black acknowledged Jones' correspondence, promising that the letter was receiving attention and a response would soon be forthcoming. Dependents Claims Service replied on September 25, 1936, asking Jones what specific information he desired. The correspondent added, "However, for your information, it may be stated that there is no existing law which provides death compensation or pension benefits to a nephew of a veteran."[2]

On December 18 Jones received a letter from the General Accounting Office, Records Division. The assistant chief of the Records Division issued the reply. He informed Jones that Carr had received all arrears and pay and allowance including $100, paid in full to March 1866, and added, "Nothing further is due."[3]

Jones, like Arthur Carr, persisted. Jones trusted there was something for him, if only the government would look. In January 1937, he appealed to President Franklin D. Roosevelt for assistance.

I thought, now here is a Black man who believed in his cause and his own worth. He showed no hesitancy about writing to the president, the man who held the highest office in the land. The typed letter was stamped "copy" by the Dependents Claims Service.

> Mr. Franklin D. Roosevelt
>
> Dear sir:
>
> I am writing again in behalves of my claim of my uncle Charley Carr. It has past in every house except the claim office. And the claim office says it been payed. Mr. Padgett told me he had never got any thing. And said he was mustered out an honorable discharge. And he said Charley Carr stopped writing. And he did not no the cause. And he gave me his address. Hartsville, S.C. I written there to the General Post Master. And he told me he was dead also his wife. That been about twenty six years ago. I am the only one living that is due two. I am seventy seven years old now myself.
>
> Mr. Roosevelt, I wish you would please look into this matter for me. You are the one that had it located for before. I had got more confidence in you than any other man I no of. Because you have did more for the poor class of people that any other man has done.
>
> Thanking you in advance
>
> I am Respectfully,
>
> (signed) Charley Jones
>
> 218 15th Ave. N
>
> Nashville, Tenn[4]

Jones' faith in Roosevelt was not surprising. Jones lived during the Great Depression. Roosevelt, with his New Deal agenda designed to get people back to work, often was viewed as a savior, perhaps a second Lincoln to poor Black people. New Deal programs such as the Works Progress Administration (WPA), later renamed the Work Projects Administration, and Civilian Conservation Corps combined employed more than five hundred thousand Black individuals. The National Youth Administration hired African American supervisors to oversee the work on behalf of Black youth. The WPA assisted in helping laborers. It set quotas for companies with government construction contracts to ensure they hired Black laborers in proportion to the 1930 labor census. Blacks were hired in the arts and theater. More than one million African Americans were taught to read through New Deal education programs.[5] Illinois Congressman Arthur W. Mitchell, the only African American in the U.S. Congress between 1935 and 1943, praised Roosevelt and his leadership and added to the Congressional Record, "the attitude of the Administration at the White House is absolutely without prejudice, insofar as the Negro citizenry is concerned."[6]

Not so, railed some Black leaders. To many, the Black community needed more than a new deal—they needed a square deal. Critics of President Roosevelt pointed out that despite policy Negroes were often forgotten, ignored, or discriminated against when the federal government disbursed relief funds and federal jobs. Black people were hired often only after long protracted struggles to get them in the door and into positions. Inequities existed in housing, economic, and agricultural programs. The National Recovery Administration not only offered whites jobs first but set up different pay scales that favored whites over Blacks. Under the Agricultural Adjustment Administration, white landowners found it more economically advantageous to reduce acreage under government rental agreement than to cultivate farms. Idle land idled Black farmworkers, leaving thousands unemployed.

The Economic Security Bill, which later became the Social Security Act of 1935, provided funds for unemployment insurance, the aged, dependent children, and social programs. However, Social Security excluded thousands employed in agriculture, as domestic workers, and as personal servants and farmers—jobs in which African Americans were employed. Closer to Jones was the Tennessee Valley Authority (TVA), which oversaw the construction of dams and produced electrical power along the Tennessee River. An early report revealed that no African Americans had been admitted to the trade school to train for the TVA program; nor were African Americans admitted in the town of Norris constructed by the TVA.[7]

To poor Blacks, many of whom were born in or right after slavery, Roosevelt and his New Deal gave hope, if not always assistance. Some waited patiently for government relief or a private pension. Former enslaved men and women living in Nashville, where Jones resided, told their stories.

To hear their voices, I turned to the WPA Slave Narratives, found online and in books. During the Depression, writers hired by the WPA's Federal Writers Project traveled in teams throughout the South to interview formerly enslaved individuals, many in their later years of life. WPA writers asked the elderly about life under slavery, work, foodways, health, leisure, family, and more. They recorded their answers and then transcribed the interviews. The interviewers were often criticized for writing and transcribing words and phrases used by older African Americans that fed into the stereotype of a bowing and bobbing slave.

Researchers and historians often look askance at the narratives, as they were recorded mostly by white workers. Some doubt that interviewees would reveal their true experiences under slavery to white workers, who in the 1930s were symbols of authority and power. It was thought that the elderly, many who lived near or worked for the former enslaver or his children, wouldn't speak against those who allowed them to stay on the land. Some interviewees probably held back, telling the white writers what they thought they wanted to hear: stories of kind masters and life better in slavery than under Jim Crow and the Depression. Others, however, told of the cruelty of slavery, of people beaten and sold. In the throes of the Great Depression, many interviewees shared how difficult it was to make ends meet, and how they were waiting on the government to assist as promised. Several elderly Black men and women in Nashville, where Jones lived, told their story of life during the Depression, allowing us to hear Black voices, even if guarded.

Cecelia Chappel told a WPA interviewer, "For a long time de relief give me a quart of milk a day, but now all I has is what my sister Harriett give me. She isn't got much work and some days we don't have much to eat. If my Missis was livin' I wouldn't go hungry."[8]

At age eighty-two, former slave Wiley Childress looked wistful, holding on to waning faith in the government: "I's not able to work now and all I have is a small grocery order that the relief give me. Dey keep promisin' to give me de Old Age Pension and I wish dey would hurry it up."[9]

Patsy Hyde shared her plight and her wait on promised relief: "After I got too feeble to do washin' and ironin' for my livin' I went to the Relief Office to get them to help me, but dey wouldn't do a thing. I han no place to go and no money to do with."[10] Narcissus Young fared better, receiving benefits from a New Deal program: "I become feeble and couldn't work out en ever since den I been come up a mountain, but now I get helps by de Social security."[11]

Whether his faith was ill placed, Jones believed in President Roosevelt and saw him as a friend of the forgotten man. However, there would be no reply from the president. The letter was forwarded to the Dependents Claims Service. Director E. L. Bailey replied January 21, noting, "Because of the multitude of pressing demands made upon the President's time, incident to his office, it is not possible for him personally to answer the many letters he receives each day; hence, he has referred to this Service for consideration and reply."

Eleven months later, November 17, 1937, Jones received a letter from the Records Division, General Accounting Office. It again was explained that Charles Carr was mustered out with the bounty of $100, with nothing further due, and added he was discharged before ten months. The office suggested that Jones write to the Veterans Administration if there were questions of payment of a pension.

As advised, Jones had someone contact the Veterans Administration. In the December 12 letter Jones inquired "information regarding the possibility of securing a pension, or compensation, said to be due my uncle Charles Carr, (deceased). I am sole, living kin of my uncle, *much* in need of the pension, and will appreciate any help, or information leading to getting the money."

I may never know how Jones knew he was Carr's last living relative. As neither Arthur nor Jones could write, the two may have had friends pen letters for them over the years. Someone must have informed Jones when Arthur died as well.

When Jones received word that there is no law that entitled the nephew of a veteran to pension benefits, Jones wrote the president again.

> I am writing, for my Uncle claim. Charley Carr. Who died and never did get any thing. He served three years in the Civil War. Mr. Padgett told me that he died and never did get anything. His wife after his death tried and could not get any thing. He said he did not no what the trouble was. They stop writing. He gave me the address and told me to write Hartsville South Carolina. I written there and got an answer from the General Postmaster. It must have been something for

> him or else he would not have been writing for it. I am not after no pension. On his discharge if anyone related to him could get what he failed to get every thing has been worked up to the claim office.
>
> The Claim office man said they payed him one hundred dollars when he was mustered out.
>
> They all got pay when they were mustered out.
>
> Mr. Roosevelt, I wish you would please look in the matter for me. I would be glad if you could do some thing for me. I think there is something there for me.

The response came January 7, 1938, and read as the previous disappointing letter: The demands on the President made it impossible for him to respond. The letter was being forwarded to the appropriate government office.

It was the last documented communication between Jones and the United States government on Carr's pension and the widow's pension claim. Perhaps Jones gave up. Perhaps he no longer had someone to write letters for him. Maybe letters written were lost, or misfiled, or ignored.

Charley Jones died November 12, 1942, in Nashville General Hospital at the age of eighty-two. Jones was the last of Carr's relatives to appeal to the U.S. government for Charles Carr's or Dianah Carr's pension. The quest for a pension—a forty-four-year ordeal—ended. There would be no compensation for the African called Charles Carr—not for being captured and shipped on the clandestine slave ship *Wanderer*, not for funds lost in the failure of the Freedman's Bank, not for the battlefield injury to his arm that caused so much pain that at times he could not work. He would live and die virtually unnoticed, with no one to rally for him except his community of family and friends. And they—Black, poor, illiterate—were no match for a system that discounted African Americans through law and custom—for a government that said "No."

EPILOGUE

No doubt there were hundreds of other survivors of the *Wanderer*, their stories untold. Yet as fate would have it, the name Charles Carr was again spoken. During the Great Depression, writers with the Savannah Unit of the Georgia Writers' Project interviewed individuals formerly enslaved in the Savannah area. Their interviews were published in 1940 in the book *Drums and Shadows: Survival Studies Among the Georgia Coastal Negroes*. Interviewers visited Tatemville, a community southwest of Savannah. One wrote that Tatemville "was inhabited by Negroes, some of whom are survivals of ante-bellum days."[1] He added, "It is interesting to note that a number of these old people in speaking of their fellow-slaves frequently prefix 'Golla' to their given name."

Golla or *Gullah* refers to the people of the Sea Islands from West and Central Africa who held on to their traditional African ways. The elders interviewed in Savannah knew the Golla were from Africa and were "different" and respected their African traditions.

I was familiar with *Drums and Shadows,* but one day I took a second look. I am glad I did. In one of the chapters, Tonie Houston, described as an old Black preacher, held much information about the Golla people. When asked by the interviewer if he remembered any of the people brought over from Africa, Houston replied, "Yas, I know heaps ub um. Deah waz 'Golla' John Wiley, 'Golla' Jim Bayfield—he wuz bought by Mahse Chahles Lamar, and he sole im to Mr. McMullen. Den deah wuz 'Golla' Jack, 'Golla Tom,' 'Golla Silvie,' 'Golla Chahles Carr,' 'Golla' Bob, Chahlotte, Cain, an Jeanette, and 'Golla' Alice. Dey wuz all bought by Mr. McMullen. . . . All duh people wut come frum Africa aw obushseas wuz call 'Golla' and dey talk wuz call 'Golla' talk."[2]

It took me a minute to decipher the words as transcribed by the interviewer, and then I began to recognize the names: John Wiley, Tom Simmons, Silvie Simmons, and Alice. They all had lived in Monteith, Georgia. They were acquaintances of Charles Carr, with Alice, the only one of them living in 1901, providing testimony in Carr and his widow's pension case. Alice gave the pensions agent detailed depositions about Carr and her mother being brought over on the *Wanderer*. Houston only knew one of the Gollas' full name: "Golla Chahles Carr." He remembered him not just as Charles, but Charles Carr. These Gollas and others likely were smuggled into Georgia aboard the *Wanderer* by their former enslavers, whom Houston identified as Charles Lamar and Montmollin.

Houston described various Golla traditions. For their meetings, Golla Tom or another would beat the drum signaling them to gather; then all would sing and dance in a circle to the accompaniment of the drum. This is an extension of the circle ritual of Black soldiers under Higginson's command and of the ring shout. The drums of death would also sound, summoning them to the "sitting up" or wake.

"Dey would have some hot drinks . . . sech as coffee an tea. Den at duh time fuh buryin duh drum would beat an all would lay flat on duh ground on dey faces befo duh body wuz placed in duh grave," recalled Houston. "Den all would rise and dance roun duh grave. When duh body wuz buried, duh drum would give signal wen all wuz tuh rise aw fall aw tuh dance aw sing."[3]

Houston gave examples of the Gollas' language. He explained *musungo* was the word for tobacco, *mulafo* for whiskey, and *sisure* for chicken. Gollas made their own utensils and dishes. "Dey would make wooden cutters for meat and vegetubble and would dress some of dem with pretty figures." He told of Dick Hamilton, a conjure man who could disappear at will (reminiscent of the enslaved Igbo who walked or flew back to Africa), and of Solomon Davis, who had not been heard from since departing for Africa some years earlier.[4]

There was something about Carr that more than thirty-five years after his death in 1895, someone would remember him. An acquaintance in Tatemville would speak his name and tell how "Golla" Africans shook off the white man's culture to gather with their countrymen, beat the drum, and bury the dead in an African ritual. Charles Carr retained remnants of his African culture and practiced them with his fellow countrymen and women with whom he shared life—from capture, to filth and disease on the slave ship *Wanderer* where in anguish they witnessed as bodies were thrown overboard. They toiled together in slavery under the watchful eye of John Montmollin. Perhaps Charles confided in them when he dared escape to join the Union army. He kept them in mind upon his discharge and returned to the community, working on nearby plantations for former enslavers. Carr would not be forgotten by them, either. Alice, Carr's niece, recalled Hester, his first wife, and after her death, his marriage to Dianah and the latter's confinement to the mental institution when living in abject poverty became too much for her to bear.

His son Arthur's determination to reopen his mother's widow's pension application, arguing he was under age sixteen when she was committed, kept Charles' name and military service alive. The Pensions Bureau rejected Arthur's appeal and that of his wife, Eliza. Years later his aged uncle, Charley Jones, wrote an appeal to the president of the United States. The letters were shuttled about by a government fed up with explaining that nothing was due.

I had to piece together Carr's story because so much information is missing. Where was Carr buried? If I knew where, I am sure I could lobby to at least have a marker at the burial site of a survivor of the *Wanderer*. What became of his sister Rose, listed on Charles' Freedman's Bank register? Charley Jones said Charles was his uncle. Jones may have been Alice Golphin's brother, as her maiden name was Jones.[5] She stated her mother was Charles' sister, but one cannot find her record of her mother's name. The death certificate for Charley Jones listed Edd Jones as his father. His mother's name was unknown. What became of Patience Small, the daughter of Alice and John Golphin? She knew "Uncle Charles" and "Aunt Hester." Patience failed to appear in any public record.

Documenting the words of the enslaved and freedmen and women is difficult, as in slavery it was a crime to teach the enslaved to read or write. Immediately after slavery, freed people sought to become literate, but not all were successful. The enslavers left diaries, wills, letters, and such telling about their slaves, but these are enslavers' interpretation of what we felt and experienced.

Our family history is often passed down through oral tradition, and we cherish the stories told by our elders. Yet if we dig, if we are fortunate, we can find records of our ancestors' lives and deeds. They married, owned land, held positions in their communities. Our challenge is to record these accounts while our elders are still with us.

Arthur Carr lived in Florida for perhaps five or more years. Was the Arthur Carr listed as a county convict on the WWI draft card found in Jackson County, Florida, the son of Charles Carr? What of Arthur's relationship with Eliza? We know very little about her or about them as a couple. Charley Jones, the aged uncle, had one daughter, Margaret Amos, who was recorded in the 1940 federal population census in Tennessee. She appeared in the 1950 census with her husband, but with no children.

Much more is known about the slave ship *Wanderer* coconspirators. Charles Lamar, owner of the vessel and mastermind of the clandestine voyage, held the rank of colonel in the Georgia Regiment of Confederate Army. Lamar was killed in 1865 in the Battle of Columbus. He is believed to be the last Confederate to die in the war, according to some, choosing death over surrender. Montmollin was killed in Savannah in 1859 in the explosion of the steamer *Lawton*. After his death, the slave pen in Savannah from which he auctioned Africans was used as a school for freedmen. E. H. Nichols, the white physician who denounced Carr's injury claim as "bosh," died in 1906. The cause of death was ruled suicide by a self-inflicted gunshot wound.

Benjamin James, the African American physician and missionary who attended Carr until his death, died in Hardeeville in 1908 after a long illness. Having remarried, James left a wife and three daughters and a community of Black and white residents to mourn his passing.

Other survivors of the *Wanderer* were noted. In 1863, in Louisiana, the brothers Wimbo Congo and August Congo related that they were brought over on the *Wanderer*. They enlisted in the Company A, 2nd Regiment Louisiana Volunteers Native Guard, also known as the Corps d'Afrique. The two were recruited by P. B. S. Pinchback, the son of a white planter and an enslaved woman. During Reconstruction Pinchback served Louisiana as a state senator in 1868, as president of the senate, and as lieutenant governor in 1871; and from December 9, 1872, to January 13, 1873, as governor, when the elected official underwent impeachment proceedings. From the *Douglass Monthly*, in April 1863, came this report:

> NEW ORLEANS, Feb. 27 1863
> Mr. Editor—In Company, A. 2d Regiment Louisiana Volunteers Native Guards, there are two privates. Wimbo Congo and August Congo, Who are natives of Africa. They were bro't here some three years ago on board of the celebrated yacht *Wanderer*, and sold as slaves to an enslaver on the opposite side of the river, and were compelled to work until the city was captured by the United States troops. As soon as Gen. Butler issued his order calling on the colored people of Louisiana to take up arms to defend their homes, these two patriotic sons of Africa threw down their hoes in the field, and marched boldly to the Touro building, and in broken language declared that they wanted to fight for the United States. Capt. Pinckback [*sic*] at first declined to enlist them because they could not speak the English language plain enough to be soldiers, but Lieut. Keeling insisted on taking them, which was done, and they proved as good soldiers as we can find in the whole three colored regiments. They are from the Congo river. They give wonderful accounts of Africa, and tell how they were stolen from there and brought to America. They speak highly of their King George's country. We want ten thousand more brave sons of Africa like these, so if the *Wanderer* and her officers would like to go into the recruiting business, we will pay two dollars for each able-bodied man they may steal from Africa and bring to the United States army....

Compiled service records exist for both brothers; however, they disappear from records, never appearing in state or federal census or on pension rolls.

In early 1900 Charles Montgomery located and interviewed survivors of the *Wanderer*. He published his work in 1908 in the *American Anthropologist*. Several survivors lived in or near Augusta, Georgia. They were fellow captives who learned to meld into American culture and become like the rest of the enslaved. None spoke the name of Charles Carr, but they spoke of an experience as freed people in America. I was glad to find their stories. Their remembrances captivated Montgomery and no doubt readers. Manchuella, known as Katie Noble, resided in Aiken County,

South Carolina. She recalled she came "from deep in Africa" but could remember no more about her native home.

The formerly enslaved African named Mabiala was called Uster Williams. He was blind and confined to the Richmond County Home in Augusta, Georgia. He believed someone put a spell on him and was trying to take his money. Although feeble in mind, he knew where he was from. He told he came from the "Bezy River" in Africa. Lucy Lanham was a child when she was captured and thrown in the hold of the *Wanderer*. She remembered nothing of her homeland. Zow Uncola, called Tom Johnson, said he came from the coast where the sun rises. It was a land, Montgomery reported, where there were no trees. Recalled Uncola, "Where I come from, you can just see the water just drippin' out o the sun."[6]

Cilucangy was given the name Ward Lee; the African Pucka Geata was called Tucker Henderson. Romeo or Tahro did not give his indigenous name. Montgomery wrote that the first names of these three bore the names of their native communities. They, along with Manchuella and Mabiala, were believed to come from the same village beyond the Congo. Their chief was Mfotila. Cilucangy lived in the village called Cowany. Taharo was from Kuluwaka. Both villages were far from the coast. Despite their forty and more years in the United States, they remembered words and customs of Africa.

As a reminder of home, Tahro built a house fashioned like those in his village. It was a straw house without a chimney or windows. There were no tables or chairs. He and others remembered their native words for produce, animals, and more. An alligator was *ngando*; baby, *muana*; doctor was *ganga*; a pipe was called *tordia*, a knife, *mbala*; fish was *golla*, chicken, was *susu*. Tahro and Cilucangy spoke their native language fluently, although some words may have been forgotten. *Ukola* meant "How do you do?" *Wenda twas mona kona keamvo* was "Carry me across the river." *Zolza ana aku*? was "Do you love your children?" *Muany yama* translated into "The sun is hot."[7]

They seemed to have settled in, accepting their new world and new country. Only two spoke longingly of Africa. When asked if he wished to return to Africa, Zow Uncola (Tom Johnson) replied, "I'm gittin' so old I'm 'fraid I couldn't git back."[8] Cilucangy (Ward Lee) tried to return home, seeking help from anyone who would give it. He had circulars printed through which he made this plea:

> Trenton, S.C. Sept. 14, 1904
> To the Public:
> Please help me. In 1859 I was brought to this country when I was a child. I cannot say just what age I was then but I have been aroused by the spirit—and I trust it was the spirit of God—on last May. One year ago it was revealed to me to go home back to Africa and I have been praying to know if it was God's will and the more I pray the more it presses on me to go and now I am trying to get ready if God be with me to go back to Africa soon as I can get off to go. And now I beg every one who will please help me. I will be glad of whatever you will give me. I have been trying to make some arrangements to go ever since it was revealed to me to go. I am bound for my old home if God be with me white or black yellow or the red I am an old African.[9]

Lee died in 1914. He was buried in Mount Canaan Baptist Church cemetery in Edgefield County, South Carolina.[10]

Old-timers in Brunswick, Georgia, paused in 1912 when "Aunt" Lucile DuBignon died. The *Macon Telegraph* reported her passing, noting that at age 110, she was probably one of the oldest negresses in the state, if not the nation, when she died. It reported, "according to her story of her history [*sic*] came to the United States from Africa when she was a young girl on the slave ship *Wanderer* . . . the vessel landed at Jekyl which [at] that time was owned by the DuBignon and slaves . . . Aunt Lucile was the last of the DuBignon slaves and was respected by all who knew her."[11]

Neither Lee, Carr, "Aunt" Lucile, nor the others interviewed returned physically to Africa, but if their folklore were true, the spirits of these Gollas made it back to the land of their birth.

Charles Carr's South Carolina communities continued to thrive. The 1890 Veterans Schedule for Beaufort County listed ten men in Yemassee (Carr was not among them) who served in the United States Colored Troops. This proud expression of Black self-determination continued. In 1924 Yemassee was home to a chapter of the Universal Negro Improvement Association (UNIA). Founded by Jamaican Pan Africanist Marcus Mosiah Garvey, the UNIA was the largest Black organization of the early twentieth century. The Brewton (Burton) Plantation where Bettie Fields, the midwife who assisted in the birth delivery of Arthur Carr lived, was purchased in 1971 by heavyweight champion "Smokin" Joe Frazier. He had grown up in the area and bought the plantation for his mother. Some criticized the purchase of the dilapidated plantation that ended up as a huge debt. Others shrugged, noting that for once in the area a Black man *owned* a plantation instead of slaving on it.

Black veterans continued facing obstacles obtaining veteran benefits. Black WWII veterans often were denied education and housing benefits and loans of the G.I. Bill enjoyed by white veterans, and which were administered by state and local officials steeped in Jim Crow. Responding to advocates of recent Black veterans, President Joe Biden signed a bill into law in November 2021 requiring the Government Accountability Office to investigate potential disparities in Veterans Affairs benefit awards based on race and ethnicity. In 2021 U.S. Representatives Seth Moulton (D-Mass.) and James Clyburn (D-S.C.) introduced the G.I. Bill Restoration Act in the house. U.S. Senator Raphael Warnock (D-Ga.) introduced the G.I. Bill in the Senate in 2023. The act would repair the economic harms experienced by Black WWII veterans and military families denied access to the full range of G.I. Bill benefits. Studies indicate that minorities may receive lesser benefits or face additional obstacles to disability payouts than their white peers. Let us not be surprised if we find out this is indeed the case.

First African (Missionary Baptist) Church where Carr and Dianah married still has an active congregation. Proud members tell their church's history on anniversary Sunday, held the third Sunday in May. Perhaps now the congregation will add the name Charles Carr, a *Wanderer* survivor and private in the United States Colored Troops, to their shining history. Today Yemassee, Hardeeville, Levy, and Savannah are included in the Gullah Geechee Cultural Heritage Corridor, one of only fifty-five federal cultural heritage areas in the United States.

Like many communities, Marianna, where Arthur and Eliza Carr resided, has had its shameful history and difficulties. Archaeological work conducted between 2013 and 2015 at the now closed Arthur G. Dozier School for Boys in Marianna unearthed fifty hidden, unmarked graves. Founded as the Florida State Reform School, the institution opened in

1900 as a place for troubled boys. It turned into a house of torture where boys were severely lashed and mentally and sexually abused and perhaps killed, if punishment went too far. In 2017, Florida State legislature issued a formal apology for the inhumane treatment the boys received at Dozier and its campus at Okeechobee.[12]

In October 2018, Hurricane Michael tore through the Florida Panhandle, with Marianna hopelessly in its path. The hurricane ripped bricks from buildings, shattered glass, tossed roofs, and splintered trees. It toppled a Confederate monument; it left standing the "hanging tree," where, according to folklore, troublesome Black property was strung up during slavery.[13]

The *Wanderer* would not fare as well as the *Wanderer* coconspirators. The yacht was seized in May 1861 by the Union and used in blockades of federal ports. After the war, a private citizen purchased the yacht as a commercial vessel for the West Indian fruit trade. In January 1871 the *Wanderer*, a once stunning pleasure yacht forever to be remembered as a wretched slave ship, sank off the coast of Cuba.

The shameful tale of the *Wanderer* continued to intrigue or perhaps delight people. In 1958, one hundred years after the slave ship landed on the Georgia coast, the Wanderer motel opened on Jekyll Island. When I read this I fumed, "Goodness people! Is nothing sacred?" A postcard, once the way to write home while on vacation, listed the motel's amenities: "Air conditioned efficiency suites, facing snow-white beach and the blue Atlantic Ocean - Swimming pool, TV, room telephones and restaurant; - Convenient to amusement area, golf course." An image of the postcard can be found in the Vanishing Georgia Photographic Collection at the Georgia Archives.[14] Advertisements boasted that, additionally, the motel's modest rates made the motel popular for business meetings, conclaves, and banquets. Later renamed the Oceanside Inn and Suites hotel, the motel that bore the name of a slave ship is now known as the Holiday Inn Resort.[15]

The mess kettle in which food was cooked to feed the enslaved brought over on the *Wanderer* is displayed at the Mosaic Museum on Jekyll Island. Hardeeville United Methodist Church notes on its website that the bell in the belfry is that from the last slave ship to enter the United States, a reference to the *Wanderer*. One study doubts that the bell is from the ship, remarking it is likely from a plantation. My guess is that both accounts hold truth and that the bell is from the Montmollin Plantation, once located near Hardeeville.

The Babcock Building on the campus of the State Hospital in Columbia, South Carolina, where Carr's wife Dianah withered and died, still stands—albeit long abandoned. It's getting new life. Although the Babcock was damaged in 2020 by fire, plans continued to convert the former asylum into luxury apartments with a campus that includes a pool, dog park, coworker space, and lounging and exercise facilities. I guess those who rent the apartments don't know the power of roaming, hurting spirits. They will.

The site of the *Wanderer*'s landing and the tale of the enslavers and the African survivors still ring. In 2008, on the 150th anniversary of the landing, the Jekyll Island Authority unveiled a memorial to honor the survivors of the voyage. On one of the descriptive panels were the haunting words Charles Carr spoke as he was examined by the physician for the Pensions Bureau: "Sometimes 15 were picked up in the morning and thrown overboard." The memorial, consisting of sail-shaped panels in metal frames, eventually succumbed to environmental elements. With the panels succumbing to saltwater corrosion and the exhibit trail overrun by vegetation, the foundation thought it was best to upgrade the exhibit; it was removed for safety reasons.

In 2018 the Authority unveiled a new memorial and sought input from the African American community. It erected a self-guided, family friendly memory trail, with interactive elements, an audio guide that recounts the tale of Africans who took to the sky, a reconstructed African hut, and artistic and interpretive panels. The trail tells of the Middle Passage and the life of slavery and freedom through the eyes of the young Umwalla, the African who in 1888 told of his capture, transport on the *Wanderer*, and enslavement. Gone are the words spoken by Charles Carr; no longer are they part of the exhibit. Yet his words are important and must be remembered as they speak of the terror of the Middle Passage that millions of Africans endured as they were brought in chains to foreign lands.

Looking back on this work, I can only imagine what went through the minds and hearts of Carr and his family. For forty-six years from 1890 to 1936, they fought to receive a pension for Carr's service in the Civil War.

For Carr, the promise of government assistance went unfulfilled. Similarly, for many African Americans today equal treatment in America seems unlikely. A 2019 Pew Research Center report on race revealed that most Americans, Black and white, believe that the legacy of slavery continues to have an impact on the positions of African Americans in this country. More than 40 percent of those surveyed said the country had not made enough progress toward racial equality. Fifty percent of African Americans said it was unlikely that Blacks would eventually have equal rights in the United States. Only 7 percent of whites held that view.[16] These were feelings expressed before the international protests in 2020 over the killing of George Floyd and others. They were feelings we harbored long before the nation acknowledged the 1921 killings and mass burial of between one hundred and three hundred Black residents of Tulsa, Oklahoma, by a white mob, accompanied by the burning of their Greenwood neighborhood.

A 2021 Pew Research Center report revealed that among Black adults, 75 percent believed heightened attention to the history of slavery and racism was a good thing while less than half (46 percent) of whites held the same position. The report found 71 percent of Black Americans believe whites benefit "a great deal" from societal advantages. Of whites, 21 percent believe the same.[17] Black and white Americans hold different views on America, access to the American Dream, or even the fulfillment of America's promises. Perhaps just giving attention to slavery and racism is not enough. Vehement reactions to teaching "critical race theory" signal that America really isn't ready to have the hard talk about racism, American history, and white privilege.

A 2024 Pew Research Center report revealed the majority of African Americans believe that U.S. institutions were designed to hold African Americans back—by intentional design. We cite prison, political, and economic systems as treating us unfairly.[18] As the presidential election neared in 2024, African American groups eyed (and planned to counter) Project 2025, which promises to "restore" and put America first. That usually means putting Black folks and other marginalized groups last.

Hope of achieving racial equality is held differently between African Americans and whites—more than four hundred years after the first Africans were brought to Comfort Point, Virginia, in 1619. It was not the first arrival of Africans brought in chains to what became the United States. Historians are now looking at evidence dating to 1526 in South Carolina, and note the arrival of free and enslaved Africans in St. Augustine in 1565. But 1619 became pivotal in defining race relations in America. The date of our forced arrival does not change what we know and feel. Our blood is mixed in this soil, our skills and genius built this nation. Respect that and allow us to reap what we've earned. Holding us back holds you back.

In 2018 I traveled to South Africa. It was transformative to touch the continent where all life began. Africa is my ancestral home; it was Carr's home before he was snatched up and crammed in the hold of the *Wanderer*. I carried some of my husband's ashes to South Africa and held them close to me as I stood along the coast where waves rush out to meet the Atlantic Ocean. A couple of months later my friend Uwimana planted a tree in Ghana in his honor. A year later she returned and found his tree lush and healthy. I guess returning to Africa may do that to Black people—revive us.

Carr never returned to the land of his birth. As Carr's family line ended with the death of his son, Arthur, there was no one to tell his story. Then Carr chose me. Discovering him, his family, and community has been exhausting, exhilarating, painful, reflective, and inspiring. It's the story of us—Black people who get up every day, take on a system that benefits the privileged, and return to our communities where we are nourished and replenished, where tears mix with laughter and hope overrides despair. Some African Americans today, as in centuries past, do not believe we can find justice in the United States. They advocate leaving America or, if remaining, building institutions that are Black-owned and -operated and that serve our interests. I find no fault with their arguments. It is a choice that every African American must make for him or herself.

Through this work Charles Carr's story is now part of a shared history. It gives insight into the life of a survivor of the *Wanderer* who fought for his freedom, prodded America to keep its promise, and held Africa in his heart. It asks America to fulfill the ideals upon which this nation was founded—that all men (and women) are created equal, that they are endowed by their Creator with certain unalienable rights, among these life, liberty, and the pursuit of happiness. Carr's story is that of Black people in America, from Africa to slavery to freedom—through joys and disappointments, through victories and setbacks. We must tell our stories. We must honor our ancestors. We must memorialize our everyday heroes and sheroes. We must remember the wisdom of the African proverb: "Until the lion has a storyteller, the hunter will always be the hero."

NOTES

Chapter 1. The Journey Begins

1. U.S. Circuit Court, Savannah, Ga., Minutes, 1857–1860 S.O. 108.

Chapter 2. The Slave Ship *Wanderer*

1. Laura A. White, "The United States in the 1850s as Seen by British Consuls," *Mississippi Valley Historical Review* 19, no.4 (1933): 525.

2. "The Yacht *Wanderer*," *New York Times*, June 12, 1859, 2.

3. "The Yacht *Wanderer*'s Mystery Explained—The Marshall Satisfied, and the Vessel Released," *New York Times*, June 12, 1858, 8.

Chapter 3. Clandestine Voyage to Congo

1. Ottobah Cugoano, *Narrative of Enslavement of Ottobah Cugoano, a Native of Africa; Published by Himself, in the Year 1787*, 126, available at Documenting the American South, https://docsouth.unc.edu/neh/cugoano/cugoano.html.

2. Sarah Pruitt, "What Part of Africa Did Most Enslaved People Come From?" History.com, accessed September 17, 2021, https://www.history.com/news/what-part-of-africa-did-most-slaves-come-from.

3. Accounts of the number of Africans brought aboard the *Wanderer* vary from 350 to 487. Wells devotes several pages in his work to the discrepancies in the numbers captured. Erik Calonius, in *The "Wanderer": The Last American Slave Ship and the Conspiracy that Set Its Sails* (St. Martin's Press, 2006), 104, places the number at 437.

Chapter 4. The Hellish Middle Passage

1. Olaudah Equiano, *The Interesting Life of Olaudah Equiano, or Gustavas Vassa, The African*, available at Public Broadcasting Service, accessed May 24, 2014, http://www.pbs.org/wgbh/aia/part1/1h320t.html. A storm of controversy swelled in 2005 regarding the birthplace of Equiano, whose autobiography was hallowed for years as a rare, firsthand account by an African who survived the transatlantic slave trade. Based on research, scholar Vincent Carretta suggests that Equiano was not African-born, but rather an African born in South Carolina. Carretta's findings raise questions regarding the veracity and intent of Equiano's writings. Nonetheless, Equiano's account is still referenced and included in the study of the slave trade.

2. "The Last Cargo of Imported Slaves," *Atlanta Constitution*, October 9, 1888, Digital Library of Georgia, https://gahistoricnewspapers.galileo.usg.edu/lccn/sn89053706/1888-10-09/ed-1/seq-1/#date1=01%2F01%2F1888&nottext=&date2=12%2F31%2F1890&words=Umwalla&searchType=advanced&sequence=0&index=0&proxdistance=5&rows=12&ortext=&proxtext=Umwalla%2C&andtext=&page=1.

3. Charley Carr (Pvt., Co K, USC inf., Civil War), Invalid pension application no. 912191 (Rejected), Case Files of Rejected Pension Applications . . . , 1861–1934, Civil War and Later Pension Files, Department of Veterans Affairs, Record Group 15, National Archives, Washington, D.C., Surgeon's Certificate, examination by E. H. Nichols, M.D., August 20, 1894.

Chapter 5. Strange Land

1. "Sale of the Yacht *Wanderer*," *New York Daily Herald*, March 13, 1859, 2.

Chapter 6. Flying Africans et al.

1. Montgomery M. Folsom, "King Mingo: A Story of the Slave Ship Wanderer," *Atlanta Constitution*, February 3, 1896, 2.

2.Georgia Writers' Project, *Drums and Shadows: Survival Studies Among the Georgia Coastal Negroes* (University of Georgia Press, 1940), 151.

3. "Poor Squash," *Weekly Sumter Republican*, July 27, 1884, 3, Digital Library of Georgia, https://gahistoricnewspapers.galileo.usg.edu/lccn/sn85033988/1884-06-27/ed-1/seq-3/#index=0&rows=12&proxtext=%22Ebo+Landing%22&sequence=0&words=Ebo+Land+Landing&page=1.

Chapter 7. Caught, Tried, Acquitted

1. This chapter draws on well-established and publicized research on the trial of the *Wanderer* coconspirators. For those interested in more details, sources include but are not limited to: Erik Calonius, *The "Wanderer": The Last American Slave Ship and the Conspiracy that Set Its Sails* (St. Martin's Press, 2006); Peter Grindal, Opposing the Slavers: The Royal Navy's Campaign Against the Atlantic Slave Trade (I.B. Tauris, 2016); and Tom Henderson Wells, *The Slave Ship Wanderer* (1968; repr., University of Georgia Press, 2009). Copious information about the trial is also found in the National Archives.

Chapter 8. Carr, Aiken, and the Weeping Time

1. Ancestry.com. Georgia, Property Tax Digest, 1793–1892, https://www.ancestry.com/search/collections/1729/rcOF107&_phstart=successSource. Original data: *Georgia Tax Digest* [1890], 140 volumes, Georgia Archives, Morrow, Ga.

2. F. D. Lee and J. L. Agnew, *A Historical Record of the City of Savannah*, (J. H. Estill

Morning News Steam Power Press, 1869), 199–200, available at https://babel.hathitrust.org/cgi/pt?id=uc2.ark:/13960/t6736n66c&seq=9.

3. Kwesi DeGraft-Hanson, "Unearthing the Weeping Time: Savannah's Ten Broek Race Course and the 1859 Slave Sale," *Southern Spaces*, February 18, 2010, https://southernspaces.org/2010/unearthing-weeping-time-savannahs-ten-broeck-race-course-and-1859-slave-sale/.

4. John Simkin, "Slave Marriages," *Spartacus-Educational*, September 1997, https://spartacus-educational.com/USASmarriage.htm.

5. Q. K. Philander Doesticks, Pierce Butler, Daniel Murray Pamphlet Colllection, and Joseph Meredith Toner Collection, *What Became of the Slaves of a Georgia Plantation?: Great Auction Sale of Slaves, at Savannah, Georgia, March 2nd & 3rd, a Sequel to Mrs. Kemble's Journal*, 12, accessed December 7, 2015, available at https://www.loc.gov/item/11003986/.

6. *What Became of the Slaves of a Georgia Plantation?* 8.

Chapter 9. Carr Among Montmollin's Slaves

1. Richland District (South Carolina) Court of Equity Petitions #593, Ex Parte H. M. R. Montmollin, R.I. 151, 1863, roll 593, South Carolina Department of Archives and History.

2. "Large Sale of Negroes," *Daily Morning News* (Savannah), April 10, 1863, 2, Digital Library of Georgia, https://gahistoricnewspapers.galileo.usg.edu/lccn/sn82015886/1863-04-10/ed-1/seq-2/#date1=04%2F01%2.

Chapter 10. Witnessing Quasi-Freedom

1. First Census of the United States, 1790 (Philadelphia, 1791), as reported by Whittington B. Johnson, *Black Savannah 1788–1864* (University of Arkansas Press, 1966), 108.

2. "Mother Mathilda Beasley," Georgia Historical Society, accessed May 7, 2015, http://georgiahistory.com/education-outreach/online-exhibits/featured-historical-figures/mother-mathilda-beasley/from-slavery-to-savannah/.

3. "An Ordinance," *Republican and Savannah Evening Ledger*, February 7, 1811, 2, https://gahistoricnewspapers.galileo.usg.edu/lccn/sn82014388/1811-02-07/ed-1/seq-2/.

4. "An Ordinance," *Daily Savannah Republican*, September 23, 1839, https://gahistoricnewspapers.galileo.usg.edu/lccn/sn87062328/1839-09-23/ed-1/seq-3/#words=badge+badges+ordinance.

5. *George J. Kollock Plantation Papers Journals, 1837–1861*, University of North Carolina Libraries, accessed July 21, 2016, http://www2.lib.unc.edu/mss/inv/k/Kollock,George_J.html#folder_5#1p2.

6. *George J. Kollock Plantation Papers Journals, 1837–1861*, 59, accessed August 14, 2016, http://www2.lib.unc.edu/mss/inv/k/Kollock,George_J.html#folder_5#p1.

7. *Kollock Plantation Papers Journals*, 10, accessed July 31, 2016, http://www2.lib.unc.edu/mss/inv/k/Kollock,George_J.html#folder_4#1p.

8. *Kollock Plantation Papers Journals*, 30, accessed July 31, 2016.

9. *Manigault Plantation Journal*, 1824–1897, 32, University of North Carolina Libraries, accessed July 29, 2016, http://dc.lib.unc.edu/cdm/compoundobject/collection/plantation/id/795/show/636/rec/1.

10. *Manigault Plantation Journal*, 33.

11. *Manigault Plantation Journal*, 36.

Chapter 11. Freedom Coming

1. Lido Brown, Claim no. 18225, Chatham County, Georgia, Ancestry.com, *U.S., Southern Claims Commission Allowed Claims, 1871–1880*.

2. *King James Version Bible* (James C. Winston Publishing Company, 1993).

3. Willie Lee Rose, *Rehearsal for Reconstruction: The Port Royal Experiment* (Oxford University Press, 1964), 146.

4. Budge Wideman, "Black Soldiers in the Civil War: Preserving the Legacy of the United States Colored Troops," National Archives, 1997, https://www.archives.gov/education/lessons/blacks-civil-war/article.html.

5. Thomas Wentworth Higginson, *Army Life in a Black Regiment* (1869; repr., Riverside Press), available via the Gutenberg Project, http://www.gutenberg.org/files/6764/6764-h/6764-h.htm#link2HCH0010.

6. While often described as pertaining solely to West Africa, the ring shout was also prevalent in Central Africa. The late, venerated professor of African American history Sterling Stuckey wrote that the ring shout was endemic to West and Central Africa, the powerful circular ritual imported from Angola-Congo was so elaborate in its exerted influence over slaves in the Carolinas. Joseph E. Holloway notes that in the Kongo the ring shout is identical to the Gullah counterclockwise dance. See Joseph Holloway, *Africa in American Culture*, 2nd ed. (University of Indiana Press, 2005), 6, 51.

7. Jacqueline Jones, "The Emancipation Proclamation Reaches Savannah," *Not Even the Past* (blog), January 1, 2013, https://notevenpast.org/emancipation-proclamation-reaches-savannah/.

Chapter 12. Raising Black Regiments

1. "Negroes and the National War Effort: An Address Delivered in Philadelphia, Pennsylvania, on July 6, 1863," available through The Frederick Douglass Papers Project, accessed December 4, 2025, https://frederickdouglasspapersproject.com/item/9183.

2. Taylor remarried after her husband's death but was widowed again within a few years. Her autobiography, *Reminiscences of My Life in Camp*, is believed to be the first book about the Civil War written by a freedwoman.

3. E. Merton Coulter, "Robert Gould Shaw and the Burning of Darien Georgia," *Civil War History* 5, no. 4 (1959): 365.

Chapter 13. General Sherman—Warrior, not Liberator

1. William Tecumseh Sherman, *Memoirs of General William T. Sherman by Himself* (Indiana University Press, 1957), 249.

2. Alfred Barnard, Southern Claims Commission Approved Claims, 1870–1880, Georgia, M1658, NARA Record Group 217, Claim #20092.

3. Sambo Jefferson, Southern Claims Commission Approved Claims, 1871–1880, Georgia, M1658, NARA, Record Group 217, Claim #17020, https://www.fold3.com/image253645165.

4. Diana Cummings, Southern Claims Commission Approved Claims, 1870–1880, Georgia, M1654, NARA Record Group 217, Claim #18091.

5. Rachel Broomfield, Southern Claims Commission Approved Claims, 1870–1880, Georgia, M1658, NARA Record Group 217, Claim #13361.

6. *A journal, kept by Emma Florence LeConte, from Dec. 31, 1864 to Aug. 6, 1865, written in her seventeenth year and containing a detailed account of the burning of Columbia, by one who was an eyewitness*, Documenting the South, http://docsouth.unc.edu/fpn/leconteemma/leconte.html, accessed December 24, 2016.

7. M. A. DeWolfe Howe, ed., *Marching with Sherman: Passages from the Letters and Campaign Diaries of Henry Hitchcock, Major and Assistant Adjunct General of Volunteers*, November 1864–May 1865 (Bison Books, 1995), 202, quoted in Jacqueline Jones, *Saving Savannah: The City and the Civil War* (Vintage Books, 2009), 208.

8. Georgiana Kelly, Claim no. 15586, Chatham County, Georgia, witness Delia Rivers, Ancestry.com, *U.S., Southern Claims Commission Allowed Claims, 1871–1880.*

9. *Memoirs of General William T. Sherman*, 2nd rev. and corrected ed., 2 vols. (D. Appleton, 1886), 2:248, available at https://babel.hathitrust.org/cgi/pt?id=nyp.33433082388863&seq=282&q1=Halleck.

10. Burke Davis, *Sherman's March* (Random House, 1980), 132.

11. Davis, *Sherman's March*, 132.

12. "Savannah Freedpeople Express Their Aspirations for Freedom," Facing History, https://www.facinghistory.org/reconstruction-era/savannah-freedpeople-express-their-aspirations-freedom, accessed December 31, 2016. From "Sherman Meets the Colored Ministers in Savannah," O.R. Series I, vol. XLVII/2 [S# 99] Union Correspondence, Orders, and Returns Relating to Operations in North Carolina (from February 1), South Carolina, Southern Georgia, and East Florida, from January 1, 1865, to March 23, 1865, #2.

Chapter 14. Private Carr Injured

1. Stephen V. Ash, *Firebrand of Liberty: The Story of Two Black Regiments that Changed the Course of the Civil War* (W. W. Norton, 2008) 39.

2. Littlefield was suspected of profiting from bounties with a total of nearly two hundred thousand dollars involved in payments to "paper recruits." See William S. Powell, "Littlefield, Milton S.," in *Dictionary of North Carolina Biography*, accessed April 16, 2017, http://www.ncpedia.org/biography/littlefield-milton-smith.

3. Marcus Maxwell, Invalid pension application no. 912,191 (Approved), Case Files of Rejected Pension Applications . . . , 1861–1934, Civil War and Later Pension Files, Department of Veterans Affairs, Record Group 15, National Archives, Washington, D.C., Pension no. 807801, Deposition May 22, 1901.

4. Isaiah Henderson: Record number 175, Savannah Bank 1866, Ancestry.com. *U.S., Freedman's Bank Records, 1865–1871*. Original data: *Registers of Signatures of Depositors in Branches of the Freedman's Savings and Trust Company, 1865–1874*, Washington, D.C.: National Archives and Records Administration. Micro publication M816, 27 rolls. No record of Virgil or Issac found.

5. William A. Dubak, accessed May 28, 2017, *Freedom by the Sword: The U.S. Colored Troops 1862–1867*, 80, http://www.history.army.mil/html/books/030/30-24/CMH_Pub_30-24.pdf, 80.

6. John Boudreau, "Breaking the Silence: Military: Were 50 Black Sailors Wrongly Convicted of Mutiny After a 1944 Explosion that Killed 320?," *Los Angeles Times*, July 16, 1991, https://www.latimes.com/archives/la-xpm-1991-07-16-vw-2465-story.html.

7. Pvt. Charles Carr, the National Archives at Washington, D.C., Washington, D.C.; *Compiled Military Service Records of Volunteer Union Soldiers Who Served with the United States Colored Troops: Infantry Organizations, 31st Through 35th*, Record Group Number 94, Microfilm Serial: M1992; Microfilm Roll, 51.

Chapter 15. Freedman's Bank Signature Card

1. "Colored Democrats Going for the Freedman's Bank Swindle," *Savannah Morning News*, September 27, 1876, 11, Digital Library of Georgia, https://gahistoricnewspapers.galileo.usg.edu/lccn/sn82015137/1876-09-27/ed-1/seq-1/#date1=09%2F01%2F1876&city=Savannah&date2=09%2F30%2F1876&words=Bank+Freedman&searchType=advanced&nottext=&index=0&sequence=0&proxdistance=5&rows=12&ortext=&proxtext=Freedman%27s+bank+&andtext=&page=1.

2. "Savings Bank Question—Meeting of Colored People," *Savannah Morning News*, July 9, 1874, Digital Library of Georgia, https://gahistoricnewspapers.galileo.usg.edu/lccn/sn82015137/1874-07-09/ed-1/seq-3/#date1=01%2F01%2F1874&nottext=&date2=12%2F31%2F1875&words=Bank+banks+freedman+Freedman&searchType=advanced&sequence=0&index=4&proxdistance=5&sort=relevance&rows=12&ortext=&proxtext=Freedman%27s+bank&county=Chatham&andtext=&page=2.

3. Susie King Taylor, *Reminiscences of My Life in Camp with the 33D United States Colored Troops Late 1st S.C. Volunteers*, 1902, Documenting the American South, 3, https://docsouth.unc.edu/neh/taylorsu/taylorsu.html.

4. *The Life and Writing of Frederick Douglass*, vol. 1, *Reconstruction and After* (International Publisher, 1955), 306–7.

Chapter 16. Hope and Dark Days Ahead

1. Records of the Assistant Commissioner for South Carolina, Bureau of Refugees, Freedmen and Abandoned Lands, 1865–1870, National Archives Microfilm Publication, M869 roll 34, Reports of Conditions and Operations, Report from Capt. A.P. Ketchum and A.D.V., to Bvt Maj Gen'l R. Saxton, Assistant Commissioner South Carolina and Georgia, Savannah Georgia September 1, 1685, accessed September 4, 2017, http://www.freedmensBureau.com/southcarolina/scoperations4.htm.

2. Major General W. T. Sherman, "Order by the Commander of the Military Division of the Mississippi," available at Freedmen and Southern Society Project, accessed December 4, 2025, https://www.freedmen.umd.edu/sf015.htm.

3. The Montmollin surname also appears as DeMontmollin.

4. "Excitement in Savannah," *Edgefield Advertiser*, October 26, 1871, 2, https://www.newspapers.com/image-view/72159060/?match=1&terms=%22Savannah%22.

5. "A Correct Account of the Affair," *Savannah Morning News*, October 25, 1871, 3, https://gahistoricnewspapers.galileo.usg.edu/lccn/sn82015137/1871-10-25/ed-1/seq-3/#words=Montmollin.

6. "The DeMontmollin Affair," *Savannah Morning News*, November 1, 1871, 2, Digital Library of Georgia, https://gahistoricnewspapers.galileo.usg.edu/lccn/sn82015137/1871-11-01/ed-1/seq-3/#words=Montmollin+Montmollin%E2%80%99s.

7. "The Meeting in St. James Square," *Savannah Morning News*, October 6, 1870, 3, Digital Library of Georgia, https://gahistoricnewspapers.galileo.usg.edu/lccn/sn82015137/1870-10-06/ed-1/seq-3/#date1=10%2F05%2F1870&nottext=&date2=10%2F07%2F1870&words=Aaron+Bradley&searchType=advanced&sequence=0&index=0&proxdistance=5&rows=12&ortext=&proxtext=%22Aaron+Bradley%22&andtext=&page=1.

8. "The American Mosaic: Colonization," Library of Congress, accessed March 20, 2025, https://www.loc.gov/exhibits/african/afam002.html.

9. "Sailing of the Golconda," *Weekly Constitutionalist*, June 5, 1867, 3, Digital Library of Georgia, https://gahistoricnewspapers.galileo.usg.edu/lccn/sn87090503/1867-06-05/ed-1/seq-3/#date1=01%2F01%2F1867&nottext=&date2=12%2F31%2F1867&words=Golconda&searchType=advanced&sequence=0&index=1&proxdistance=5&rows=12&ortext=&proxtext=Golconda&andtext=&page=1.

Chapter 17. Wife Dianah and Help for Veterans

1. Dianah Carr, widow's pension application (hereafter, WO pension application) no. 638231 (Rejected) for service of Charles Carr, National Archives in Washington, D.C., Christmas Graham, Deposition G, August 9, 1901, 25–26.

2. Tenth Census of the United States, Year: 1880; Census Place: Yemassee, Beaufort, South Carolina; Roll: 1221; Family History Film: 1255221; Page: 323D; Enumeration District: 051.

3. *Agriculture Schedules (South Carolina) 1850–1880*, Microfilm F 600204, 15 rolls, South Carolina Department of History and Archives, Columbia, 1870, Agricultural Census South Carolina, Beaufort County, St. Peter Parish, 21.

Chapter 18. Pension Application and the Terrible Voyage

1. Charley Carr (Pvt., Co. K, USC Inf., Civil War), Invalid pension application no. 912191 (Rejected), Case Files of Rejected Pension Applications, 1861–1934, Civil War and Later Pension Files, Department of Veterans Affairs, Record Group 15, National Archives, Washington, D.C., U.S. Pensions Application letter to bureau, February 20, 1893.

2. E. H. Nichols, Surgeon's Certificate, Charley Carr, pension claim no. 912191 (Rejected).

3. Kelly M. Hoffman, Sophie Trawalter, Jordan R. Axt, and M. Norman Oliver, "Racial Bias in Pain Assessment and Treatment Recommendations, and False Beliefs About Biological Differences Between Blacks and Whites," *Proceedings of the National Academy of Sciences* 113, no. 16 (2016): 4296–4301.

4. "Prejudice and Policy: Racial Discrimination in the Union Army Disability Pension System 1865–1906," *American Journal of Public Health* 100, Suppl. 1 (2010): S56–S65.

5. "VA Disability Benefits: Actions Needed to Further Examine Racial and Ethnic Disparities in Compensation," U.S. Government Accountability Office, Washington, D.C., July 26, 2023, https://www.gao.gov/products/gao-23-106097.

Chapter 19. Carr's African American Physician

1. Daniel Smith Lamb, *Howard University Medical Department Washington, D.C., A Historical, Biographical and Statistical Souvenir* (1900; repr., Books for Libraries Press, 1971), 183–85.

2. WO pension application no. 638231, Benjamin James, M.D., Deposition B, 10 August 1901, 9–10. Also Charley Carr (Pvt. Co. K USCT, Union, Civil War), Invalid pension application no. 912191 (Rejected) Department of Veteran Affairs, RG 15.

3. "Africa: Our New Missionaries," *American Missionary* 32, no. 2 (1878): 48.

4. "Africa: The Mende Mission: Death of Mrs. Dr. James," *American Missionary* 32, no. 8 (1878): 246. Note: Daniel Lamb wrote that Mrs. James and their newborn child perished. Dr. James then sent their surviving two children back to Baltimore.

5. Benjamin James, MD, "The Day—School, Christmas Entertainment—Knives and Forks," *American Missionary* 32, no. 3 (1878): 83.

6. Caulker is an influential family in Sierra Leone descending from Thomas Corker, an agent of the Royal African Company, and a duchess or princess of Ya Kumba of the

Sierra Leone peninsula. See "Cleveland Tombstone," Sierra Leone Heritage, accessed December 2, 2025, https://www.sierraleoneheritage.org/sites/monuments/cleveland.

7. Benjamin James, MD, "A Heathen Bundoo Dance and a Retreat," *African Missionary* 33, no. 4 (1879): 118.

8. James, "Heathen Bundoo Dance," 119.

Chapter 20. Dianah Seeks a Widow's Pension

1. WO, pension application no. 638231, Medical Evidence, Affidavit of Dr. Benj. James. Received by the Pension Office July 20, 1897.

2. WO, pension application no. 638231, General Affidavit, Dianah Carr, September 14, 1898.

Chapter 21. The Church Where They Married

1. WO pension application no. 638231, Josephine Graham, Deposition H, August 9, 1901, 26–27.

2. WO pension application no. 638231, Chrismas Graham, Deposition G, August 9, 1901, 23–24.

3. WO pension application no. 638231, John Howard, Deposition D, August 14, 1901, 15–16.

4. WO pension application no. 638231, Enoch Johnson, Deposition C, August 14, 1901, 12.

5. The church where Charles and Dianah married is today known as First African Missionary Baptist Church (formerly Jonesville Baptist), Levy, South Carolina. According to the written church history, the church was established in 1872 and named Jonesville Baptist. Reverend J. H. Johnson was chosen as a leader and pastor. Rev. J. W. Coles was the second pastor, serving until he passed in 1927. The church was renamed under the leadership of Reverend J. J. Jenkins of Bluffton, S.C., who served from 1928 to 1961, until his passing. However, additional documentation accompanying the marriage certificate reveals the name First African was used as early as 1900, under the leadership of Pastor Coles.

6. WO pension application no. 638231, marriage certificate. C. B. Boyd, notary, Beaufort County, State of South Carolina, writes that Rev. J. W. Coles certifies that the information is true, January 22, 1900.

Chapter 22. Their Community Speaks

1. WO pension application no. 638231, Enoch Johnson, Deposition C, August 14, 1901, 12–14.

2. WO pension application no. 638231, Enoch Johnson, Deposition C, August 14, 1901, 13.

3. WO pension application no. 638231, John Howard, Deposition D, August 14, 1901, 15–16.

4. Enoch Johnson, Deposition C, August 14, 1901, 13.

5. Chrismas Graham, Deposition G, August 9, 1901, 23.

6. WO pension application no. 638231, Josephine Graham, Deposition H, August 9, 1901, 26.

7. WO pension application no. 638231, Frank Brown, Deposition I, August 9, 1901, 30–31.

8. Josephine Graham, 26–28.

9. WO pension application no. 638231, Samuel Bennett, Deposition A, August 8, 1901, 6.

10. Enoch Johnson, Deposition C, August 14, 1901, 13.

11. WO pension application no. 638231, Marcus Maxwell, Deposition E, August 8, 1901, 18–19.

12. John Howard, Deposition D, August 14, 1901, 15–16.

Chapter 23. Arthur's Birth

1. Fanny Kemble, *Journal of a Residence on a Georgian Plantation, 1838–1839* (Harper & Brothers, 1863).

2. WO pension application no. 638231, Frank Brown, Deposition I, August 9, 1901, 30.

3. WO pension application no. 638231, Josephine Graham, Deposition G, August 9, 1901, 27.

4. "Earthquake," *Yorkville Enquirer* (Yorkville, S.C.), September 8, 1886, *Chronicling America: Historic American Newspapers*, Library of Congress, http://chroniclingamerica.loc.gov/lccn/sn84026925/1886-09-08/ed-1/seq-2/.

5. WO pension application no. 638231, General Affidavit of Bettie Fields, June 1, 1897.

6. For more information on Gullah Folklore, see William Bascom, *African Folktales in the New World* (Indiana University Press, 1992).

Chapter 24. Carr's African People

1. WO pension application no. 638231, Enoch Johnson, Deposition C, August 9, 1901, 13–14.

2. WO pension application no. 638231, Alice Golphin, Deposition A, December 14, 1901, 2–3.

3. WO pension application no. 638231, John Golphin, Deposition B, December 14, 1901, 4–5.

4. WO pension application no. 638231, Patience Small, Deposition C, December 14, 1901, 6.

Chapter 25. Death in an Asylum

1. wo pension application no. 638231, Josephine Graham, Deposition H, August 9, 1901, 27.

2. wo pension application 638231, Jacob Martin, Deposition F, August 14, 1901, 21.

3. "Columbia State Lunatic Asylum," Genealogytrails.com, accessed December 9, 2017, http://genealogytrails.com/scar/state_institution.htm.

4. "Report on Asylum Is Made," *Herald and News*, January 25, 1920, 6, https://chroniclingamerica.loc.gov/lccn/sn86063758/1910-01-25/ed-1/seq-6/#date1=1910&index=7&rows=20&words=hospital+Hospital+Hospitals+hospitals+State&searchType=basic&sequence=0&state=South+Carolina&date2=1910&proxtext=%22state+hospital%22&y=5&x=13&dateFilterType=yearRange&page=1.

5. "Columbia's Forgotten Cemeteries," *Post and Courier* (Columbia, S.C.), May 16, 2019, https://www.historiccolumbia.org/tour-locations/2091-slighs-avenue.

Chapter 26. Arthur Appeals for Reparations

1. For more information, see Spires Liggans, "Purdee Made History as Lawyer, Jackson County Floridian," *Dothan Eagle*, accessed June 23, 2018, https://www.dothaneagle.com/jcfloridan/news/local/Black-history-month-profile-purdee-made-history-as-lawyer/article_85b623a2-8de2-56bf-92b6-8a95e6134347.html.

2. Curley Spires Potter, "Purdee Relatives on Mission to Fulfill His Dream," *Jackson County Floridan*, February 7, 2018, 6, http://ufdcimages.uflib.ufl.edu/UF/00/02/83/04/02091/02-07-2018.pdf.

3. "Amusements," *Pensacola Journal* (Pensacola, Fla.), May 1, 1913, http://chroniclingamerica.loc.gov/lccn/sn87062268/1913-05-01/ed-1/seq-1/.

4. wo pension application no. 638231, correspondence to commissioner of pension, Marianna, Florida, April 15, 1915. (Note: letters are transcribed as written, including spelling and grammar errors.)

5. wo pension application no. 638231, correspondence from Commissioner, Civil War Division, Washington, D.C., to Mr. A. Purdee, Marianna, Florida, May 3, 1915.

6. wo pension application no. 638231, correspondence from C. F. Williams, MD, Superintendent, State Hospital for the Insane, Columbia, South Carolina, October 20, 1915.

7. wo pension application no. 638231, correspondence between C. M. Saltzgaber, Commissioner, to Arthur Carr, November 20, 1915.

8. Full text of "Digest of Decisions of the Department of the Interior in Appealed Pension and Bounty-Land Claims; PENSION AND BOUNTY-LAND CLAIMS. Insane Widow—Charity not Dependence. Dependence—Widow—Act June 27, 1890—Charitable institution (Margaret Morman, insane widow), vol. 12, 1901–1902, P. D., 40, 191.

9. Registration State: *Florida*; Registration County: *Jackson*; Roll: *1556858*, Ancestry.com, *U.S., World War I Draft Registration Cards, 1917–1918.*

10. "How Florida Handles Her State Convicts," *Pensacola Journal* (Pensacola, Fla.), December 18, 1910, http://chroniclingamerica.loc.gov/lccn/sn87062268/1910-12-18/ed-1/seq-21/.

11. "Lagoon Road Work to Begin Immediately," *Pensacola Journal* (Pensacola, Fla.), August 18, 1916, http://chroniclingamerica.loc.gov/lccn/sn87062268/1916-08-18/ed-1/seq-1/.

12. "Guard Shoots Prisoner in a Hard Fight," *Pensacola Journal* (Pensacola, Fla.), March 1, 1911, http://chroniclingamerica.loc.gov/lccn/sn87062268/1911-03-01/ed-1/seq-2/.

13. "Chas. Jones Dies in Convict Camp," *Pensacola Journal* (Pensacola, Fla.), January 18, 1915, http://chroniclingamerica.loc.gov/lccn/sn87062268/1915-01-18/ed-1/seq-2/.

14. "Guard Shoots J. Underwood," *Pensacola Journal* (Pensacola, Fla.), October 3, 1914, http://chroniclingamerica.loc.gov/lccn/sn87062268/1914-10-03/ed-1/seq-3/.

15. J. C. Powell, *The American Siberia: Or, Fourteen Years' Experience in a Southern Convict Camp* (Homewood Publishing, 1893), 22, available at http://palmm.digital.flvc.org/islandora/object/ucf%3A7756#page/22/mode/2up.

16. Powell, *American Siberia*, 21.

17. Catherine Kim Gyllerstrom, "2,000 Trees a Day: Work and Life in American Naval Stores Industry, 1877–1940" (PhD diss., Auburn University, 2014), 105–6, available at https://holocron.lib.auburn.edu/handle/10415/4437.

Chapter 27. The Women and Continuing the Fight

1. WO pension application no. 638231, Correspondence from H. T. Vicks, Campbellton, Florida, on behalf of Liz Carr to War Department, Washington, D.C., March 10, 1920.

2. WO pension application no. 638231, Correspondence from H. T. Vicks, Campbellton, Florida, to the Bureau of Pensions, Washington, D.C., December 12, 1922.

3. WO pension application no. 638231, Correspondence from H. T. Vicks, Campbellton, Florida, to Bureau of Pensions, Washington, D.C., February 10, 1923.

4. WO pension application no. 638231, Correspondence from H. T. Vicks, Campbellton, Florida, to Hon. Duncan U. Fletcher, United States Senate, Washington, D.C., December 1, 1923.

5. WO pension application no. 638231, Correspondence from Commissioner (location of office not indicated) to Hon. Duncan U. Fletcher, United States Senate, Washington, D.C., December 10, 1923.

Chapter 28. Tennessee and the Last Word

1. WO pension application no. 638231, Correspondence from Charley Jones, 218 15th Ave. N., Nashville, Tenn., to Office of Adjutant General, Widow Division, Washington, D.C., August 10, 1936.

2. WO pension application no. 638231, Letter from E. L. Bailey to Mr. Charley Jones, September 25, 1936.

3. WO pension application no. 638231, Letter from P. L. Fallon to Charley Jones, December 18, 1936.

4. WO pension application no. 638231, Letter from Charley Jones to Mr. (President) Roosevelt, January 3, 1937.

5. For a brief overview of the benefits of the New Deal to African Americans, see "African Americans and the New Deal: A Look Back in History," Roosevelt Institute, accessed September 10, 2018, http://rooseveltinstitute.org/african-americans-and-new-deal-look-back-history/.

6. Herbert Aptheker, ed., "Congressman Mitchell on the New Deal," *The Negro People in the United States 1933–1945* (Citadel Press Book, 1974), 182.

7. John P. Davis, "A Black Inventory of the New Deal," in Aptheker, *Negro People in the United States*, 171–72.

8. Cecelia Chappel, interviewed in *Federal Writers' Project: Slave Narrative Project*, vol. 15, *Tennessee, Batson-Young* (1936), 8, https://www.loc.gov/item/mesn150/. Interviewers of the Federal Writers' Project chose to pen the narratives mimicking the dialect of former slaves. I chose to rewrite the narrative using more standard English so the reader would not be distracted by trying to decipher the wording.

9. Wiley Childress, interviewed in *Federal Writers' Project*, 10.

10. Patsy Hyde, interviewed in *Federal Writers' Project*, 36.

11. Narcissus Young, interviewed in *Federal Writers' Project*, 81.

Epilogue

1. Georgia Writers' Project, *Drums and Shadows: Survival Studies Among the Georgia Coastal Negroes* (University of Georgia Press, 1940), 151.

2. *Drums and Shadows*, 66.

3. *Drums and Shadows*, 67.

4. *Drums and Shadows*, 66–67.

5. *Georgia, Marriage Records from Select Counties, 1828–1978*, Ancestry.com, https://www.ancestry.com/search/collections/4766/records/218118. Original data: County Marriage Records, 1828–1978, Georgia Archives, Morrow, Ga.

6. Charles J. Montgomery, "Survivors from the Cargo of the Negro Slave Yacht *Wanderer*," *American Anthropologist*, n.s., 10, no. 4 (1908): 613.

7. Montgomery, "Survivors," 616–18.

8. Montgomery, "Survivors," 613.

9. Montgomery, "Survivors," 621.

10. Memorial Page for Ward Lee, Find a Grave Memorial Idaho 110178730, *U.S., Find a Grave Index, 1600s–Current*, accessed May 25, 2025, http://www.findagrave.com/cgi-bin/fg.cgi.

11. "Old Negress Dies at Home in Brunswick," *Macon (Georgia) Telegraph*, December 1, 1912, 2, available at https://www.newspapers.com/image-view/825581709/?match=1&terms=negress.

12. Jim Turner, "Search for Bodies Isn't Over at Florida's Infamous Dozier School for Boys," *Orlando Sentinel*, August 29, 2019, https://www.orlandosentinel.com/politics/os-ne-dozier-schools-bodies-20190827-yw2rmsgimra3rm7hlacti2skcq-story.html.

13. Patricia Sullivan and Frances Stead Sellers, "On Land of Former Slaves, a Sturdy Home Gives Shelter from Hurricane Michael," *Washington Post*, October 1, 2018.

14. Historic Postcard Collection, RG 48-2-5, Georgia Archives, https://vault.georgiaarchives.org/digital/collection/postcard/search.

15. "New 155-Bed Holiday Inn Resort Coming to Jekyll Island," *Florida Times-Union*, March 18, 2013, https://www.jacksonville.com/story/business/2013/03/18/new-155-bed-holiday-inn-resort-coming-jekyll-island/15834610007/.

16. Pew Research Center, "Race in America," April 2019, https://www.pewresearch.org/social-trends/2019/04/09/race-in-america-2019/

17. "Deep Divisions in Americans' Views on the Nation's Racial History—and How to Address It," Pew Research Center, August 12, 2021, https://www.pewresearch.org/politics/2021/08/12/deep-divisions-in-americans-views-of-nations-racial-history-and-how-to-address-it/.

18. Kiana Cox, "Most Black Americans Believe U.S. Institutions Were Designed to Hold Black People Back," Pew Research Center, June 15, 2024, https://www.pewresearch.org/race-and-ethnicity/2024/06/15/most-black-americans-believe-u-s-institutions-were-designed-to-hold-black-people-back/.

INDEX

Page numbers in italic refer to images.

www.ingramcontent.com/pod-product-compliance
Lightning Source LLC
LaVergne TN
LVHW040505011026
849280LV00024B/226
* 9 7 8 1 5 8 8 3 8 5 8 3 3 *